Information Technology Industry in India

INFORMATION TECHNOLOGY INDUSTRY IN INDIA

Dr. Tapan Choure
Dr. Yogeshwar Shukla

Publications

KALPAZ PUBLICATIONS
DELHI - 110052

INFORMATION TECHNOLOGY INDUSTRY IN INDIA

Rs. 850

ISBN : 81-7835-312-1

Published in 2004 in India by
Kalpaz Publications
C-30, Satyawati Nagar,
Delhi-110 052
Email : kalpaz@hotmail.com

Lasertype Setting by: *Tact Computer Graphics*, Delhi
Printed at: Mehra offset press, Delhi

Contents

प्रोफेसर ए.डी.एन.बाजपेयी
कुलपति
Professor A.D.N.Bajpai
Vice-Chancellor

Fax : 07662- 242175,230819
Ph : 230819 (O.)
: 242175,251952(R.)
e-mail : adnbajpai@yahoo.com.
vcapsu@lycos.com.
अवधेश प्रताप सिंह विश्वविद्यालय,
रीवा – 486 003 (म.प्र.)
Awadhesh Pratap Singh University,
Rewa – 486003 (M.P.)

Foreword

After the industrial revolution of Britain, the greatest technological revolution in modern history has been the revolution brought in the lives of the common man as well as of the elite by information technology. Our most natural and spontaneous behaviour today was not even thought of a decade back. Computers, mobiles, data collection devices, internet-the magic toys in the hands of present generation were not even conceivable when we were children. The speed of the mind has gone fast. The arena of thought has expanded. The conversion of wish into reality is rapidly becoming as everyday penomenon. I take these changes as the growth and evolution of the human race. The human existence has a natural tendency to go from hard work to comfort, from physical labour to more and more mental labour. These changes indicate this basic tendency of our race.

We, as the intellectuals of India must see to it that the potential and concerns of our country and our region in particular are not neglected in the global scenario. The present book is extremely useful as it provides a conceptual framework to IT industries in India and Madhya Pradesh. It provides a rational approach for understanding the constraints as well as their remedies of the this important sector.

(A.D.N. Bajpai)

Acknowledgements

It is our pleasure to thank all the IT experts and professionals; those are help for our work. We are grateful to Prof. ADN Bajpai, Vice-Chancellor; APS University, Rewa and Mahatma Gandhi Gramodya University, Chitracoot for a foreword for this book. On this occasion we are very thankful to Prof. Ram Rajesh Mishra; Vice-Chancellor, Vikram University, Ujjain for his congenial support and suggestions. We also thanks Prof. Nageshvar Rao; Dean, Faculty of Information Technology, Vikram University, Ujjan and Prof. G.K. Parakh, Head, School of Studies in Economics, Vikram University, Ujjan for their valuable help for line of direction.

We are hopeful that, this book will be widely used by different sections of the IT sectors and scholars. On this opportunity, we are also giving our thanks to our family members for their cooperation. Now lastly, we are thanks to our publisher; Kalpaz Publications, Delhi.

Ujjain

Dr. Tapan Choure
Dr. Yogeshvar Shukla

1
Introduction

1.1 Conceptual framework of Information Technology and Information Technology Industry

Since the drawn of civilization, people have required information to aid them; in their personal battle of survival as well in their attempts to manage their organisations. Through for the centuries man live without keeping recórds, latter it become necessary to do so with the growth of the social organisations. Distortions have traced some type of record keeping and data processing back to about 3500 B.C. Today all of us still keep records and process data, but the technology by which data are processed has made a quantum leap forward in the last twenty to thirty years. (Sumita[1], 2001). India used to harp on its civilization and tradition, perhaps due to its cursed medievalism and missed modernism can now legitimately pride itself-thanks to Information Technology (IT) Sector - at the threshold of the new millennium. A decade half ago, a PC generated at best curiosity and at worst mystique even amongst the educated Indians. But the rapid strides of Information Technology, both in sophistication and expansion, especially during the Rajiv Gandhi[2] regime and later has been truly revolutionary. Be it home or office, school or university, the ubiquity of a small sized box processing, evaluation and churning out information at the press of button is not an uncommon sight today.

Concepts of Information

No doubt computers have done wonder in our lives by enhancing out abilities and increasing our efficiency. Even people who have been using computers for years still marvel at what they can do: how at lightning speed and with amazing accuracy they get their work done- be it sorting a mailing list, balancing a ledger, type-setting a book, sending a document miles across (e-mail) [3] or any other processes (converts) data[4] and informaiton[5] World is changing at enormous speed and every aspect of it is getting affecting by it. Civilisation today has become complex and sophisticated and the demand of the time is competition. One has to be competitive to survive in this sophisticated and complex world. And to competitive, one has to be well informed of all type of happenings in the society. With the advent of the educational reforms in society, mankind is surrounded with a vast amount of data. Modern business management needs a system for bulk collection of data from various sources which needs to be rearranged in a fashion so that it can utilized with minimum possible time. All this requires a huge storage space and proper maintenance. (Computerisation has eased all this to a great extent). When huge amount of data are to be utilized with minimum possible time, it is possible if only it is converted into required information. The urge for converting facts into meaningful information is the root cause of information need. Information is an important ingredient of our day-to-day life. It plays various important roles in our lives. The strong needs of information is supported by the following information usage (Sumita[6], 2001):

1. **Addition to Knowledge**—Information certainly adds to knowledge. More information one has, more is he capable of applying it in various contexts. In today's information sensitive world, information is needed
    - To have knowledge about the surroundings and happenings in the society.
    - To know about the rules and regulations and byelaws of society, government, industry etc.

Ignorance was never bliss and it might cost human life. Thus, it pays to be information sensitive.

2. **Decision Making Aid**—Information is a crucial decision making aid. It is the information that plays a key role in decision making. Information is significant for a manager and policy makers as it can add to his knowledge in planning the operations to help him in discharging their responsibilities. Information is important to business man, researchers, policy makers, etc as it tells them what do?, when do?, how to do?, etc. In fact, information is important for each and every person of the society even though his or her needs

each and every person of the society even though his or her needs and roles may differ.

3. **Impact on Society**—Information plays a key role in the formation and structure of societies. Man is said to have gone through three ages: agriculture, industrial and information. These were periods of emphasis or focus on agriculture, industry or information- with their own particular characteristics. In each of these ages, information was the main ingredient, though the type of information required was different. We are now in information age where everything revolves around information i.e., the primary resource is information, transforming resource is information, computer, communications, technology is information, intellectual technology, strategic resource is information knowledge and so on. In this information age, the computers and communication combine to from Information Technology (IT), by which the use of information becomes far more efficient. This more efficient use of information can affect society and management. In fact, this will have an effect an aspects of life. IT is one of the most pervasive technologies and hence, has effects on practically everything we do. For instance, if we argue upon "How can people living in villages/rural areas possibly be affected by computers?", we have following points to support:
   - Using IT, weather may be predicted and communicated to rural areas thereby helping them decide and live accordingly.
   - Using IT (computer) analysis of various crops, fertilizers may be done and the people living in rural areas may be suggested over these and numerous other matters thereby helping them earn more, live better.
   - Using IT, people living in these areas can be made more aware of the technologies and their usage thereby helping them raise their life styles.
   - Using IT, literacy rate may be improved thereby improving the life styles, living standard etc.

As information can do miracles in society transformation, it is very important to be informed, remain informed.

4. **Increase in Productivity**—Information availability plays a very important role in increasing productivity. Productivity is directly

related to the information available, its value in the related context. The information availability can increase productivity as a result of that. For instance, exception reports (information) can quickly signal out-of-control conditions requiring corrective action when actual performance deviates from what was originally planned. New plane and actions can then be implemented to take corrective measures thereby increasing productivity.

- A properly report (information), given a manager the ability to evaluate more possible alternatives and to consider the internal and external variables that may have a bearing on their outcome. The manager can do a better job of identifying and assessing the probable economic and social effects of different courses of action and hence can draw a better implementation plan to increase productivity.

IT or Information Technology has the potential to change the face of India. Networking of villages, blocks and districts to the state and the national capitals is bound to give a tremendous boost to Indian's developmental effort. Information Technology has the potential to generate massive employment. Infect India has the largest pools of Information Technology manpower and the Indian IT Diaspora is spread far and wide internationally. Countries like Germany and Japan have fallen short of IT manpower. Indian has readily filled the vacuum. For a country like India IT can be a good source of earning foreign exchange. India is fast emerging as a great software-exporting nation. As we know that India has a new mantra - Information Technology (IT) - and almost everyone has started chanting it. This IT mantra has its roots in the "passionate and strategic infection" spread by the unrivalled success of India's export led software industry. This passionate infection has not only made the software sector as one of the high value-addition and net foreign exchange earning industry, but has created history of sorts on the Indian stock exchanges. The potential of its high capacity to generate wealth, foreign exchange and employment has already caught the imagination of India's businessmen, citizens, economists, bureaucracy and politicians, alike. Software driven IT industry is today at the top of India's national agenda as an instrument and a model, for the modernisation of India's economy.

In India, there has been a gradual shift towards usage of IT in government, public sector, private sector as well as public services and education. However, usage of computers is yet to reach many homes in the country. Undoubtedly, it was the computerisation of railway passenger reservation system in 1986- that brought computers closer to masses. And, in the last two years - it is the power of Internet, E-Commerce as well as Government of India's thrust - which is bringing IT in daily life of a common person in India. Pioneering work done by Indian software companies using the high-speed datacom links brought in new paradigm of offshore software development. In fact, Indian software industry has been recognised as representing one of the most successful business models that can help to sustain high growth and competitiveness. Thus, with software as the driving engine, since early 90's, the Indian IT industry has been growing at a phenomenal growth rate. What's more, India's software industry is torchbearer for not only India's IT industry but even Indian economy's global ambitions. It is a way to build competitiveness in technology-driven service economy.

India has many advantages to become an important player in the global IT industry. By marshalling its vast human, industrial and technological resources, especially with expansion of its software sector - the engine of the IT Industry. India can raise productivity of domestic manufacturing and services. Obviously, this will lead to IT in governance, IT in industry and IT for every citizen of the country. There are even talks of infusing tangible productivity gains amongst various sectors and communities through use of IT. The domestic opportunity is evident.

Today everyone talk about Information Technology, weather they belong to engineering field, medical field, business, commerce, science and social science fields. Every stream of knowledge wants to shower under the spring of Information Technology. Now the question arises that what is Information Technology: -

'IT' means any representations or instruction, data, sound, image and can be transferred from one place to another through the high-tech machine like Computer, Radar and Satellite.

Important definition of Information Technology[7]

"IT Software" means any representation of instruction, data, sound, image including source code, object code recorded in a machine, readable form and capable of being manipulated or providing interactively to use by means of automatic data processing machine falling under head "IT products".

"IT service" is defined as any service which results from the use of any IT software over system of IT products for realising value addition.

"IT products" would include computer, digital data communication and digital data broad-casting products as notified by the Ministry of Finance, Government of India or Central Board of Excise and Customs.

· "IT industry" would include development, production and services related to IT products, IT software and IT services.

IT *pundit* proclaim with legitimate pride that IT is not just sunrise industry but an Information Technology revolution that is being unleashed. The marriage of computers and communication has given to what is now called Information Technology (IT) which bids fair to be the technology of the future[8]. The use of Information Technology promises improved performance for organisations. The benefits of Information Technology can usually be measured in terms of enhanced processing speed, transmission rates and access time[9]. The introduction of micro and minicomputers has enabled greater decentralisation of information systems[10]. Recent innovations, such as local area network, make possible the linking of task, groups and managerial work processed[11]. These capabilities are likely to impact culture, structure and work practices[12].

A Model of Function of Information Technology

What can we do with Information Technology? What function does it serve and does it serve them better than the old technology? The fundamental function served by the technology is that it enhances our ability to communicate information. Whereas traditional technologies serve to magnify physical ability, the intent of Information Technology is to augment and magnify human mental abilities; and information science must provide the necessary knowledge base [13]. "New Information Technology is at our service to enable us to store, collect, select, transform, send or display, information". What are the characteristics of a model that helps us to explain the function of Information Technology? Firstly, it must be a two-way model, the channels within it must allow for two-way traffic. Secondly, it must include all the functions and thirdly, it must shows how these functions can be integrated. It should be capable of exhibiting principal functions; making, sending/rendering, storing and displaying. Making is sub-divided into creating, collecting, selecting and transforming. Receiving of course complements sending. We can look at each of these functions in turn and examine their interrelationships (figure 1.1).

Information Technology Services

Information Technology (IT) is emerging as dominant industry in the global economy. It offers a variety of services, products and technologies, which acts as drivers to enhance productivity and in turn helps to improve the GNP of the Nations. As an industry, IT perhaps is the largest, fastest growing and the most profitable industry in the world today and India is well placed to exploit the competitive advantage it enjoys in the same.

In the Indian context, the potential leverage of IT is enormous especially in the Software sector. Government identified this as an area extreme of focus and announced a policy in 1986 making "Software Export, Software Development and Training" as a major thrust area. Government further identified some of the factors impending the growth of the software industry and formulated "Software Technology Park"(STP) scheme with a view to boost software exports for the country. To meet this objective, a suitable framework was formulated covering aspects like simplifications/ rationalisation of procedures, providing single-point-contact services to the industry, providing basic common amenities needed for export operations within a very short gestation period and share captive infrastructural facilities like computing resources and data communication services in a cost effective manner[15].

The framework was designed to help software export industry in general and Small and Medium Enterprises (SMEs) in particular and enables them to remain competitive in the global market. Government of India on May 22, 1998 also constituted a "National Task Force on Information Technology and Software Development" to recommend steps to remove bottlenecks in the path of rapid development of Information Technology and to give a boost to Information Technology and Software Industry[16].

Various Information Technology development institution and Software Parks have been developed with the help of Union and Strate Government and Private Sectors. Software Technology Parks of India (STPI) was set-up to implement the STP Scheme and to promote software exports by providing infrastructural facilities including High Speed Data Communication (HSDC) links.

Software Technology Parks of India (STPI)

Software Technology Parks of India was established and registered as a Society under the Societies Registration Act 1860, under Ministry of Information Technology (formally the Department of Electronics), Government of India, on 5th June 1990 with an objective to implement STP scheme, set-up and manage infrastructural facilities and provide other services like technology assessment and professional training. As on 31th March 2000 STPI had set-up 15 STP centers in the last nine years as per details under[17]. (Table 1.2)

These centres act as "single-window" in providing services to the software exports. The centres are equipped with basic facilities like back-up power, EPABX, security, training aids, library, photocopier, fax etc. with a built-up space of over 2,00,000 sq.ft. all over India. STPI also provides incubating infrastructure to SMEs enabling them to commence operations without any delay.

STPI is working closely with the respective State Governments/local authorities for creation of more space, equipped with state-of-the-art infrastructure facilities, for development of the software industry and increasing exports.

Software Technology Parks (STP) Scheme

Software Technology Parks (STP) is a 100 Per cent export oriented scheme for the development and export of computer software including export of professional services using communication links or physical media. This scheme is unique in its nature as it focuses on one product/sector, i.e. computer software. The scheme integrates the concept of 100 per cent Export Oriented Units (EOUs) and Export Processing Zones (EPZs) of the Government of India and the concept of Science Parks/Technology Parks as operating elsewhere in the world[18].

The unique feature of STP scheme is the provisioning of Single-Point Contact Services for the member units enabling them to conduct export operation at a pace commensurate with international practices. The STPI also acts as a resource centers for the member computer software exporting units by offering general infrastuctural facilities like ready to

STPI also acts as a resource centers for the member computer software exporting units by offering general infrastuctural facilities like ready to use built-up space, centralised computing facility and High Speed Data Communication (HSDC).

Highlights

- Approval under single window clearance mechanism.
- 100 per cent foreign equity permitted.
- Imports by STP units are completely duty free.
- Second hand capital goods may also be imported.
- Exemption of local taxes for domestic purchases.
- The sales in the domestic market are permissible upto 50 per cent of the exports.
- Exemption from corporate income tax till 2009-2010.

The export obligation on net foreign exchange should be 0.25 m $ or 5 times the CIF value of the goods imported, whichever is more, to be fulfilled over a period of 5 year.

Spectrum of IT Enabled Services

Amongst others, the spectrum of IT enabled services applications already evident in India include the following broad segments:

Customer Interaction Services, Business Process Outsourcing Management; Back Office Operation, Insurance Claims Processing, Medical Transcription, Legal Databases, Digital Content, Online Education- Customer Interaction Services, Back Office Operations, Data Digitisation / GIS, Payroll / HR Services.

Table–1.1 India's Irresistible and Sustainable Value Proposition

Country	*Workforce*	*Market Access*	*Local Market*	*Infra-structure*	*Cosmo politan*	*Cost base*
New Zealand	2	2	-	2	3	2
Kuala Lumpur	1	2	-	2	2	2
Japan	1	2	1	3	1	3
Hong Kong	1	2	2	2	2	2
India	3	2	2	2	3	1

1 denotes low; 2 denotes average; 3 denotes high

Source—Nasscom.

Table–1.2. STPI Centres

Place	*Year of set-up*	*Place*	*Year of set-up*
Bangalore	1990	Chennai	1995
Puna	1990	Jaipur	1998
Bhubaneswar	1990	Navi Mumbai	1998
Hyderabad	1991	Coimbatore	1998
Noida	1991	Manipal	1999
Gandhinagar	1991	Mysore	1999
Thriuvananthapuram	1991	Indore	2000

Source–STPI.

Figure 1.1: A Model of Function of Information

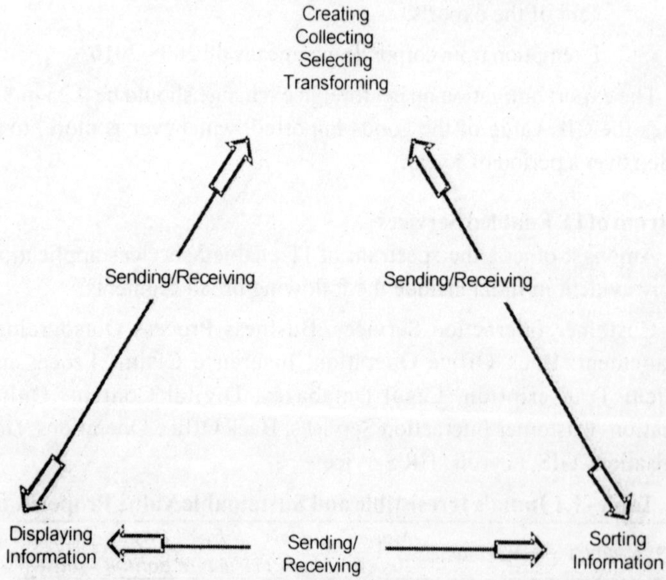

Web site Services Customer Interaction Services[19]—Customer Interaction Services, including call centres, combine the use of highly effective and empowered company representatives with a service framework that relies heavily on state of the art communications and information technologies. A call centre is sometimes defined as a telephone-based shared service centre for specific customer activities. It is used for a number of customer related functions like marketing, selling, information dispensing, advice, technical support etc. Thus, a call centre is a service centre that has adequate telecom facilities, trained consultants, access to wide database, Internet and other online information support infrastructure to provide information and support to customers. It operates round the clock to provide year round service, i.e., 24 × 365 service.

As per industry estimates, there are more than 100,000 call centres worldwide and this is expected to grow to 300,000 by 2002 employing approximately 18 million people. By the year 2003, a sum of US$ 60 billion is expected to be spent on call centre services, further driven by e-commerce.

Business Process Outsourcing / Management; Back Office Operations[20]—Industries such as Banks and Airlines require large-scale data processing and data based decision-making capabilities. For instance, for revenue accounting and other back office accounting operations, paper documents / raw data are sent to remote locations, which are used for data entry and necessary reconciliation. Using high-speed datacom links for their back-office and data processing operations, these banks, airlines and other organisations with extensive data turnover and customer interface, are able to save costs and valuable resources. The prime concern of these companies is 100 per cent availability of data and uptime of facilities. This can be ensured through high-speed datacom links from India to the parent country. In other words, such a centre could be realised simply as an offshore extension of existing information and back office operations promising constant availability. Over the last few years, there has been a steadily growing trend to outsource these services to major IT enabled service providers with contracts running into decades. The prime criteria for such projects are quality of organisational processes, availability of abundant manpower and ability to dedicate resources to clients' needs. India stands to gain from such a trend, as Indian software industry has been able to make a mark and also has access to a huge pool of skilled as well as semi-skilled professionals with relative cost advantage.

Insurance Claims Processing[21]—Large insurance companies get myriads of claims. With the help of well laid down rules on how they a large number of are to be processed, such processing can be done anywhere, as long as there is availability of a large number of graduates who can read and write English, a few doctors and a few accountants. As a result, to save costs, large insurance companies in the US are now outsourcing a lot of such work. Thus this can prove to be another good opportunity area.

Insurance companies have two basic activities that require internal efforts, i.e., creating and setting up an insurance policy and then processing the large volume of insurance claims and accounting for the insurance claims.

Apart from processing, there is a large amount of logistics involved in this activity. But the guidelines to the process are well established and hence can be easily performed remotely.

In this business also, there is an element of help desk, providing annual appraisal update service by maintaining an updated database of all property records, creation of low cost property value estimates and providing for claims reporting centres round the clock.

Medical Transcription[22]—Medical Transcription is the process through which one accurately and swiftly transcribes medical records dictated by doctors and other healthcare professionals. It is the method of translating the dictation (that forms the basis of providing healthcare) into a format suitable for inclusion in a medical record (hard copy or electronic)

In countries like the USA, doctors' time is at high premium. The current practice is for doctors to simply record their findings through a dictaphone or some such device. These sound tracks are then sent through datacom lines to overseas companies (where costs are much lower) that employ "medical transcriptionists" who hear these recordings, transcribe them into reports and send them back electronically through datacom lines. Information and communication technologies are used to send the voice recordings on satellite lines to far-off, low cost locations, where these recordings are transcribed into reports that are again sent back to the hospitals or clinics digitally through the same lines and printed as reports locally. Turn around time is often as low as two hours and, therefore, is often better than what the hospital may have achieved if it had done all of it in-house.

Legal Databases[23]—There is a constant need for lawyers, who counsel cases, to go through relevant laws, rulings and precedents in order to build-up their case. Very junior lawyers in legal firms usually do this. However, in the US and other developed countries, even junior lawyers' services are highly priced. One of the ways to get around this hurdle is to have a readily accessible source of well-managed and intelligent information. And one of the most promising and low cost ways of having ready access to information is Information Technology. Therefore, many legal firms have started to outsource this work to organisations that have a large English speaking, lower-priced workforce of trained lawyers. The job comprises of working closely with the firms to create a database of their existing records, indexing on the basis of various useful and common understood criterion, keeping track of new documents being created and incorporating them into database as per well established parameters. Lawyers can then simply use their computers to draw up a history of like cases and draw a clear plan of action. Once again, the rules are clear and only average qualifications and ability are required.

Digital Content Development[24]—Digital Content development is emerging as one of the fastest growing service segments in the global IT enabled services industry. It caters to needs of web site management, production of content for new media such as Compact Disk, Digital Versatile Disk and products of convergent technologies such as Internet-enabled TV. It offers a large emerging potential; as more and more offices, homes, institutions, students and professionals realise an ever-growing need to have easy access to information that can also be suitably fused with other media. The process consists of -

- Compilation and development of digital content for intra-organisation dissemination,
- Cross-institution usage,
- Collaborative projects,
- Public domain information,
- Programs for public / specialised education,
- Web content development and management,
- Developing animated movies and

It typically involves defining a set of rules and norms for collection of data; collating various unorganised sources of data; sorting; indexing and sifting; compilation; conversion into digital format and disseminating to various users.

In other types of digital content development, there is usually a contract between content provider and developer to review project on an ongoing basis such as cartoon movies, etc. Opportunities also include acting as an offshore content developer for organisations such as Internet media companies and advertising organisations where there is a constant need for content development.

There are several other such areas where the potential is high. The acceptability of outsourcing such work to distant countries and the recognition of the cost savings is rapidly growing.

Online Education[25] —The online education market is booming all over the world and is currently considered a rapidly growing sector. In fact, surveys conducted by leading global research firms have indicated that online education will follow an upward moving graph and that more and more organisations and individuals will implement this mode of training.

Some interesting statistics on the size of the online education market across the globe, put forth by US based IDC point out that the online education or e-learning market will grow from US$ 1.1 billion in 2000 to US$ 11.4 billion in 2003.

Online education or Web-based training implies that courses are delivered partly or completely via the Internet, an intranet or an extranet. The factors that are driving demand for virtual education are essentially need and availability. More than 1,600 companies including nearly half the Fortune 500 have built corporate universities. Nearly all such programs offer at least some classes in the traditional-way based on set schedules and led by instructors in the classroom. But 90 per cent have gone virtual, offering at least some classes online, primarily through the Web, but also via video-conferencing, CD-ROM and other technologies.

The online education market in India is showing marked potential and is expected to be a significant revenue earner for the industry in the years to come. Some of the developments taking place in the online education market include -

- Growth in education at home market segment,
- Distance learning; foreign university-Indian training institute tie-ups,
- Collaborations between Indian universities and Indian training houses,

- Collaborations between some IITs, CMU, IIITs and IISc for imparting distance education, are expected to provide impetus for Indian audience.

Data Digitisation / GIS[26]—Digitisation is the process by which physical or manual records such as text, images, video and audio are converted into digital forms. This is of paramount importance when projects need directions based on already established facilities and the implementing agency needs to find the scope for expansion. Digitised data offers the following benefits -

- Long term preservation of documents,
- Orderly archiving of documents,
- Easy and customized access to information,
- Easy information dissemination through images and text, CD-ROMs, Internet, intranets and extranets.

Data Digitisation offers a very good opportunity for the Indian market place, due to relatively lower costs and the technical skills available. Many overseas companies like Bechtel have set-up engineering design centres in India.

Geographic Information System[27]—Geographic Information System (GIS) is a compendium of tools and methods that are used in a digital environment for the study of spatial information. Traditionally, this spatial information was presented as maps on paper. Today, its counterpart is the digital map.

IT enabled services in GIS offer business opportunities in Europe and the US. Today, in these countries, there is a need for digitising vast number of maps on different themes and also processing an enormous amount of Remotely Sensed (RS) data. The IT services that create suitable digital input for GIS require skilled technical manpower of which there is a large pool in this country. Further, many of these processes are labour intensive and it is this that gives India a cost advantage over other countries in providing services for GIS.

Payroll / HR Services[28]—HR services are another area that has immense potential in the field of IT enabled Services. HR service components include:

- Recruitment screening,
- Administration and relocation services,

- Payroll processing,
- Compensation administration,
- Benefit planning,
- Administration and
- Regulating compliance.

Web Services [29]—Internet and the wide use of the Web has accelerated the growth of remote services and created opportunities of its own. Some of the Web services include email management; Internet security; web page designing and updating; managing of Internet commerce, acting as an exchange of data, payment and clearance; EDI supply chain management; Internet data centres etc.

India's irresistible and sustainable value proposition on the path of Information Technology related services not enjoys the pick position as compared to Europe and United State. By outsourcing IT-enabled services, overseas companies can not only achieve significant improvements in cost, quality and time but also create platforms for building new businesses. Overall, these benefits are due to the advantages offered by skill-surplus economies. India has currently the best value proposition of all IT-enabled services hubs.

India's value proposition is already leading IT-enabled services hubs such as Ireland and Singapore to back-end their operations in India, since skilled labour is becoming an increasingly scarce resource in these countries. Seizing the opportunity, several companies in the financial service sector, for example, have saved at least 50-60 per cent of their process costs. Additionally, the process redesign that comes with out location provides additional cost savings[30].

A comparison amongst some countries in Asia Pacific based on these factors highlights the following (ratings are on a scale of 1 to 3, with 1 being the lowest and 3 the highest) Table 1.

IT-enabled service centres in India are able to deliver superior quality because of specialisation and scale benefits. India already has a large and rapidly growing number of IT-enabled service providers collectively covering a wide range of services with different levels of complexity and value added. Yet another compelling rationale for IT-enabled services is that it allows companies to capitalize on time zone differences and to provide services round-the-clock, every-day of the week (24x7 service). For example, doctors in the US can have transcribed records of their notes at the start of the next day by sending them to medical transcription services in India who will start work at the end of their working day in the US[31].

Finally, companies can discover new business opportunities in the skills they learn from operating IT-enabled services. GE Capital, one of the largest IT-enabled services operators in the financial services arena, is now planning to extend it services beyond GE group companies to external customers. It is planning to expand its IT-enabled services operation in India to over 10,000 employees. Additionally, there are already a large number of smaller Indian companies that provide services in many areas of the business system.

The sustainability of the value proposition makes it irresistible. India will continue to offer a large talent pool and favorable economics for some time to come. These advantages are buttressed by the significant number of IT-enabled services set-ups in the country that they can learn from.

The proliferation of IT-enabled Services and its continuing demand-led growth may well emerge to be a strong opportunity for India, both in terms of generating employment and export.

As evident, IT-enabled Services is a major boon for India as it provides tremendous potential to provide employment opportunities and attract foreign investments. Amongst others, the benefits include:

- Generation of new direct or indirect investment,
- Earning of foreign exchange leading to higher earnings of local staff,
- More revenues to telecom carriers,
- Introduction of new technology,
- Transfer of skills to India,
- Increase in competitiveness,
- Improved parity of income levels in and far flung areas and remote states.

India Offers Many Advantages

India offers many advantages to serving as an IT-enabled Services destination for major global companies. These include:

- A virtual 12-hour time zone difference with USA and other major markets for IT-enabled Services.
- A huge pool of English speaking and computer literate graduate manpower who can continue to cater to the growing demand for professionals for IT- enabled Services. These professionals are skilled as well as quality conscious.
- Cost of qualified personnel is amongst the lowest in the world.
- India provides income tax holiday till 2010 for export of IT-enabled Services.
- Stable legislative and economic framework.
- Support of Government of India for all IT-led industries
- Government of India has announced a special policy for call centres in India.
- Many State Governments in India offer special incentives and infrastructure for setting up IT-enabled Services.
- Thrust by Government of India to make India an IT-driven nation with a focus on services sector where potential for value addition and thus premium is higher.
- India enjoys very strong brand equity in major markets, thanks to its growing and globally competitive software industry.

Information Technology Industry

The role of Information Technology industry, well described by Churchill[32] (1999), is pervasive: "... effective decision making depends on the quality of information input and marketing research plays an essential role in providing accurate and useful information" (p. 4). All businesses are information businesses in the sense that they use information to guide strategy and operations. So what is the Information Technology industry?

If we are going to talk about an information industry, we should know how to define it. What are its boundaries? How is it distinct from other industries? Empirical studies in industrial organisation begin with at least an implicit definition of an industry. (Thomas W. Miller[33], 2000). In practical terms, this might translate into a Standard Industrial Classification (SIC) code or a group of codes. Though, as we can see from Exhibit 1, it is hard to define the information industry with SIC codes

Think of the information industry as a service industry, distinct from computer and Information Technology services and distinct from many other professional services. Marketing has its four "Ps": product, promotion, price and place (distribution). The information industry has its four "Gs." Firms in this industry Generate, Gather and Group information and then Give (sell) information to other firms.

Generate Information—Firms generate information when they develop new scales and coding schemes, specify models, set priors, or provide a theoretical organisation for research. Interpreting textual data from in-depth interviews or focus groups and writing research reports—these are creative, generative processes. Firms also generate information, quite literally, when they employ computer-intensive statistical methods, resampling techniques, or data augmentation. It is their styles of information generation that often distinguish one research firm from another. Successful firms in the information industry are creative firms.

Gather Information—Central to the information industry is the process of gathering information. Research firms gather primary information from business managers and consumers. They also gather information from a variety of secondary sources. Traditional modes of gathering include face-to-face and telephone interviews and focus groups, mail surveys and observational studies. Today's methods of gathering include the additional methods of online research. Successful information industry firms are efficient gatherers.

Group Information—George A. Miller[34] (1956) called it "chunking." It is easy to be overwhelmed by the data, by the gigabits of information that come our way each business day. To learn from data, firms organise, aggregate and process those data. They use model-based or data-adaptive statistical methods to transform, smooth, or reduce data. They convert data into summary statistics, parameter estimates and probability statements. Although analysts may not reduce data down to what Miller[35] (1956) called "the magic number seven, plus or minus two" chunks of information, their grouping activities should yield a more manageable, more understandable organisation of the data. Successful information industry firms group information in meaningful ways.

Give Information to Others—All types of firms are involved in information generating, gathering and grouping. But for the firms in the information industry, the information providers, information generating, gathering and grouping are primary activities. Information providers make and sell information. Information clients buy and use information. Successful information industry firms provide long-term value to their clients. The information industry includes firms from conventional lists of the largest marketing research firms (Honomichl[36], 2000). It also includes small firms and independent agents. A nonfiction writer or an anthropologist describing social trends that affect consumers, giving lectures and writing books, is just as much a part of the information industry as is the large firm that gathers scanner data from supermarkets. It seems appropriate to consider firms at various points along the information supply chain. It seems appropriate to include firms engaged in business-to-business as well as business-to-consumer research, database as well as field research and secondary as well as primary research.

Level of aggregation or generalization should not be the deciding factor for including firms in the Information Technology industry. Information products can focus upon individual consumers, consumer segments, or markets. They can focus upon individual products, categories, or classes of products. At broad levels of aggregation, information products and services can deal with nationwide or worldwide markets and consumer cultures.

Information Technology Industry Analysis

A former student of economics and industrial organisation, Michael Porter[37] (1980), provided a useful model for industry analysis and competitive strategy. Let's apply his model, as shown in Figure 1.2, to today's information industry.

Suppliers—Information industry firms do research. They convert physical and human resources into information products. Physical inputs to the information production function include computer and communications hardware and software, offices and office equipment. Human resources, especially important to information production, include clerical personnel, technical writers, telephone and face-to-face interviewers, focus group moderators, database and business analysts, management consultants, statisticians, field researchers and, of course, survey respondents and focus group participants. Because there are many suppliers of labour (many highly mobile information workers) and many suppliers of information services, individual suppliers have little bargaining power.

Traditional research is labour-intensive; online research is less labour-intensive. Changes in Information Technology imply changes in the information production function. When today's firms want to learn about business and consumer markets and learn about them quickly, they use computers and communications technologies to generate, gather and group information. They work with customer databases and conduct online research. Accordingly, information systems suppliers are an important component of the information supply chain.

Figure 1.2: Information Technology Industry analyses

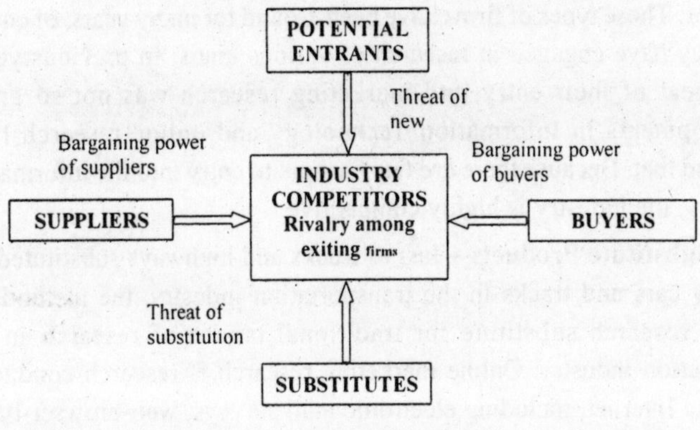

Source: Porter (1980)

Figure 1.3. An Information Technology Industry Supply

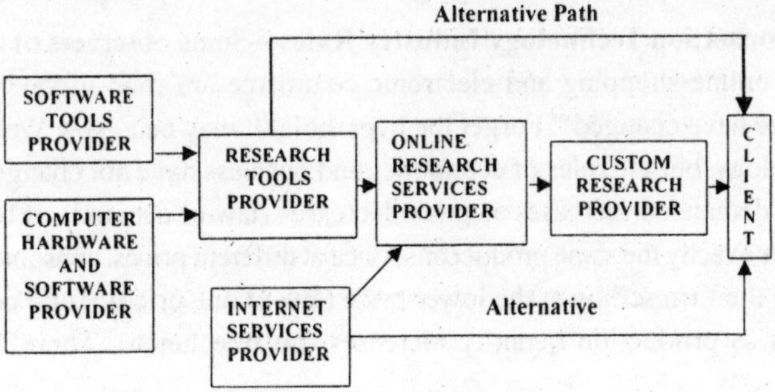

Buyers—Custom research addresses the needs of individual clients and there are many clients. General-purpose research also serves the needs of many clients. There are times when information buyers and sellers lock themselves into multi-year contracts, but it is more common for buyers and sellers to set up short-term contracts on a project-by-project basis. Because there are so many potential buyers of business and economic information, individual buyers have limited bargaining power.

Potential Entrants— Traditional marketing research firms be warned. Potential entrants into the information industry include technology and information systems manufacturers and consulting firms, accounting and financial services firms and political, social and public opinion research firms. Advertising, media and publishing firms can also supply research services. These types of firms have been around for many years, of course and they have engaged in research of various kinds. In previous years, the threat of their entry into marketing research was not so great. Developments in Information Technology and online research have changed that. Because there are few barriers to entry into the information industry, the industry is highly competitive.

Substitute Products—Just as trucks and highways substituted for railway cars and tracks in the transportation industry, the methods of online research substitute for traditional modes of research in the information industry. Online marketing research is research conducted over the Internet, including electronic mail surveys, web-browser-based surveys, distributed survey applications, online interviews, bulletin boards and focus groups. Online research is more than just a new way to gather information, more than just a new modality of research. It represents a technological and cultural change. What we do as researchers and how we think about research are changing because of what we can do online.

Information Technology Industry Rules—Some observers of the Internet, online shopping and electronic commerce are fond of saying, "The rules have changed." Forget the hyperbole. It may be a New World of technology, but the rules of economics and business have not changed. Quantity demanded increases as price decreases (law of demand). If two firms offer exactly the same product or service at different prices, consumers buy from the firm selling at the lower price (law of one price). Total cost increases as production quantity increases (no free lunch). There are economies of scale and economies of scope in production, just as surely as there are diminishing returns associated with the use or over-use of a single factor of production. Total cost is still the sum of fixed and variable costs and profit equals revenue minus cost.

If the rules haven't changed, what has changed? The parameters. Firms that set up their own web sites for online surveys incur higher fixed costs and lower variable (per participant) costs than firms that conduct traditional surveys.

Communication over the Internet is faster than communication through mail. Traditional research is time- and paper-intensive. The time to complete a traditional study, a cross-sectional survey of 1,000 consumers done by Thomas W. Miller[38], for example, is measured in weeks or months. The time to complete an online study is often measured in hours or days. The parameters of information production change with technology. Economic agents, consumers and firms, are subject to the rules of information economics. These information rules, as described by Shapiro[39] and Varian[40] (1999), may be less widely understood than the law of demand or the definition of profit. But they are no less important to understanding the structure of the information industry and changes in the information supply chain.

The Information Supply Chain

Client firms are at the far end of the information supply chain. Clients need business and consumer information to make decisions; they need information to run their businesses. How shall they get this information? They can make it or buy it. To make information, firms set-up in-house research departments. To buy information, firms set up contracts with research providers, firms in the information industry. All firms both make and buy information. What distinguishes firms from one another along the information supply chain is how much information they make and how much they buy. In past years it may have been reasonable to characterize information supply chains as being limited to individual research provider and client firms.

Information providers would design studies, collect data and write research reports on behalf of clients. Information generation, gathering and grouping were customized for each client. A variation upon this theme would include initial providers of interviewing, tabulation, or syndicated database services (information gathering) selling to intermediate providers of research design, analysis, interpretation and consulting (information generating and grouping) who would work with clients.

Just as many businesses are being transformed by the e-business revolution, as described by Amor [41] (2000), marketing research is being transformed by online research. The automation of information generation, gathering and grouping activities can lead to the development of a more complex information supply chain. Figure 1.3 shows an information supply chain in which providers of information gathering software (survey or research tools) sell to intermediate providers of online research services. These providers of online research services, in turn, sell to custom research providers, who sell to clients. As we move from providers of general-purpose tools and services to providers of more specialized services, there is value added through information integration and customization.

Evans and Wurster [42] (2000) describe how changes in Information Technology affect the "richness versus reach trade-off." In a business-to-business context, "richness" refers to the quality of information, its accuracy, currency, customization and relevance to the client. "Reach" refers to the number of clients who can easily access information. Consider how Evans and Wurster's [43] (2000) analysis relates to the information supply chain:

"Until recently, it has been possible to share extremely rich information with a very small number of people and less rich information with a larger number, but it has been impossible to share simultaneously as much richness and reach as one would like. . . . The trade-off between richness and reach is based on the existence of information channels: physical infrastructures or behavioural patterns that support limited movements of information. But the existence of channels implies that some have privileged access and others do not: channels imply asymmetries. Some can get rich information only through an intermediary who has access to the channel and who extracts the value of his informational chokehold. Eliminate the richness/reach trade-off, make the channel universally accessible and the asymmetry collapses."

Referring again to Figure 1.3, we see how alternative information flows can develop. There can be disintermediation. A vendor of general-purpose research tools can offer its products and services directly to clients at the far end of the information supply chain. To the extent that these general-purpose research tools are customizable, intermediate information providers, including providers of custom market research, may be eliminated from the supply chain. Traditional provider-to-client channels are unnecessary when clients can get rich information by using customizable research tools and when clients have worldwide reach through the Internet.

Our attempt to place research within the broader context of the Information Technology industry suggests that there will be increased competition among the providers of research services. Competition could just as easily come from information systems providers and consulting companies as from businesses included in conventional lists of marketing research firms. Because information systems and services are central to the research function, marketing research will be part of a large and growing information industry.

The positive role the IT industry is playing in our lives is no longer a debatable issue. Most countries today are beginning to understand the value add that Information Technology is bringing to economies - introducing both efficiency and benefits. And businesses around the globe have been investing heavily in the IT hardware and software infrastructure. As communication within companies and users occurs more rapidly, with more customized information, greater security and interactivity and timeliness than before, business strategies and even the structures of companies and industries are being transformed.

India - the world's largest democracy and home to a billion people is also rapidly emerging as of IT. The IT revolution has become the new mantra in the economic landscape here. The high potential of IT to generate wealth, foreign exchange and employment has already caught the imagination of India's businessmen, citizens, economists, bureaucracy and politicians.

A gradual shift towards the usage of IT is happening in the Government, public as well as the private sector all over the country. And in the last two decades, Software Engineering, Web-based Services and E-commerce Solutions have emerged as the new jewels of the Indian economy. The year 1999-2000 particularly witnessed a concerted effort to trickle the benefits of IT to the common masses in the country.

Information Technology is the fastest growing sector of the Indian industry and Sunrise industry and the area of growth for the millennium. During the Eighth Plan, the electronics industry has achieved a cumulative annual growth of 20 per cent in production and over 40 per cent in exports. The Indian electronics production during the year 1999-2000 was Rs. 52,450 crore. A goal of annual electronics production of Rs. 1,38,350 crore has been set for the terminal year of the Ninth Plan (2001-02), representing a growth rate of 39 per cent[44].

Consumer electronics sector has achieved a production level of Rs. 11,200 crore during 1999-2000. Colour TV industry continued to witness phenomenal growth and has crossed a production of 57 lakh nos. during the calendar year 1999[45]. However the stage of hardware and electronic industry of IT sector is not good as compare to Japan and United States, but in the case of software industry of IT sector there is high degree of prospects and possibility in India.

1.2 Review of literature

Over the one and half decade many scholars, researchers, economist have done prominent work in the field of Electronic industry, Communication and Information Technology Industry. A review of the available resources on Information Technology Industry can underline the major trends of the research in Information Technology Industry studies as the scope for further research on the problem of development of Information Technology Industry.

Bajpai and Dokeniya[46] observe that, this is more importantly on the success with which IT is applied for economic growth and productivity generally. They point out that while the application of information and communication technology to government and industry is a demand side issue, establishing a local IT, the Indian and Chinese immigrants who have studied work in the US, while maintaining their base in their adopted country, are playing growing role in linking US technology businesses to those in their countries of origin. According to Jeffrey D Sachs[47] and Bajpai Note that venture capital, which is key nurturing new industries, is very weak in India. Paper by Nagy Hanna[48] in the world Bank discussion Explain that the future prospect of IT and IT industry in India, She also point out the exploiting IT for development in India.

According to Navi Radjow and Nirupam Bajpai[49] reveals in their research work that, In the emerging knowledge-based global economy, the sustainable competitive advantage of nations will reside not in their possession of natural resources or cheap labour force, but in their countries intellectual asset. As such, the knowledge revolution offer a unique chance to leapfrog entire stage of development. They argue that in order to make such a leap Tamil Nadu needs to initiate a knowledge-led development policy that build on the states successful IT industry. Their work proposed a road map to raise the global competitiveness of Tamil Nadu's IT industry, through strengthening both demand and supply. According to S Mahalingam[50] , EVP at TCS and head of CII-TN's IT panel, This vision document highlights the positive social transformations that could be realised through intelligent use of IT and internet .Bartlett, Ghospal and Prahalad[51] comment that "trapping into international markets means more then accessing new customer. It also means accessing new talent knowledge, information and experience (what ever they exist)". For them, the 'next phase' of globalisation involves creating and leveraging multiple sources of innovation. This point was made by S Mahalingam[52] Who thinks that the state's comparative advantage are 'real'; unlike some rival states where "reality does not match hype". Shastri and Bajpai[53] Further propose that data generated in this cell should be available on a day-to-day basis to the highest officials and government personnel dealing with software policy. According to Advait Aundhkar, Nalini Vaz, Geeta A Pillai, DLN Murty , S S Thakur[54]: A team of researcher from CIDCO conducted, A detailed study of the prevalence of teleworking in three sectors - software, financial and banking and media-reveals that current regulatory mechanism operating in the IT industry and the inadequate infrastructure services are major hurdles in the growth of teleworking and teletrade. Bresnahan and Greenstein[55] (2001) after a careful study observe that, By what process does technical change in Information Technology (IT) increase economic welfare? How does this process result in increases in welfare at different rates in different countries and regions? This paper considers existing literature on measuring the economic benefits from Information Technology, emphasizing comparative issues and user studies. Oliner and Sichel[56] (2000) has studies that, The performance of the US. economy over the past several years has been remarkable, including a rebound in labour productivity growth after nearly a quarter century of sluggish gains. To assess the role of Information Technology in the recent rebound, this paper re-examines the growth contribution of computers and related inputs with the same neoclassical framework that we have used in earlier work. Our results indicate that the contribution to productivity growth from the use of Information Technology - including computer hardware, software and communication equipment - surged in the second half of the 1990s. In addition, technological advance in the production of computers appears to have contributed importantly to the speed-up in productivity growth. All in all, we estimate that the use of Information Technology and the production of computers accounted for about two-thirds of the 1 per centage point step-up in productivity growth between the first and second halves of the decade. Thus, to answer the question posed in the title of this paper, Information Technology largely is the story.

Renu Budhiraja[57] (2000) by her ultimate analysis observes that, the electronic governance wave has started worldwide. With the technologies to implement electronic governance already available/understood by us, managerial issues are of key importance. Change in the mindset of the people particularly at the top levels in the bureaucracy and policy making is important because it is they who provide the leadership. This change in the mindset can be brought about by focused organisation development interventions and training programs. Once this is done, there should be a corresponding trickle down effect right through the spectrum of government. The future is e-homes with e-services at the doorsteps .

Manjeet Kripalani[58] (2000) in his studies observes that, India has reached a pivotal moment. Just once before, when they achieved independence from Britain in 1947, have Indians had such an opportunity to remake themselves. "The '80s were the Asian Tigers' decade; the '90s, China's. The IT revolution will make this decade India's," says New Delhi economist Surjit Bhalla. Given India's many false starts, it's too early to declare success. But as the benefits of joining the global IT revolution become ever more apparent, India may be ready at last for its moment on the world stage.

Pohjola and Roponen[59] (2001) in their working Project work, which concentrated on the impacts of Information Technology on productivity and economic growth. In his contribution to this project, Danny Quah argued forcefully that the most profound impact of the IT revolution is that it makes modern economies increasingly weightless or dematerialized in the sense that an increasingly greater fraction of gross domestic product comes to reside in economic goods with little or no physical manifestation. Such a weightless group of commodities includes all products and services that can be expressed in digital form -encoded as a stream of bits - such as computer software, telecommunications, biological algorithms, financial services, electronic databases and libraries, media entertainment and Internet delivery of goods and services. The thesis of dematerialization is that economic value will increasingly be created by producing and distributing bits of logic rather than atoms of physical material. This work confined to the economic effects of the 'digital', 'Internet', 'weightless' or 'new' economy.

The Economist, John Browning[60] (1990) wrote: "Information Technology is no longer a business resource; it is the business environment." His statement is not far from truth. Ongoing advances in Information Technology (IT), alongwith increasing global competition, are adding complexity and uncertainty of several orders of magnitude to the organisational environment. One of the most widely discussed area in recent business literature is that of new organisational network structures that [supposedly] hold the promise of survival and growth in an environment of ever-increasing complexity (Bradley, Hausman and Nolan[61], 1993; Byrne[62], 1993; Davidow and Malone[63], 1993; Eccles and Nolan[64], 1993; Jarillo and Ricart[65], 1987; Malone and Rockart[66], 1993; Miller, Clemons and Row[67], 1993; Naisbitt[68], 1982, 1985; Toffler[69], 1985). How can IT help the organisations in responding to the challenges of an increasingly complex and uncertain environment? How can IT help the organisations achieve the "flexible" organisation structure? So many works have been observed a strong trend of convergence of the technologies of computing and telecommunications (McFarlan and McKenney[70], 1983). Changing technology economics, merging of formerly disparate technologies with different managerial traditions and the problems of managing each of the phases of IT assimilation in different ways calls for a major reappraisal of the organisation structures designed for yesteryears.

Researchers have expressed time and again that technological change poses the greatest challenge to their research (Teng and Galletta[71], 1991). Dickson and DeSanctis[72] (1991) mentioned that not much attention has been given to the integration of technology or its use as a coordinating mechanism for organisational units. It is our contention that IT should be studied as an independent variable affecting the organisational structure. Huber[73] (1990) recommends a reassessment of certain components of organisation theory, which are affected by the tremendous changes that have occurred in the capabilities and forms of communication technologies. This article will attempt to contribute to the development of these issues.

Bayes, Abdul and Von Braun, Joachim[74], explain the validity impact of IT and IT industry in rural economy of Bangladesh. Bonder, Seth,[75] 1997, explain the Changing the paradigm for Telemedicine Development and Evaluation. Bradsher, Monica[76], 1995, comment on prospects and strategies for Improving Basic Education in Developing Countries through the use of computer-based Information Technologies.

Coyne, R[77]., Lamberton, D. [78], Bruce, H. [79], Strand, J.R. [80], MacDougall, S. [81], Ogden, M.R[82], Layton, S. [83],Molnar, H. [84] Wells, D. [85], Chatwin, D. [86],Wickramanayake, E. [87] and Boaden, C. [88], 1995, Information Technology and Development. This discussion, spread over 11 papers, questions the widely held assumption that improved communication systems and the free flow of information and knowledge carry positive benefits for developing countries. It is becoming increasingly apparent that information technologies do not necessarily support beneficial change. Rather promote the disparity between the rich and the poor and the developed and developing countries. Coyne argues that vast information of often conflicting nature available on the Internet has led to scepticism about professional expertise and greater pressure on the individual to decide what to do. In the next paper . Lamberton considers the emergence of electronic colonialism because of inappropriate or incomplete information infrastructures. Bruce focuses on the considerable barriers many developing countries face because of their involvement with the internet. The dramatic impact of the new technologies on libraries and the ways in which large statistical databases ate stored, accessed and utilized is discussed by Chatwin. The other papers examine the following; telecommunications and economic development (Strand); Pacific Islands and Information Technology (Ogden); the Coconet Wireless which operates between the pacific Islands (Layton); issues relating to the development of communications in the South Pacific; the utilisation of computers by NGOs in development programs (Wells); and the use of computers in rural development planning in Thailand (Wickramanayake).

Hame, Hagy, Guyy Ken and Arnold, Erik[89], This study reports on the experience of Canada, Germany, Ireland, the Netherlands, Sweden, the United Kingdom, the United States and Japan in designing, implementing and adapting Information Technology(IT) diffusion programmes in the 1990s. the study examines the determinants of effective IT diffusion and analyzes national IT policy portfolios to draw lessons and trends. Programmes should consider technology life cycles, the business needs of potential users, their technological sophistication and their current exposure to international best practices. The study concludes buy suggesting roles for governments, private sector and aid agencies to accelerate the benefits of IT diffusion for development.

Gurmukh Gill, Kan Young, Dennis Pastore, Jesus Dumagan and Isaac Turk[90] (1997), explain the Economy-Wide and Industry-Level Impact of Information Technology. Sandra Black and Lisa Lynch[91] (1998). Focus the light on the impact of workplace practices and Information Technology on procuctivity. Dean Parham, Paul Roberts and Haishun Sum[92] (2001), reveal the Information Technology and Australia's productivity surge. Robert Merquez and Robert Hauswald[93] (2002), explain about Information Technology and financial services competition. Thomas Peince[94] (2000), explain Information Technology and Hospital Closures. Amir Ziv[95] (1999), reveals the Information Technology and optimal firm structure.

Notes and References

1. Sumita Arora (2001). "*Informetics Practices*". Dhanpat Rai and Co. (Pvt.) Ltd., New Delhi, pp.1.
2. Rajeev Ghandhi was first Prime Minister in India during ninth decade of twentieth century who has done pivotal work for the promotion of Information Technology and computer education in India.
3. E-mail (electronic mail) is sending and receiving messages through computers.
4. Data are set of isolated, unrelated, interpreted raw facts?
5. Information refers to meaningful data, or in other words, information is a set of organised, validated, corrected and collected data.
6. Sumita Arora (2001). "*Informetics Practices*". Dhanpat Rai and Co. (Pvt.) Ltd., New Deihi, p.3.

7. Journal of Electronics Information Planning, MIT, New Delhi.
8. Kulkarni,M.R., *Industrial Development*, National Book Trust, New Delhi, 1998, pp. 327.
9. Grover V and Segars A.H (1996), *The relationship between Organisational Characteristics and Information System Structure: An International Survey.*, International Journal of Information Management.
10. Olson, M.H. and Chervany N.L.(1980), *The Relationship Between Organisational Characteristics and the Structure of the Information Services Function*, MIS Querterly, 4, 57-68.
11. Venkatraman N (1991), *IT-Induced Business Reconfiguration*, Oxford University Press, New York.
12. Doherty NF and King M (1998), *The Importance of Organisational Issues in Systems Development*, Information Technology and People, 11(2), 104-123.
13. Subhash B (2000), *Information and Communication Technology in Development: Cases from India*, Sage Publication, New Delhi.
14. Hawkridge (1980), *Information Technology and its facets*, National Book Trust, New Delhi.
15. Software Technology Park of India. Website: www.stpi.net.
16. Advantage India, MIT, New Delhi.
17. See Software Technology Park of India centers in http://www.stpi.net.
18. See Software Technology Park of India exported oriented zones in http://www.stpi.net.
19. See the detail of consumer Interaction Services in www.nasscom.org\it_enable_services.html.
20. See the detail of Business Process Outsourcing/Management; Back Office operation in :www.nasscom.org\it_enable services.html
21. See the detail of Insurance Claims Processing in :www.nasscom.org\it_enable_services.html.
22. See the detail of Medical Transcription in :www.nasscom.org\it_enable_services.html.
23. See the detail of Legal Database in : www.nasscom.org\it_enable_services.html.

24. See the detail of Digital Content in : www.nasscom.org\it_enable_services.html.

25. See the detail of Online Education- Customer Interactive Services in : www.nasscom.org\it_enable_services.html

26. See the detail of Back Office Operations in :www.nasscom.org\it_enable_services.html

27. See the detail of Data Digitisation / GIS in :www.nasscom.org\it_enable_services.html

28. See the detail of Payroll/ HR Services in :www.nasscom.org\it_enable_services.html

29. See the detail of Web sites services in :www.nasscom.org\it_enable_services.html

30. Software Technology Park of India. www.stpi.soft.net\itenable.htm

31. *Ibid.*

32. Churchill, G. A., Jr. (1999). *Marketing Research: Methodological Foundations* (7th Ed.). Orlando, FL: Dryden.

33. Miller, G. A. (1956). The Magic Number Seven, Plus or Minus Two: Some Limits on Our Capacity for Processing Information. *Psychological Review*, 63, 81-97

34. Miller, Thomas W. (2000). "Marketing Research and the Information Industry." *CASRO Journal 2000*.

35. *Ibid.*

36. Honomichl, J. (2000, June 5). Business Report on the Marketing Research Industry. *Marketing News*, H1-H36.

37. Porter, M. (1980). *Competitive Strategy: Techniques for Analyzing Industries and Competitors*. New York: The Free Press.

38. Miller, Thomas W. (2000). "Marketing Research and the Information Industry." *CASRO Journal 2000*.

39. Shapiro, C. (1999). *Information Rules: A Strategic Guide to the Network Economy*. Boston: Harvard Business School Press.

40. Varian, H. R. (1999). *Information Rules: A Strategic Guide to the Network Economy*. Boston: Harvard Business School Press.

41. Amor, D. (2000). *The E-business (R) evolution: Living and Working in an Interconnected World*. Upper Saddle River, NJ: Prentice-Hall.

42. Evans, P. , ans Wurster, T. S. (2000). *Blown to Bits: How the New Economics of Information Transforms Strategy.* Boston: Harvard Business School Press

43. Ibid

44. Ministry of Information Technology http://www.mit.gov.in/dbid/producti.html

45. Ministry of Information Technology http://www.mit.gov.in/dbid/producti.html

46. Bajpai and Dokeniya, IT-led growth Policies : A case study of Tamil Nadu. Harvard Institute of International Development , Harvard University.

47. Jeffrey D Sachs and Bajpai ,'Strengthening India's strategy for economic growth' , Development Discussion paper No- 641, Harvard Institute for International Development , Harvard University.

48. Nagy Hanna ,World Bank Discussion (1995) , Newyork

49. Navi Radjow and Nirupam Bajpain. 'Raising Global competitiveness of Tamil Nadu's IT industry' EPW , Vol XXXV No-6 , 2000, A Sameeksha trust publication , Mumbai

50. S Mahalingam, EPW , Page No-465 , Vol XXXV No-6 A Sameeksha trust publication , Mumbai.

51. Bartlett and Ghospal and Prahalad , Managing Across Borders : The Transnational Solution , Harvard Business School press , Bosten.

52. S Mahalingam, EPW , Page No-465 , Vol XXXV No-6 A Sameeksha trust publication , Mumbai.

53. Shastri and Bajpai, EPW , Page No-465 , Vol XXXV No-6 A Sameeksha trust publication , Mumbai.

54. Advait Aundhkar, Nalini Vaz, Geeta A Pillai ,DLN Murty , S S Thakur: *Teleworking in India,* CIDCO, New Delhi.

55. Timoty F. Bresnahan and Shane M. Greenstein 'The Economic Contribution Of Information Technology: Towards Comparative And User Studies', National Bureau of Economic Research (NBER); Department of Economics, Journal of Evolutionary Economics, Vol. 11, No. 1, 2001

56. Stephen D. Oliner and Daniel E. Sicner 'The Resurgence of Growth in the Late 1990s: Is Information Technology the Story?'Board of Governors of the Federal Reserve System, U.S.A. ,2000.

57. Renu Budhiraja 'Electronic Governance - A key issue in the 21st century', Electronic Governance Division, Ministry of Information Technology, Govt. of India, New Delhi. Email: renu@mit.gov.in

58. Manjeet Kripalani and Mark L. Clifford 'Information Technology is lifting the economy and the politicians are backing it.' Business Week, Asian Edition, Hyderabad, Feb 21, 2000.

59. Matti Pohjila and Liisa Roponen, 'Production, Employment and Income distribution in the Global Digital Economy.' WINDER, U.S.A. 2001.

60. Browning, J., "Information Technology: The Ubiquitous Machine," The Economist, (June 16, 1990), p. 5.

61. Bradley, S.P., Hausman, J.A. and Nolan, R.L., "Global Competition and Technology," in S.P. Bradley, J.A. Hausman and R.L. Nolan, Globalisation Technology and Competition: The Fusion of Computers and Telecommunications in the 1990s, Harvard Business School Press, Boston, MA, 1993, 3-31.

62. Byrne, J.A., "The Virtual Corporation: The Company of the Future will be the Ultimate in Adaptability," Business Week, (February 8, 1993), 98-103.

63. Davidow, W.H. and Malone, M.S., The Virtual Corporation, Harper Collins, New York, 1992.

64. Eccles, R.G. and Nolan R.L., "A Framework for the Design of the Emerging Global Structure," in S.P. Bradley, J.A. Hausman and R.L. Nolan, Globalization Technology and Competition: The Fusion of Computers and Telecommunications in the 1990s, Harvard Business School Press, Boston, MA, 1993, 3-31.

65. Jerillo, J.C. and Ricart, J.E., "Sustaining Networks," Interfaces, 17, 5, (September-October, 1987), 82-91.

66. Malone, T.W. and Rockart, J.F., "How Will Information Technology Reshape Organisations?: Computers as Coordination Technology," in S.P. Bradley, J.A. Hausman and R.L. Nolan (Eds.), Globalisation, Technology and Competition: The Fusion of Computers and Telecommunications in the 1990s, Harvard Business School Press, Boston, 1993, 37-55.

67. Miller, D.B., Clemons, E.K. and Row, M.C., "Information Technology and the Global Virtual Corporation," in S.P. Bradley, J.A. Hausman and R.L. Nolan (Eds.), Globalisation, Technology and Competition: The Fusion of

Computers and Telecommunications in the 1990s. Harvard Business School Press. Boston. 1993. 283-307.

68. Naisbitt. J., Megatrends: Ten New Directions Transforming Our Lives. Warner Books. New York. 1982.

69. Toffler. A., The Adaptive Corporation. McGraw Hill, New York. 1985.

70. McFarlan. F.W. and McKenney, J.L., Corporate Information Systems Management: The Issues Facing Senior Executives. Irwin. Homewood. IL. 1983.

71. Teng. J. C. and Galletta. D.F., "MIS Research Directions: A Survey of Researchers' Views," DataBase. 22. 1, (1991). 53-62.

72. Dickson, G.W. and DeSanctis, G., "The Management of Information Systems Research Status and Themes," Research Issues in IS: Agenda for the 1990s. 1991. 45-81.

73. Huber. G.P.. "A Theory of the Effects of Advanced Information Technologies on Organisational Design, Intelligence and Decision Making," Academy of Management Review. 15 (1990), 47-71.

74. Bayes, Abdul and Von Braun, Joachim, Village Pay Phones and Rural Poverty: Insights from a Grameen Bank Initiative in Bangladesh. http:\\www.zef.de\zef_deutsch\f_first.html.

75. Bonder. Seth. 1997. Changing the paradigm for Telemedicine Development and Evaluation: A Prospective Model-based Approach. Socio-Economic Planning sciences.

76. Bradsher. Monica. 1995. Prospects and Strategies: Improving Basic Education in Developing Countries through the use of computer-based Information Technologies. Aguirre International. Arlington. VA, Development Infrastructure, Arlington, VA, World Learning Inc., Washington. D.C., USAID. Centre for Human Capacity Development, Washington. D.C.

77. Coyne. R.. 1995. Information Technology and Development. Development Bulletin Vol. 35 pp. 3-39.

78. Lamberton. D.. 1995. Information Technology and Development. Development Bulletin Vol. 35 pp. 3-39.

79. Bruce. H.. 1995. Information Technology and Development. Development Bulletin Vol. 35 pp. 3-39.

80. Strand, J.R., 1995, Information Technology and Development, Development Bulletin vol. 35 pp. 3-39.

81. MacDougall, S., 1995, Information Technology and Development. Development Bulletin vol. 35 pp. 3-39.

82. Ogden, M.R, 1995, Information Technology and Development, Development Bulletin vol. 35 pp. 3-39.

83. Layton, S., 1995, Information Technology and Development, Development Bulletin vol. 35 pp. 3-39.

84. Molnar, H., 1995, Information Technology and Development, Development Bulletin vol. 35 pp. 3-39.

85. Wells, D., 1995, Information Technology and Development, Development Bulletin vol. 35 pp. 3-39.

86. Chatwin, D., 1995, Information Technology and Development, Development Bulletin vol. 35 pp. 3-39.

87. Wickramanayake, E. 1995, Information Technology and Development., Development Bulletin vol. 35 pp. 3-39.

88. Boaden, C., 1995, Information Technology and Development., Development Bulletin vol. 35 pp. 3-39.

89. Hame, Hagy, Guyy Ken and Arnold, Erik[92], 1995, The Diffusion of Information Technology-Experience of Industrial Countries and Lessons for Developing Countries, World Bank Discussion Paper 281, Washington D.C., IDRB/World, p. 207.

90. Gurmukh Gill, Kan Young, Dennis Pastore, Jesus Dumagan and Isaac Turk, Economy-Wide and Industry-Level Impact of Information Technology, U.S. Department of Commerce , U.S. Department of Commerce , U.S. Department of Commerce , U.S. Department of Commerce and U.S. Department of Commerce Date Posted: June 26, 1997

91. Sandra Black and Lisa Lynch, *How to Compete: The Impact of Workplace Practices and Information Technology on Productivity*, University of California, Los Angeles and Tufts University , January 13, 1998.

92. Dean Parham, Paul Roberts and Haishun Sun, *Information Technology and Australia's Productivity Surge,* Productivity Commission , Productivity Commission and Productivity Commission ,October 24, 2 001.

93. Robert Merquez and Robert Hauswald, *Information Technology and Financial Services Competition,* University of Maryland and Indiana University January 11, 2002.

94. Thomas Prince, *Information Technology and Hospital Closures,* American Bankruptcy Institute Law Review, Vol. 8, pp. 115-123, 2000.

95. Amir Ziv , *Information Technology and Optimal Firm Structure,* Columbia Business School, November 23, 1999.

2

Scenario of Information Technology Industry in India

2.1 Historical background of Information Technology Industry in India

The Land—India is the second largest country in Asia it is a land of lofty mountains and mighty rivers covering an area of some 3 million square kilometers with age old traditions of culture and tourist attractions in every region of the country and the software all over.

The Federal Capital is at New Delhi.The financial and commercial nerve center is Mumbai (Bombay). Bangalore is India's "Silicon Land", home to a number of large software development centers and nerds. Other cities with significant IT presence are Hyderabad, Chennai (Madras), Pune, Trivandrum (Thiruvananthapuram) and Bhubaneswar[1].

India has a tropical monsoon climate: the year being divided into two broad seasons: summer - from mid-March to mid-September - is wet, hot and humid; winter somewhat cooler 12°C to 20°C Temperatures vary by region and altitude. Mumbai, for example, experiences fairly constant temperatures of about 28°C to 32° C in summer and 21 °C to 32°C in winter, while Bangalore's temperatures range from 16°C to 33°C in summer and 15°C to 26° C in winter.[2]

The People—India is the biggest democracy in the world, with a population of one billion made up over 100 ethnic groups. There are fifteen official languages, with English and Hindi being the link languages. English is used for business, legal and political purposes, The universality of English makes India particularly accessible to international investors compared to other countries in the region or for that matter globally.

India is organised into 28 States and 7 Union Territories, based predominantly on linguistic division. The head of each State is the Governor, who is advised by a Council of Ministers headed by the Chief Minister. Each State government consists of a Legislative Assembly (of elected members) and a Legislative Council (of nominated members).

India Bound—The Embassy Office of India (EOI) in our country provides advice and guidance to our prior to visiting India. In addition, there are a number of private consultants with in-depth knowledge of India, who can support our companies and provide introductions to suitable Indian business partners in the IT sector. In an initial visit, Indian will want to cover a lot of ground and meet as many company representatives as possible. However, to make the visit as productive as possible and to gain maximum benefit from the Consular office in the EOI. We should clearly set out the objectives of our visit before we go - the type of companies we would like to see, the products or businesses we are interested in, the cities or technology parks Indians would like to visit - and set the agenda and duration of any meetings. Ministry of Information Technology would be able to help us to identify a suitable associate in India. It will take considerable planning to identify the companies we would like to meet [3].

Smart Sourcing

India's reputation as a center for world-class IT and software development destination has grown steadily over the past decade. The Indian software companies generate close to 75 per cent of the total revenues from off-shore development. In 1999-2000, 270 of the Fortune 1000 companies out sourced requirements from India with 180 coming from top 500. The US accounted for more than 60 per cent of this. It is no wonder therefore, that no IT icon of this world has not visited India in the past one year-weather it is Bill Gates or John Chambers.The leading lights are Craig Barett, Jorma Ollila, Negro Ponte and many others [4]. All of them in addition to heads of such global giants like GE's Welch have established research and development centers for smart sourcing the Indian knowledge workers. In fact, companies around the world are gaining competitive advantage by using Indian software services that offer high quality, cost effectiveness, time savings, state-of-the-art technologies and above all reliability. [5]

A virtual 12-hour time zone difference between India and USA and 4-5 hours with West Europe and Japan offers cost and time savings with little down time for the customer.

- A huge pool of English speaking and computer literate graduate workforce who can continue to cater to the growing demand of professionals worldwide. In addition there is a building pool of professionals in major European and Oriental languages.
- With more than 145 ISO 9000 certified and with 22 out of 32 companies having achieved SEI CMM Level 5 ultimate quality advantage.
- Indian software companies believe in highest adherence to delivery schedules and customer satisfaction by using sate-of-the-art technologies.
- E-Business and web based solutions: Indian companies offer the-most cost-effective, innovative and extensive web-based solutions.

Exodus, Hotmail, Junglee, Who where are some of the examples of Indian innovativeness. This is in addition to the number of new start ups engineered like - Vinod Khosla's Juniper Networks and Sidhu's [6].

The Government of India has pursued policies of economic liberalisation during the past decade. The industrial, trade and fiscal policies introduced by the Government since 1991 have paved the way for greater technological advancement and international competitiveness of the Indian Electronics and Information Technology Industry. Restrictions on the private sector have been relaxed significantly and promotion of India's international trade has gained increased importance in the national economy since then. Industrial licensing has been virtually abolished for the electronics sector with the exception of manufacturing electronic aerospace and defence equipment. The Indian Electronics and Information Technology Industry is poised to play a major role in the Indian Economy and has emerged as the fastest growing segment of Indian industry both in terms of production and exports. During the Eighth Plan (1992-97), the electronics industry has achieved a cumulative annual growth of 20 per cent in production and over 40 per cent in exports. The production at the end of the Ninth Plan (1997-2002) is targeted at about Rs. 1,380 billion, with a growth rate of 37 per cent and exports at about Rs. 490 billion with a growth rate of 52 per cent.[7]

Technological revolutions sometimes bring unexpected opportunities for countries. India, a relative laggard among developing countries in terms of economic growth, seems to have found such an opportunity in the Information Technology revolution as an increasingly favored location for customized software development.

Early success has led to speculation about how long the Indian software industry can sustain its growth. It has also led to the hope that software and Information Technology can be the engine of growth for poor, labour abundant countries.

Currently, software exports contribute to around 5 per cent of India's total exports. The industry association also indicated a target of garnering 23 per cent of customized software market and 5 per cent of products and packages market in the global IT economy by 2003. Nasscom also projects that software exports will constitute about 25 per cent of India's total exports by 2003. These projections are likely to be excessively rosy.[8] The Indian software industry faces a number of challenges as the labour cost advantages diminish and competition from other countries with supplies of educated and underutilized workers increases. However, even if the projected goals are only partially achieved, the Indian software industry will still have achieved a substantial role in the world software industry, especially in customized software and software services. If the projected trends in demand for skilled workers hold, demographics alone should continue to ensure the survival and growth, albeit perhaps at a reduced rate of the Indian software services industry[9].

The Indian success story has, for the most part, been a combination of resource endowments (created in part by a policy of substantial investments in higher education), a mixture of benign neglect and active encouragement from a normally intrusive government and good timing. By the late 1980s, India was graduating approximately 150,000 English-speaking engineers and science graduates, with only a limited demand for their services from the rest of the economy[10]. By the late 1980s as well, India's economic liberalisation was also well under way. Around this time, the Information Technology revolution in the developed world had begun to take root and shortages of skilled programmers and IT professionals were beginning to develop. By this time a number of Indians were working in very substantial numbers in US firms. Some of them played an important, although as yet undocumented role, in bridging the gap and matching the buyers in the US with the suppliers in India. Responding quickly to the growing demand, a number of Indian firms arose in quick time. Contrary to its normal practice, the State encouraged this growth by considerably simplifying the process for obtaining the numerous clearances and permits that any firm in the organized sector in India typically needs[11].

Software development can be broadly categorized into custom developed software and packages or generic software products. Customized software development involves close interaction between the development team and the end-user. Typically, software companies that provide customized software concentrate on particular vertical market segments or domain areas, like retail, banking and manufacturing. The software developed is specific to those clients or domains. Software products may be targeted to a vertical segment or may cut across segments, but rarely to a specific user. In some cases, business software products, such as ERP packages that manage the flow of inputs, work in process and shipments in a company, are very large and complex. These require a great deal of customization before they can be used. Often, this customization is done by outside software consultants. Information Technology consultants, such as Anderson Consulting, provide "solutions", which may involve some combination of custom developed software and commercial off-the-shelf software and hardware products.

Software development involves a number of stages: Conceptualization, requirement analysis, high-level design, low-level design, coding, testing and support. These stages roughly correspond to stages described in the waterfall model of software development [12] (Figure 2.1) (Royce[13] 1970). The value added is typically greater in earlier stages of development - namely requirement analysis and high level design. Traditionally firms have designed the software in-house and outsourced the coding and support. However, increasingly, consulting firms are undertaking all stages of software development. As we discuss Indian software firms largely provide services rather than products. Further, Indian software exports consist largely of low-level design, coding and maintenance services.

A Historical Perspective

The Indian software industry consists of a large and growing number of firms: Using NASSCOM membership as a measure, the number of Indian software firms has grown from around 430 in 1996-97 to over 620 in 1997-98. Table 2.2 shows that many of these firms entered the industry during or just before the economic liberalisation in 1991 and few have exited. A few big companies, with a large fringe of small and medium sized companies dominate the industry. According to NASSCOM figures, the top 25 companies accounted for 58.67 per cent share of software exports revenue in 1997-98. Nearly one fourth of companies have sales of less than Rs.10 million (about $250,000).

The market leaders in the Indian software firms are, for the most part, relatively new themselves. What is more, with a few exceptions, notably Wipro and Satyam, these firms specialize in software alone. This is in marked contrast to early entrants into the industry, who had close links with computer hardware development. Heeks[14] (1996, p. 69) notes that Tata Consultancy Services, (TCS) was the first firm to agree to export software in return for being able to import hardware, in 1974. TCS, currently the largest Indian software firm, employs around 9000 people.[15] Once software exports took off, a large number of firms entered the industry. Entry barriers were low because firms could start small, since initial investments required were fairly small, little more than office space and communication facilities. With the growing need for maintenance services many firms began by providing these services, often by sending software programmers to the client on a temporary basis.

The entrants were of two types. The first type were existing firms diversifying into software. These included computer hardware firms, such as HCL and Wipro, as well as firms with large in-house data processing and system integration capabilities such as Larsen and Tubro (LTITL). There were others such as BFL, Sonata, Satyam and Birla Horizons that were, before their metamorphosis as software firms, divisions of large and medium industrial groups.[16] The other type of entrants was new start-ups, such as PCS, Datamatics, Infosys and Silverline. Current managers at a large number of software firms worked in these companies earlier in their career. Indeed, one of the best-known software exporters, Infosys was founded by a group of seven PCS managers who broke away from PCS. Infosys's first contract was a support and maintenance contract with a client in the apparel industry for whom PCS had finished a large project.

Entry strategies varied and not all firms entered to provide software export services. Some firms entered to develop packaged or shrink wrapped products, as well products for specific industries or products such as enterprise resource planning products, but by the early to mid 1990s, software service exports increased greatly in importance. The result was a great deal of turnover among the leading software firms in India, as shown by the table 2.1-2.2 below. Over the last couple of years, signs of maturity are appearing. Although entry in the industry still appears to be strong, there are suggestions that the market leaders are beginning to identify niches and areas of specialization, in terms of technologies or functions, as well as vertical domains (industrial sector). More recently, a couple of Indian firms, BFL and IIS Infotech, have been acquired by a Dutch bank and a British software service company respectively. However, a major consolidation still appears to be sometime away, in large measure because demand is still growing rapidly and economies of scale are relatively unimportant, particularly for low level coding and maintenance.

Contrary to popular belief, as table 2.3 shows, the industry is not concentrated in Bangalore, although Bangalore is certainly a very prominent location for firms in the industry. Instead, locations such as Mumbai, Pune, Chennai and Hyderabad are important as well. However, with the exception of the region around Delhi, there are no noticeable clusters in the northern or the eastern regions of India. The distribution of engineering colleges, concentrated in the western and southern regions, closely mirrors the distribution of the software industry. As table 2.4 shows, engineering colleges are heavily concentrated in these two regions, which also account for the greater part of employment in the Indian software industry.

The Brief International Comparison

The Indian industry is comparable to that of the Irish and Israeli software industries in terms of revenues and exports. However, the level of earnings per software professional appears to be substantially below that in Israel and Ireland. All three, India, Ireland and Israel, have some common characteristics including an abundant supply of manpower from a highly educated and relatively inexpensive, English speaking work force. Each country also has some special characteristics that have enabled it to emerge as significant players in the world software markets, albeit in different types of activities and domains. Table 2.5 shows the growth in exports and total revenues for the Israeli software industry. Israel has emerged as a source of entrepreneurial firms developing software *products* in areas such as security and anti-virus technology. There are about 300 software houses in Israel, employing nearly 20,000 people, with total revenue of over $1.5 billion. Many of these firms receive venture capital financing from the US and some are listed on the NASDAQ. A large fraction of the firms are engaged in developing software packages, often technically highly sophisticated, for export markets. Many of the world's largest computer companies including Microsoft, IBM, Digital, Hewlett Packard, National Semiconductor, Motorola and others have set up software development centers in Israel. IBM employs 300 scientists and engineers at its design facility in Haifa, while also in Haifa, Microsoft set up its first research and development facilities outside of the U.S. Motorola and National Semiconductor have major design centers in the country, while Intel is currently investing in its largest RandD center worldwide in Israel.

These features reflect the large number of technically skilled people with high entrepreneurial drive available in Israel. Reportedly, about 20 per cent of Israel's population consists of those who arrived in the last five years. These immigrants doubled the number of technicians, engineers and scientists. Israel now has 135 engineers and technicians for every 10,000 people[17], compared with only 18 for the U.S[18]. And venture capital has flowed. There are said to be over 50 venture capital funds operating in Israel and more than $4 billion was invested in high technology start-ups in Israel in 1998. Table 2.6a and 2.6b provide data on the growth in exports, total revenues, firms and employment in the Irish software industry. The Irish industry employs over 18,000 people, with 1997 revenues of over $1.5 billion as well. The software sector comprises more than 600 companies, of which about a fifth are overseas firms. The relatively high degree of foreign ownership, particularly among the larger establishments is consistent with Ireland's emergence as a favored location for multinational firms. Apart from a relatively large, relatively inexpensive, English speaking workforce, the attractions of Ireland include a variety of tax incentives and Ireland's membership in the EU (convenient for exports to other EU countries). As one might expect, nearly 70 per cent of Irish exports are to the EU, of which more than half are directed to the UK. Technology based sectors, notably electronics and software and chemicals account for 43 per cent and 25 per cent of Irish exports. The Irish software industry develops software products as well as provides a variety of software development and support services. A few Irish software firms are listed on NASDAQ and almost all the ancillary/support companies are accredited to the highest international standards, such as ISO 9000. With some exceptions, however, the Irish software industry does not appear to be as innovative or entrepreneurial as Israel.

Note that India has the largest number of people working in the industry as well as apparently the highest rate of growth of revenue, but also the lowest revenues per employee. Whereas the Irish and Israeli firms appear to earn as much as $100,000 per employee or more, firms in the Indian software industry earn only about $15,000- $20,000. This difference is a matter of some concern for managers and policy makers in India. The difference is particularly intriguing when one compares the Irish and Indian case. The Irish industry also appears to have a significant focus on software services and contract software development, somewhat similar to the Indian industry. Some of the difference may be due to the greater cultural similarity between Ireland and the US and Western Europe and the ability of Irish firms to operate in higher value added stages of the software development cycle. It may also be that the Irish software firms have been able to differentiate their services through domain or technological expertise, as compared to Indian firms, which have, until recently, been unable to distinguish themselves from their competitors.[19] If true, this would imply lower price cost margins and hence, lower revenues per employee for Indian firms. The low revenue per employee figure for Indian firms suggests that their customers are able to capture a substantial fraction of the value generated from the outsourcing.[20]

Specialised Organisations and Facilities of Information Technology Industry in India

NIC National Informatics Centre—Provides infrastructure and content for all Governmental activities. Connects all the administrative regions of the country upto microlevel.

NCST National Centre for Software Technology—High end Software Development and Training institution CDAC Centre for Development of Advanced Computing - Specialised in Very Massive Parallel Advanced Computing Technology up to 1 Trillion Tera Floating Operations Per Second (TFLOP).

CMC Limited—Premier Government Organisation for Software Products and Services - Established skills and products in Railway Reservations, Power sector management, Stock Exchanges and Banking products.

SCL Semiconductor Complex Limited—Specialising in Very Large Scale Integrated (VLSI) Circuit Design and Manufacture.

STQC Standardisation, Testing and Quality Certification agency—Institution dedicated to Standardisation and Quality Certification of IT products - Accreditation with over 13 countries globally including France, USA, Germany, Japan.

STPI Software Technology Parks of India—17 Specialised Zones for dedicated export of Software from the country - 1204 Exporting Units established - High Speed Data Communication Facilities upto 2 GBPS with 17 International Gateways.

ERNET Education and Research Network—Provides Network Services to Indian academic and research community.

ERDCI Electronics Research and Development Centre of India—Research organisation for development of new products and technologies in electronics.

Table 2.1: India: Growth in Domestic, Export and Total

Year	*Export in $M*	*Domestic Revenue $M*	*Total $M*
1993-94	330	227.9	557.9
1994-95	485	340.8	825.8
1995-96	734	515.4	1249.4
1996-97	1085	680.8	1765.8
1997-98	1800	900	2700
1998-99	2650	1250	3900
1999-00	4000	2000	6000
2000-01	6200	2060	8260
2001-02	8500	2700	11200

Source—NASSCOM

Table 2.2: India: manpower and Revenues/man-year

Year	*Manpower*	*Revenue/employee ($)*
1993-94	90000	6198.5
1994-95	118000	6998
1995-96	140000	8924.5
1996-97	160000	11036
1997-98(Est.)	180000	15000

Source–NASSCOM and CMU Software dataset.

Figure 2.1– The Waterfall Model of Software

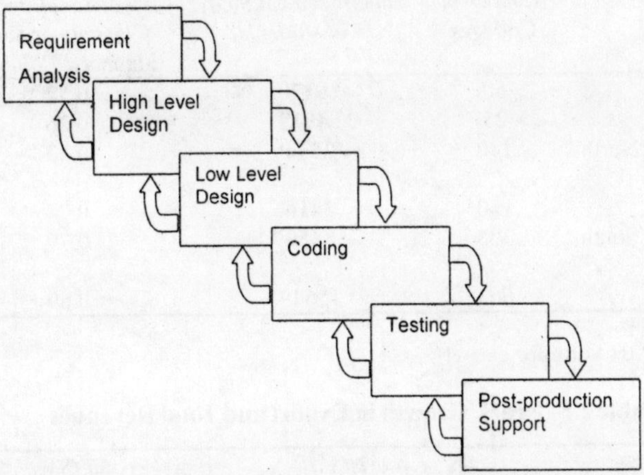

Source– Heeks[14](1996)

Table 2.3–Revenue distribution of Nasscom member firms (n=405) by geographic region, in 1997

Region	*Revenue($M)*	*Number*
Mumbai	539.8	86
Bangalore	323.6	84
New Delhi	152.9	72
Noida and Gurgaon	132.9	23
Chennai	130.9	34

Cont/.....

Region	*Revenue($M)*	*Number*
Hyderabad	62	21
Pune	57.7	21
Calcutta	44.8	26
Gujarat	3.1	13
Kerala	1.4	7
Other	8.3	18

Table 2.4–Number and capacity of Engineering Colleges in India, Approved up to 1998-1999, by region

Region	*Number of Colleges*	*Sanctioned Capacity (# of students)*	*% of Sanctioned Capacity at Self-Financed Colleges*
Central	50	9470	0.52
East	25	4812	0.26
North and North-West	140	25449	0.42
West	140	34165	0.74
South and South-West	308	82597	0.79
Total	663	156493	0.69

Source– CMU Software dataset.

Table 2.5–Israel: Growth in Export and Total Revenues

Year	*Exports($M)*	*Total ($M)*
1989	65	380
1990	89	450
1991	110	540
1992	135	600
1993	175	700
1994	220	800
1995	300	950
1996	400	1100
1997	540	1300
1998(Est.)	700	1500

Source– Israeli Association of Sotware Houses, Israel.

Table 2.6a– Ireland: Growth in Export and Total Revenue

Year	Exports($M)	Total ($M)
1991	2266.3	2436.7
1993	2594.5	2805.7
1995	3959.3	4221.3
1997	5942.5	6283.3

Source–National Software Directorate, Ireland.

Table 2.6b–Ireland: Employment and Number of firms

Year	No. of Firms	Total Employment
1991	365	7,793
1993	417	8,943
1995	483	11,784
1997	679	18,300

Source–National Software Directorate, Ireland.

Indian Federal Ministry of Information Technology

Over the last decade, the Indian Information Technology (IT) industry, particularly the software sector has grown in leaps and bounds. Industry revenues in this sector have grown more than ten fold from a mere US$ 50 million in 1988-89 to US$ 5.7 billion in 1999-2000. As a result, India has been acknowledged the world over as an important base for the growth and development of the IT industry.

In order to give a concerted and focused approach to developing this sector further, the Government of India has set-up a new Ministry of Information Technology (MIT) on October 15, 1999 to be the nodal institutional mechanism for facilitating all the initiative in the Central Government, the State Governments, Academia and the private sector for all round growth of Information Technology in the country. The Ministry of Information Technology seeks to play a role of being a pro-active facilitator, motivator, promoter and launch initiatives to ensure spread of IT to the masses, which would be the key for enabling speedy IT-led development[21].

Accordingly, the Ministry has targeted to implement a comprehensive action plan to make India an IT Superpower in the late part of this decade and achieve a target of $ 50 billion in software exports by 2008. It would take focused initiatives to accelerate the Internet revolution in India, emphasizing the creation of useful contents in Indian languages, IT-enabled services, IT education, electronics and computer hardware manufacturing and exports, silicon facility, E-Commerce and Internet based E-Businesses.

Vision of MIT— To make India a Global Information Technology power and one of the largest generators and exporters of software in the world by the year 2008. The vision translates into a mission - 'Move works to India'. The vision objectives are[22] :

1. Creation of Wealth,
2. Employment Generation,
3. IT led Economic Growth.

Time is of essence to accomplish our mission and the role of the Ministry of Information Technology would be to became a:

1. Pro-active facilitator,
2. Pro-active motivator,
3. Pro-active promoter,
4. Spread of IT to masses speedily and
5. To ensure speedy IT led development.

Key Responsibility—The key responsibilities of the Ministry relating to realisation of the Vision are :

1. All Policy matters relating to IT,
2. Promotion of Knowledge based Enterprises, Internet, e-Commerce, IT education and IT based education,
3. Development of Electronics,
4. Development of Microelectronics and Silicon facility,
5. Promotion of Information Technology and Standardisation,
6. National Informatics Centre (NIC),
7. Electronics and Computer Software Export Promotion Council (ESC).

Recent Initiatives to Accomplish the Vision Policy

Measures: A number of key initiatives have already been taken with regard to the fulfilment of the set vision. This started with the setting up of the National Task Force on Information Technology and Software

Development and a Special Subject Group on Knowledge-based Industries under the Prime Minister's Advisory Councils. This has been closely followed by a wide array of policy measures crafted to provide a vibrant enabling environment for the growth of Information Technology in the country. Some of the key initiatives taken with a view to leverage the Indian capabilities into an 'Advantage India' [23]strategy relate to financial sector reforms like liberalised norms for investments of upto 100 per cent foreign equity with full repatriation benefits, tax holiday for IT units to be set up in Software Technology Parks upto 2010, providing a complete pass through mechanism with single-point taxation for Venture Capital funds, encouragement to RandD through tax holiday of up to 10 years, growth of companies through acquisitions by ADR/GDR of up to 10 times the exports value, sweat equity, stock options and minimal taxation of these at a single point only, enhancemed rate of depreciation on computers, separate guidelines for sanction of working capital finance to the software industry, setting up of IT Venture Capital Fund, fast-track clearance of goods imported by manufacturers of electronic goods, simplification and liberalisation of Export and Import policy and procedures for implementation of the export oriented schemes.

A number of initiatives have also been taken in the telecom sector so as to enable commensurate growth of the telecom infrastructure, for growth of Information Technology. Some key steps are participation of the private sector in providing fixed, mobile and satellite based communication infrastructure in the country, revenue based sharing with up to 74 per cent equity investment in satellite based projects, liberalised access to foreign satellites, opening up of international gateways and laying of optic-fibre network for promoting broad-band internet services[24]. The focus is on to enable concerted convergence of IT, telecom, consumer electronics and entertainment media. Opening up of international and national long distance to the private sector is also a key agenda for the immediate future.

A target of achieving PC penetration of 20 per thousand, TV penetration of 225 and fixed telephony penetration of 125 per thousand has been set to be achieved by the year 2008. The entire effort required would open up widespread opportunities for investment and markets. It is estimated that the country would require investment of close to US$ 16 billion with a total equipment requirement of US$ 160 by the year 2008[25].

Advisory Committee for Ministry of Information Technology

An Advisory Committee for the Ministry comprising of well known professionals from Indian IT industry was set up on January .17, 2000 under the Chairmanship of Minister of Information Technology. The Advisory Committee is to assist Ministry of Information Technology to identify thrust/emerging technology areas and to suggest measures/ policies/actions for making Indian IT industry a Global Superpower.

A Select Group comprising of successful and well known IT professionals based at Silicon Valley has also been formed under the Chairmanship of Minister of Information Technology. The Group will advise the Government on various issues relating to development of IT, telecommunication infrastructure and software export from the country.

Electronic Commerce - Information Technology Bill

Electronic Commerce permits individuals and companies to directly make all financial transactions electronically. Electronic Commerce is growing at a rapid pace. To facilitate Electronic Commerce, MIT has drafted an 'Information Technology (IT) Bill'. The Bill provides legal framework for recognition of electronic contracts, prevention of computer crimes, electronic filing of documents, etc. Amendments have been proposed in the Indian Evidence Act, Indian Penal Code and RBI Act. The mechanism of digital signature has been proposed to address the issues of jurisdiction, authentication and origination. The Information Technology Bill has been introduced in the Lok Sabha on December 16, 1999 and referred to Standing Committee. It is likely to be passed in the Budget Session of the Parliament.

A series of initiatives have been taken to develop road map for India initiative in e-Commerce. These include - Information and Communication technology infrastructure, Legal and Regulatory Framework, Technology for e-commerce including test-beds, IPR, issues related to international domain names, etc. To set up the mechanism and infrastructure for implementation of Cyber laws, Ministry of Information Technology has funded a project to develop technology for issue of digital signature certificate and procedure for certification authorities and other security guidelines. A project on electronic copyright system is underway to develop image water marking technology.

The Semiconductor Integrated Circuits Layout Design Bill

Government of India has ratified the Agreement on Trade Related aspects of Intellectual Property Rights (TRIPs) of the World Trade

Organisation (WTO) as a result of the Uruguay Round of Multi-Lateral Trade Negotiations. As a part of the TRIPS, a law has to be enacted with regard to Layout-Designs of Integrated Circuits. Ministry of Information Technology has evolved the Semiconductor Integrated Circuits Layout-Design Bill which is a sui-generis legislation. The Bill was introduced in the Rajya Sabha on December 20,1999. It is likely to be passed in the Budget Session of the Parliament[26].

Venture Capital Fund

Recognising the importance of Venture Capital Funding, the Ministry of Information Technology has set up a National Venture Fund for Software and IT Industry with a corpus of Rs. 100 crores[27] in association with Small Industries Development Bank of India (SIDBI) and Industrial Development Bank of India (IDBI). The aim of the Fund is to provide Venture Capital to start up software professionals and IT units in the small scale sector. The Venture Capital Fund was launched on December 10, 1999 by the Prime Minister. The Fund has a two-tier structure with a separate Trustee Company and a professionally managed Asset Management Company (AMC)[28].

Electronic Governance

The trends in Information Technology have brought about a new set of services and has transformed the traditional services in terms of fast delivery. Governments around the world have used advances in IT to provide better services to citizens and businesses. The Ministry of Information Technology has initiated institutional mechanisms to facilitate initiatives towards greater utilisation of IT as an enabling tool for efficiency and effectiveness in Government. Three test-beds in the area of electronic governance have been initiated in close association with Government of Andhra Pradesh. Experience of these test-beds in Andhra Pradesh could be used by other States for replication.

National Task Force on Information Technology and Software Development

The National Task Force on Information Technology and Software Development set up by the Prime Minister's Office in May, 1998 submitted the reports in three parts. The first report of 108 recommendations was accepted by the Government. These recommendations relate to telecommunication policies and procédures, cyber laws, labour laws for IT industry, fiscal incentives and financial matters, promotion of IT in schools and rural areas, increase in computer literacy and computer penetration in the country. Out of the 108 recommendations, 56 have already been implemented and 22 are in the nature of 'ongoing' and are being implemented in phases[29]

Moving up in the Value Chain

India's strength is well recognised in customised software development. In order to make a significant impact in the area of development of products and packages, the thrust shall be on technology adoption programs, setting up of Innovation Centers/ Development Centres and high end manpower development.

IT Enabled Services

IT Enabled Services have been recognised as a major opportunity for employment and foreign exchange earning for India. The IT Enabled Services include On-line information and help support through Call Centres; Medical Transcription; Back Office Operations, Revenue Accounting and other ancillary operations; Insurance claims processing; Legal databases; Content development; Payroll and Logistics management, besides others. India offers many advantages to serving as an IT Enabled Services destination for major global Companies, which includes a virtual 12-hour time zone difference with USA and other major markets for IT Enabled Services, a huge pool of English speaking and computer literate graduate manpower, the cost of qualified personnel being amongst the most competitive in the world.

PC Penetration

Penetration of personal computers is an indicator of the diffusion of IT in various sectors of the economy. It is planned to increase PC penetration in India from the present level of 3.43 per thousand to 20 per thousand by 2008[30]. To meet this objective, personal computers have been made freely importable, customs duties on import of PCs are being lowered and the MIT is promoting development of IT tools in various Indian languages.

Human Resource Development

In order to enable an export of US$ 50 billion of computer software and IT enabled services by the year 2008, a work force of over two million

IT professionals will be required. The country today produces nearly 2,00,000 [31] graduate Engineers in all disciplines. Promotion of Human Resource Development is being achieved through implementation of the National Software Capability Enhancement Programme, National Centre for Software Technology (NCST), Centre for Electronics Design and Technology (CEDT), Setting up of Indian Institutes of Information Technology (IIITs), Special programme for generation of trained manpower in the area of VLSI design, Higher-end human resource development for Information Technology, IT enabled distance education for IT Sector, DOEACC Scheme and Project IMPACT (Industry oriented Manpower with Appropriate Competence and Training) [32].

Software Capability Enhancement

For upgrading the quality of Indian Software industry to international standard, the Ministry of Information Technology has initiated a programme for Software Capability Enhancement namely, Soft Cap in association with Carnegie Mellon University (CMU), USA.

Infrastructure

The Ministry of Information Technology has initiated a national focus on National Information Infrastructure with the aim of promoting use and proliferation of Information Technology. Strengthening of infrastructure is being achieved through major expansion and growth of international gateways by the Software Technology Parks of India (STPI); Advanced Technology Programme in Computer Networking (ATPCN), Society through network for distance learning programme, test-bed for applications like E-Commerce and Electronic Governance, installation of VSATs and the seven Gateways; and Standardisation, Testing and Quality Certification Directorate (STQCD), which provides one-stop solution to all quality related requirements of electronics industry through its 22 Labs spread all over the country [33].

Internet Bandwidth

The bandwidth requirement for Internet is estimated to be 4000 Mbps by 2001 and 15000 Mbps by 2008. Another 10000 Mbps bandwidth would be required by 2008 for software exports and IT enabled services. In comparison to this, bandwidth available today is only a few hundred Mbps. No single service provider or media (Terrestrial/Satellite) can meet this demand. There is a need for enhancement in Terrestrial and Satellite infrastructure and multiple service providers. Internet Service Providers (ISP) have been permitted to set-up international gateways and hire bandwidth on foreign satellites. This will enable the increased availability of Internet bandwidth and will facilitate Internet expansion in the country.

Technology Development

The MIT has been giving high priority to technology development in the country. The technology development programme of the MIT has resulted in development of state-of- the-art parallel supercomputer (PARAM), Gigantic Radar for atomospheric dynamic studies, Data handling and security system covering Radar and communication, Global positioning system components, Linear Accelerator for cancer therapy, Instrumentation for semiconductor industry such as Molecular Beam Epitaxy, Fingerprint analysis and criminal tracking system, Commissioning of HVDC line of 200 MW/200 KV, Automatic drip irrigation system, Agri-instrumentation systems, Water treatment plant automation, IT tools for watershed development, Low cost multimedia content creation and Technology Development for Indian languages, besides others. The Ministry of Information Technology organises an Exhibition-cum-Seminar (ELITEX) for showcasing the technologies/products/services developed by various organisations of the Ministry. ELITEX' 2000 was organised from January 31-February 1, 2000.

Application Development

Promotion of applications of electronics and Information Technology has been the thrust area of MIT. Significant achievements have been made under the Industrial electronics promotion programme, Transport and power distribution programme, Electronics in power/energy sector programme, Electronics and healthcare programme, Development programme on intelligent manufacturing systems and Electronics for rural/social/agri/water sector programme of the Ministry.

2.2 IT Policies of India and States

The Indian government recognizes that Information Technology will influence economic development extensively in the future. In view of its importance, the government instituted a task force- National Task Force on Information Technology and Software Development. The task force was given the responsibility to recommend the steps that the government needs to take to remove bottlenecks and boost IT within the country.

The continuing liberalisation and economic reforms programme of the Government of India since 1991 aims at rapid and substantial economic growth and integration with the global economy in a harmonised manner. The new policies have made governmental procedures transparent, eliminated licensing in almost all sectors and provide encouragement to entrepreneurship through market friendly systems.

Industrial Approval Policy[34]

1. Industrial Licensing has been virtually abolished in the electronics sector except for manufacturing electronic aerospace and defence equipment.
2. There is no reservation for public sector enterprises in the electronics industry and private sector investment is welcome in every area.
3. Electronics industry can be set up anywhere in the country, subject to clearance from the authorities responsible for control of environmental pollution and local zoning and land use regulations.
4. Industries exempted from licensing are only required to file information in the prescribed Industrial Entrepreneurs Memorandum (IEM) with the Secretariat for Industrial Assistance (SIA), Ministry of Industry, Government of India.
5. For the aforesaid licensable electronic industries, all applications have to be made in prescribed format and sent to :

The Entrepreneurial Assistance Unit (EAU)— Secretariat for Industrial Assistance (SIA), Department for Industrial Policy and Promotion Ministry of Industry, Udyog Bhawan, New Delhi-110011

Foreign Investment Policy—Government of India facilitates Foreign Direct Investment (FDI) and investment from Non-Resident Indians (NRIs) including Overseas Corporate Bodies (OCBs), predominantly owned by them, to complement and supplement domestic investment. Foreign technology induction is encouraged both through FDI and through foreign technology collaboration agreements. Foreign Direct Investment and Foreign technology collaboration agreements can be approved either through the automatic route under powers delegated to the Reserve Bank of India (RBI) or otherwise by the Government.

Automatic Approval—In pursuance of Government's commitment to early implementation of the second phase of the economic reforms and with a view to further liberalising the FDI regime, all items/ activities have been placed under the automatic route for FDI/NRI and OCB investment, except the following:

(i) All proposals that require an Industrial Licence which includes (a) the item requiring an Industrial Licence under the Industries (Development and Regulation) Act, 1951; (b) foreign investment being more than 24 per cent in the equity capital of units manufacturing items reserved for small scale industries; and (c) all items which require an Industrial Licence in terms of the locational policy notified by Government under the New Industrial Policy[35] of 1991.

(ii) All proposals in which the foreign collaborator has a previous venture/tieup in India.

(iii) All proposals relating to acquisition of shares in an existing Indian company in favour of a foreign/NRI/OCB investor.

(iv) All proposals falling outside notified sectoral policy/caps or under sectors in which FDI is not permitted and /or whenever any investor chooses to make an application to the FIPB and not to avail of the automatic route.

All proposals for investment in public sector unit, as also for EOU/ EPZ/EHTP/STP units would qualify for automatic route subject to the above parameters. The modalities and procedures for automatic route would remain the same and RBI would continue to be concerned agency for monitoring /reporting as per existing procedure. FDI/NRI/OCB investment under the automatic route shall continue to be governed by the notified sectoral policy and equity caps[36].

Foreign Technology Collaboration Agreements—RBI also gives automatic approval for foreign technology collaboration agreements in all areas of Electronics and Information Technology, except electronic aerospace and defence equipment, provided:

(i) Lump sum payment of the price of the technology does not exceed USD 2 million.

(ii) Royalty payments do not exceed 5 per cent for domestic sales and 8 per cent for exports. (The royalty rates are net of taxes).

The payments are subject to an overall ceiling of 8 per cent of total sales over a period of 10 years from the date of agreement or over 7 years period from the date of commencement of commercial production, whichever is earlier.

Government approval— The FDI/ Foreign technology collaboration agreement proposals which do not conform to the guidelines for automatic approval require Government approval through the Foreign Investment Promotion Board (FIPB). The Government has set up a special 'Foreign Investment Promotion Board' (FIPB) as a fast track mechanism to invite and facilitate foreign investments in large projects in India, which are considered beneficial to the Indian economy but are not covered by the automatic approval process and norms under which SIA is authorised to grant investment approvals.

Export - Import Policy

As per the current export-import Policy, effective for 5 years from April 1, 1997, capital goods, raw materials, intermediates, components, consumables, spares, parts, accessories, instruments and other goods may be imported without any restriction except to the extent such imports are regulated by the book titled 'ITC (HS) Classification of Export and Import Items'. Import of the restricted items is allowed against an import licence. Specified items can be imported against Special Import License (SIL) issued to the exporters of electronics and telecommunication goods and services including software and also to Export Houses/Trading Houses/Star Trading Houses/Super Star Trading Houses against their export performance.[37]

Export Promotion Schemes

Special Schemes for Electronics Hardware and Software—Special schemes are available for setting up Export Oriented units for the electronics sector. Foreign Investment of upto 100 per cent is permitted in units set up solely for exports. Various incentives and concessions are available for export oriented units. These schemes are:

- 100 per cent Export Oriented Units (EOUs)/Export Processing Zone (EPZ) Scheme.
- Electronics Hardware Technology Parks Scheme (EHTP).
- Software Technology Parks Scheme (STP).

Export Promotion Capital Goods (Epcg) Scheme—To encourage export of goods and services, capital goods are allowed to be imported at 5 per cent customs duty subject to an export obligation equivalent to 5 times CIF value of capital goods on FOB Basis or 4 times the CIF value of capital goods on NFE basis to be fulfilled over a period of 8 years, reckoned from the date of issuance of licence.[38]

Deemed Exports—The following categories of supply of goods by the main/sub-contractors shall be regarded as 'Deemed Exports' under the Export-Import Policy, provided the goods are manufactured in India[39]:

(a) Supply of goods against duty free licences/DFRC under the Duty Exemption / Remission Scheme.

(b) Supply of goods to Export Oriented Units (EOUs) or units located in Export Processing Zones (EPZs) or Special Economic Zones (SEZs) or Software Technology Parks (STPs) or to Electronic Hardware Technology Parks (EHTPs).

(c) Supply of capital goods to holders of licences under the Export Promotion Capital Goods (EPCG) scheme.

(d) Supply of goods to projects financed by multilateral or bilateral agencies/funds as notified by the Department of Economic Affairs, Ministry of Finance under International Competitive Bidding in accordance with the procedures of those agencies/ funds, where the legal agreements provide for tender evaluation without including the customs duty.

(e) Supply of capital goods, including in unassembled/ disassembled condition as well as plants, machinery, tools, dies and such goods which are used for installation purposes till the stage of commercial production and spares to the extent of 10 per cent of the FOR value to fertilizer plants.

(f) Supply of goods to any project or purpose in respect of which the Ministry of Finance, by a notification, permits the import of such goods at zero customs duty coupled with the extension of deemed export benefits to domestic supplies.

(g) Supply of goods to the power and refineries not covered in (f) above and coal, hydrocarbon, rail, road, port, civil aviation, bridges and other infrastructure projects provided minimum specific investment is Rs. 1000 million or more.

(h) Supply of marine freight containers by 100 per cent EOU (Domestic freight containers-manufacturers) provided the said containers are exported out of India within 6 months or such further period as permitted by the Customs.

(i) Supply to projects funded by UN agencies.

Duty/Tariff Structure—In the 2000-01 Budget for the Electronics and IT sector, Customs Duty has been rationalised by reducing 5 slabs of ad-valorem rates to 4 slabs of 5, 15, 25 and 35 per cent. The Special Additional Duty (SAD) @ of 4 per cent continues. The capital goods and most of the raw materials and components required by the electronic industry are allowed to be imported under concessional rate of customs duty. Maximum tariff duty levied on electronic equipment is 35 per cent. Customs duty on specified capital goods for semiconductor manufacture is 5 per cent or nil. IT software continues to be exempt from Customs Duty. Computer software has also been exempted from service tax. In addition to the basic customs duty, imports are also subject to a Countervailing Duty (CVD) and Surcharge on basic duty @10 per cent, wherever applicable. The tariff levels are gradually being brought in line with the average international levels in a phased manner. India is also signatory to the Information Technology Agreement (ITA). The Central Excise duty has been rationalised to a single slab rate of 16 per cent.

Incentives to Electronics and IT Sector[40]

- Export Promotion Capital Goods scheme (EPCG) has been rationalised and extended uniformly to all sectors without any threshold limit on payment of 5 per cent duty. Units in electronics and software sectors have option to apply for EPCG Licence to the competent authority on the basis of self-declaration regarding the nexus between the CG to be imported with the items to be exported.
- Foreign investment of upto 100 per cent is permitted in units set up solely for exports on automatic route. Various incentives are available for export-oriented units, which include duty free imports of capital goods, raw-materials, components and other inputs, tax holidays against export and access to the domestic market. Such units can be set up under any of the schemes,

viz., Electronics Hardware Technology Park (EHTP), Software Technology Park (STP), Export Processing Zone (EPZ) and 100 per cent Export Oriented Units (EOUs).

- EHTP and STP schemes are implemented under the aegis of the Ministry of Information Technology through a single window mechanism of the Inter-Ministerial Standing Committee (IMSC).
- In order to provide single window service, powers of approval of the Designated Officers of MIT for implementation of STP/EHTP schemes have been further enhanced. They can now approve setting up of STP/EHTP units where foreign exchange required for import of capital goods (net of taxes) is upto US$ 20 million.
- Special Economic Zones shall be set up enabling hassle free manufacturing and trading for export purposes. The units in these zones shall be treated as being outside the customs territory of the country. The units in these Zones shall not be subjected to any pre-determined value addition, export obligation, input output/wastage norms. Sale in Domestic Tariff Area by the units in these Zones will be permitted only on payment of full Customs Duty.
- Import of second hand capital goods which are less than 10 years old will be allowed to be imported without obtaining any licence, on surrender of SIL.
- A special stock option scheme for Indian Software Companies linked with ADR/GDR offerings by these companies, as an instrument to enable these companies to provide incentives to retain their highly skilled professionals, has been notified. Employee Stock Option Plans (ESOPs) shall be taxed @10 per cent at the time of their sale only. The capital gains tax would be applicable on the difference between the sale price and the issue price.
- RBI has framed Guidelines for sanction of working capital finance to Information Technology and software industry.
- Provision for issue of Sweat Equity by companies has been introduced in the Companies (Amendment) Act, 1999.

- A National Venture Fund for Software and IT Industry (NFSIT) has been set up with a corpus of Rs. 100 crore, out of which MIT's contribution is Rs. 30 crore.
- Accelerated depreciation norms for computers and computer peripherals for electronic units under Export Oriented schemes (EOU/EPZ/STP/EHTP) enhanced in the EXIM Policy applicable w.e.f 1.4.2000. These shall stand depreciated to overall limit of 90 per cent over a period of 3 years instead of around 5 years earlier.
- EOU/EPZ/STP/EHTP units are exempted from payment of Income Tax on export profits, upto 2010.
- DTA access upto 50 per cent of the FOB value of export is permitted for electronics hardware units under EOU/EPZ/EHTP schemes and the software units under EOU/EPZ/STP schemes. Broadbanding is permitted in the DTA sales of Hardware manufactured by EHTP units for items covered in the Letter of Permission.
- The procedures for operation of the units in the EHTP/EOU/EPZ/STP schemes have been simplified considerably and a number of operations have been permitted on the basis of self certification.
- Manufacturers - importers of Electronics goods having investment of Rs. 3 crore and above and units in EPZs/EHTP and STP are eligible for fast-track clearance of goods imported by them.
- Post-export duty free replenishment licence scheme for enabling import of inputs on the basis of input-output norms introduced in the Exim policy applicable w.e.f 1.4.2000. The Scheme would be available for more than 5000 such items where input output norms exist and on the basis of uniform value addition of 33 per cent.
- Value addition norms for Rupee exports to Russia reduced from 100 per cent to 33 per cent under Advance Licensing Scheme.
- The Depreciation on Computers has been allowed @ 60 per cent.

- In the 2000-01 Budget, Customs duty on Computers and Peripherals has been reduced from 20 per cent to 15 per cent. The Customs duty on all storage devices, integrated circuits, microprocessors, Data display tubes and Deflection components of colour monitors has been reduced to NIL rate.
- Information Technology Software is exempted from Customs Duty.
- Definition of Computer Software, as in Section 80 HHE of the Income Tax Act has been widened to include transmission of data.
- Benefit of Section 80 HHE is available to supporting software developers.
- Exemption of withholding tax on interest on External Commercial Borrowings (ECBs) has been extended to the IT sector.
- Computer systems are freely importable.
- The donation of computers, imported duty free by EOU/EPZ/STP/EHTP units to recognised non-commercial educational institutions, registered charitable hospitals, public libraries, public funded research and development establishments, etc., two years after their use by the said units has been permitted.
- The second-hand computers and computer peripherals donated by an outside donor to Government schools have been exempted from customs duties.
- Income by way of dividends or long-term capital gains of a Venture Capital Fund or Venture Capital company from investment made by way of equity shares in a Venture Capital Undertaking, which has been expanded to include the Software and IT sectors, will henceforth not be included in computing the total income.
- To give thrust to Venture Capital finance, SEBI has been made the single point nodal agency for registration and regulation of both domestic and overseas venture capital funds.
- There will be no tax on distributed or undistributed income of Venture Capital Funds. The income distributed by the VCFs

will only be taxed in the hands of the investors at the rates applicable to the nature of the income.

- Under policy on portfolio investment, Foreign Institutional Investors (FIIs) are permitted to invest in a company upto an aggregate of 24 per cent of equity shares, extendable upto 30 per cent subject to approvals. This limit has been raised from 30 per cent to 40 per cent in the Budget 2000-01.
- Under the Employee Stock Option Scheme, income tax payable on income from GDRs purchased in foreign currency by a resident employee of IT software and service companies, shall be at a concessional rate of 10 per cent.
- To induce more investment for RandD activities, a weighted deduction of 125% on the sums paid to any university, college or an institution or a Scientific research association for the purposes of scientific, social or statistical research has been provided.

Revised Exim Policy and Procedures for Electronics and IT Industry[41]

The revised EXIM Policy and Procedures, 1997-2002 have come in force w.e.f April 1, 2000. The highlights of the revised EXIM Policy and Procedures for the Electronics and Information Technology Sector are as under:

Special Economic Zones shall be set up enabling hassle free manufacturing and trading for export purposes. The units in these Zones shall not be subjected to any pre-determined value addition, export obligation, input output/wastage norms. The units in these zones shall be treated as being outside the customs territory of the country. Sale in Domestic Tariff Area by the units in these Zones will be permitted only on payment of full Customs Duty.

- Export Promotion Capital Goods scheme (EPCG) rationalised and extended uniformly to all sectors without any threshold limit, on payment of 5 per cent duty. Earlier, software units were allowed import of capital goods above Rs. 10 Lakhs (cif) at Nil duty and for hardware units the CG import limit for Nil duty was Rs. 1 crore (cif). No additional customs duty/countervailing duty is required to be paid. In all cases, export obligation fulfilment period has been extended to 8 years.

- Import of second hand capital goods not more than 10 years old has been allowed without obtaining any licence, on surrender of SIL.
- Pre-export DEPB scheme and Special Advance Licensing scheme for export of electronic products abolished because very few exporters were using these schemes.
- Quantitative Restrictions (QRs) removed on 714 Tariff lines. The QRs on remaining 715 tariff lines shall be removed w.e.f 1.4.2001. The grant of SIL will be discontinued after 31.3.2001. All items which are under SIL will now be importable on surrender of SIL equivalent to 5 times of CIF value of imported goods.
- Prominent Electronic items which have been made freely importable are CD players, Colour Picture Tubes, Populated PCBs, Microwave Ovens, Pocket sized radio cassette players, Projection TVs, Loudspeakers and Push button telephones, etc.
- Import restrictions continue on Colour TVs, BandW TVs, Cassette players, Radio receivers, Car radios/cassette players, Amplifiers, etc.
- Powers of Designated Officers for approval of units under STP/EHTP schemes enhanced to projects involving US$ 20 million worth of imported capital goods, from US$ 10 million.
- EOU/EPZ/STP/EHTP units have been permitted import of Diesel Generating Sets, Uninterrupted Power Supplies, Air-conditioners, Computer furniture, Security systems, Office equipment including PABX, Fax machines and Video projection systems. Earlier these were being permitted on a case-to-case basis.
- Accelerated depreciation norms for computers and computer peripherals for electronic units under Export Oriented schemes (EOU/EPZ/STP/EHTP) enhanced. These shall stand depreciated to overall limit of 90 per cent over a period of 3 years instead of around 5 years earlier.

- EOU/EPZ/EHTP/STP units may install personal computers not exceeding two in number, imported/procured duty free in their registered/administrative office subject to the guidelines issued by Department of Revenue in this behalf.
- Post-export duty free replenishment licence scheme for enabling import of inputs on the basis of input-output norms introduced. The Scheme would be available for more than 5000 such items where input output norms exist and on the basis of uniform value addition of 33 per cent.
- Advance Licence for physical exports, Advance Licence for domestic supply and Advance Licence for intermediate supply for exports will be subject to actual user condition and non-transferable. The Advance Licence for physical export and for intermediate supply for exports will be exempted from payment of all kinds of duties like Basic, ACD, SAD, Antidumping, Safeguard duty. Advance Licence for annual requirement will continue.
- The post-export Duty Entitlement Pass Book (DEPB) would continue till 31.3.2002, i.e. by 2002, the DEPB Scheme would be subsumed into the Drawback Scheme. The threshold limit of Rs. 200 million for fixing new DEPB rates stands removed, thereby making DEPB more accessible. For all products, DEPB rates of 15 per cent or more value caps would be prescribed, but value caps would not apply to products being exported under brand names approved by an Inter-Ministerial Committee.
- Double weightage would be granted on FOB or NFE on exports made by units having ISO or equivalent status for granting status certification.
- A small group would be set up to look into various policy and procedural changes that are required to be introduced, so as to step up the growth of electronics hardware sector.

Procedural Simplifications

- Duty exemption licence facility on the basis of self-declaration extended to deemed exports as well as intermediate supplies.

- Registration-cum-Membership Certificate shall now be required to be filed once in 4 years instead of with each application.
- Powers to issue Trading House Certificate delegated to regional licensing authorities.

The Government of India has announced IT as a thrust area. Accordingly, it provides for more liberal policy framework for the sector. The following are some of the important policy notifications. They have been classified into following categories:

- Customs (Import Duty) related issues
- Income Tax related issues
- Exim Policy related issues
- Reserve Bank of India related issues
- Excise rates related issues
- Indian Copyright Act, 1957 (and as amended in 1994/95)

One of the major factors of excellent and consistent growth of Indian software industry can be attributed to continuous liberalisation of policies of Government of India. The industry (Nasscom) and the government has worked together in close cooperation. During 1991, Nasscom lobbied with the Government and for the first time, secured income tax exemption from profits of software exports. Later, Government, systematically and gradually, reduced import duty on computer software from a high 114 per cent to nil. Copyright laws were also amended. We are enlisting here, some of the fiscal and non-fiscal incentives provided by the Government of India to IT software and services industry.[42]

Customs (Import Duty) Related Issues

1. Zero Import Duty on Computer Software—There is NIL customs duty on import of I.T. Software into India. Further, there is no applicability of Special Additional Customs Duty (SAD) on I.T. Software. Also, since there is no duty on "I.T. Software", there is no applicability of surcharge. For this purpose, I.T. Software has been defined as under: "Information Technology Software means any representation of instructions, data, sound or image, including source code and object code, recorded in a machine readable form and capable of being manipulated or providing inter-activity to a user by means of an automatic data processing machine."[43]

2. Zero Import Duty on Computer Software License—Department of Revenue, Ministry of Finance, Customs Notification No.46/98 dated 16 July 1998. Exim Policy 1998, incorporated a new entry for "Licence to Use" of computer software as "all documents of title for use of software issued by software company" under the ITC HS Classification No. 4907 00.20.

1. "Licences" of computer software can now imported separately (if desired with or without the software on media) without any import licence from DGFT.
2. Books, magazines and periodicals on CD-ROM are exempt from Import Duty. CD-ROMs containing books of educational nature, journals, periodicals or newspapers are exempt from import duty or SAD.[44]
3. Donation of computers and peripherals from EOU/EPZ/STP/EHTP at zero duty. Units in EOU/EPZ/STP/EHTP can donate (at zero import duty) computers and peripherals after two years of import and use to recognised non-commercial educational institutions, registered charitable hospitals, public libraries, public funded research and development establishments, organisations of Government of India, or Government of State or Union Territory.[45]
4. Duty is exempted on import of second hand computers and peripherals received by schools as donation from a donor outside India.[46]

Income Tax[47]

5. Profits derived from export of software (including some of IT Enabled services) are exempt from Income Tax under Section 80HHE of the Income Tax Act. Accordingly, computer software and software developed through on-site, off-shore and physical exports are exempted subject to various provisions contained in Section 80 HHE of the Income Tax Act. The definition of "Computer Software" in Section 80 HHE of the Income Tax Act, was further amended during 1998 enlarging its scope. According to this section of Income Tax Act, "Computer Software" means any computer programme recorded on any disc, tape, perforated media or other

information storage device and includes any such programme or any customised electronic data which is transmitted from India to a place outside India by any means." I.T. enabled services like data entry, revenue accounting, back office operations, medical transcription etc. may now claim 100 per cent tax exemption under Section 80 HHE of the Income Tax Act.

6. Benefits under Section 80 HHE of Income Tax Act is also available to sub-contractors.[48]

7. A ten year income tax holiday is available under Section 10A/10B of Income Tax Act. Accordingly, units which have begun or begins to manufacture computer software commencing on or after April 1, 1981 in any free trade zone, or commencing on or after April 1, 1994 in any electronic hardware technology park or software technology park or commencing on or after April 2001 in any special economic zone may avail of Income Tax holiday. No deduction under this section will be available from the assessment year 2010-11 onwards. Existing units which commenced operations prior to April 1, 2000 and were entitled to exemption under this section up to the assessment year 2000-01, are entitled to exemption under the new provisions for the unexpired period. For the purposes of Section 10A and 10B, 'Computer software' means

   - Any computer program recorded on any disc, tape, perforated media or other information storage device; or
   - Any customised electronic data or any product or service of similar nature, as may be notified by the Board.

which is transmitted or exported from India to any place outside India by any means. The definition of 'computer software' has been broadened and includes IT Enabled services like data processing, call center operation etc.

8. Depreciation on computers at 60 per cent. Central Board of Direct Taxes, Department of Revenue, Ministry of Finance Notification dated 4 September 1998. Government of India has raised the maximum depreciation for computers to 60 per cent. Therefore, as per the written down value method, 84 per cent of cost of the computers can be depreciated in first 2 years.

9. Incentives for Venture Capital Fund and Venture Capital Company. Accordingly, a complete pass through has been provided on distribution of income as well as undistributed income by the Venture Capital Company or Venture Capital Fund under Section 115U. Further, any income on any investments made in Venture Capital Undertaking will qualify for exemption under Section 10(23FB).
10. Beneficiary of Employee Stock Option Plan to be taxed only at the time of sale as Capital Gains. In case of ESOP/ESOS, the beneficiary will be taxed only at the time of sale and that also as Capital Gains. However, ESOP will attract Capital Gains even if it is given as gift. In this connection, revised Section 17 and 48 of the Income Tax Act refers.

Exim Policy Related Issues

11. Exim Policy 1999 allows import of all kinds of computers in India without obtaining any licenses. Prior to 1999, this was not allowed.
12. Definition of "Services" to include all tradable services covered under General Agreement on Trade in Services (GATS). Exim Policy 1999. "Services" to include
    (a) consultancy services related to installation of computer software
    (b) Software implementation services
    (c) Data processing services
    (d) Database services
    (e) Others

"Service Provider" defined as providing

(a) Supply of a service from India to any other country
(b) Supply of a service from India to the service consumer of any other country in India
(c) Supply of a service from India through commercial or physical presence in the territory of any other country.

13. Capital goods can be imported free of cost or on loan from clients for approved activity by EOUs and units operating in EPZ/STP/EHTP. (Exim Policy 1997-2002 announced on 1st April 1999).
14. 5 per cent Duty EPCG Scheme for software sector (minimum threshold of capital goods of Rs.10 lakhs removed). (Exim Policy 1998). The Exim Policy allows for a 5 per cent duty Export Promotion Capital Goods (EPCG) scheme for computer software units. Thus, software units set up anywhere in India can import all their requirement of capital goods at 5 per cent customs duty subject to signing export obligation of six times the c.i.f. value of the the imports to be made in a period of 8 years on F.O.B. basis; whereas on N.F.E. basis, it is 5 times the c.i.f. value of capital goods imported. However, no additional customs duty or countervailing duty is required to be paid.
15. Encouragement to export of quality goods or services for getting status certification. Exim Policy 1997-2002 announced on 31 March 2000. The Government will recognise software companies who have acquired ISO 9000 series or IS/ISO 9000 Series or ISO 14000 Series or HACP or WHO-GMP or SEI CMM Level 2 and above accreditation/certification. Double weight age will be given on FOB or NFE exports made by such units for granting status certification (e.g. Export House, Trading House, Star Trading House, Super Star Trading House).
16. DTA Sales by units in EOU / EPZ / STP / EHTP units enhanced to 50 per cent of f.o.b. value of total revenues of previous year Exim Policy 1999.
17. Duty free imports of capital goods on loan by units located in EOU / EPZ / STP / EHTP units. Exim Policy 1999. Units located in EOU / EPZ/ EHTP /STP are permitted to import goods, including capital goods, free of cost or on loan from their clients, subject to various stipulations of re-export.
18. Import of second hand capital goods by units located in EOU / EPZ / STP / EHTP allowed. Exim Policy 2000. Government has now permitted import of second hand capital goods which are less than 10 years old without obtaining any license on surrender of SIL.

19. Units located in EOU / EPZ / STP / EHTP may obtain RCMC Certificate from Development Commissioner or Administrative Authority. Exim Policy 1997.

RBI Related Issues

20. SOFTEX Form for Computer Software Exports made much simpler. It must be noted that SOFTEX form needs to be filled by all non-physical exporters of software and services.[49]
21. ADR/GDR Linked option for employees of software companies in India. RBI has permitted Indian software companies to offer ADR / GDR Linked Stock Option Scheme to their non-resident as well as resident permanent employees (including Indian and overseas working Directors). By exercising the option, each resident employee will be permitted to remit up to US$ 50,000 in a block of 5 years to ADRs / GDRs.[50]
22. Import of software up through Internet is permitted. RBI permits remittance towards import of software through Datacom Channels / Internet subject to production of documentary evidence in support of the remittance e.g. invoice of the foreign supplier, user's licence etc.[51]
23. Reproduction of software in India. An Indian company can sign an agreement with overseas copyright holder which allows the Indian company to reproduce software in India. The payment of royalty would be on the basis of Indian Published Price. Remittance of royalty upto 30 per centof the Indian Published Price in respect of legally duplicated/ reproduced in India to overseas copyright holder is permitted without reference to RBI. Where the royalty exceeds 30 per cent of Indian Published Price, the applicant is required to obtain specific approval from Department of Electronics, Government of India.[52]
24. Export of computer software services, repatriation of income. Individuals, firms and companies executing service contracts in "computer software" abroad, are required to repatriate to India, income equivalent to at least 30 per cent of the contract value. They may utilise income up to 70 per cent of contract value for meeting contract related expenses abroad.[53]

25. Remittances towards ISO certification, remittance towards advertisements abroad, import through courier. RBI permits, without limit, remittance towards fee payable to accredited agency abroad for ISO certification.[54]
26. Indian direct investment in Joint Ventures (JV) / Wholly Owned Subsidiaries (WOS) abroad. RBI and Ministry of Commerce have outlined the conditions and procedures for making remittance out of EEFC account towards participation by Indian companies in a JV/WOS overseas under normal route, fast track window and in respect of large investments.[55]
27. Liberalised mechanism for acquisition of software companies in the overseas markets. IT software and services companies in India can now acquire companies overseas through ADR/GDR stock swaps without prior approval as under[56]:
    - Upto US$ 100 million.
    - Ten times the exports earnings of the previous year.
    - For acquisition of values above US$ 100 million, blanket approval is also provided.
28. Use of International Credit Cards for import of software etc. RBI permits use of International Credit Card (ICC) for import of software through Internet (upto US$ 15,000) in advance even before the software is downloaded, payment of services rendered through Internet (e.g. training or education of scientific / technical nature availed through Internet) and software engineers going abroad on assignment.[57]

The commercial transformation that began not more then five year ago. The IT policy of India can accelerate Indian IT industry as well as Indian economy. The Prime Minister of India formed a National Taskforce on Information Technology and Software Development to formulate a long-term National IT policy for the country and also remove impediments for the growth of the infotech industry in May 1998. The main objective of this was to help India emerge as an IT software superpower. The Taskforce submitted three key reports to the government - suggesting various measures to build India's infotech industry and proliferate use of IT in the country.

State IT Policies

The Government has conventionally been recognized as a key driver of the domestic IT market in India and around the world. For example, in the US, about 23 per cent of total domestic IT spending is derived from government and public sector units.

The sectors within the Indian Government that took serious initiatives to adopt and implement IT were the Central/State administrations, insurance companies, financial institutions, the defense segment, the public tax system, ports, customs, telecom and education institutions.

A number of state Governments also implemented e-governance initiatives aimed at cost effectively taking various facilities to citizens. Innovations in the areas of land records, taxation, procurement, etc. were witnessed in the sector, with Internet pervading significant Government transactions.

In the last few years, 18 state governments have announced IT policies. These policies focus on the key issues of infrastructure, electronic governance, IT education and providing a facilitating environment for increasing IT proliferation in the respective states. We have provided the IT policy of 18 states, alongwith details on some key contacts and useful links. The states IT policies are almost as National IT policy. (Table 2.7)

Table 2.7 : IT policies adopted by Indian States

S.No.	*State*	*Key Contacts*	*Useful Links*
1.	Andhra Pradesh	Chief Minister: N.Chandrababu Naidu Chief Secretary : P. V.Rao IT Secretary : J Satyanarayana Director. STP : Col M. Vijay Kumar	IT in Andhra Pradesh Government of Andhra Pradesh Software Technology Parks of India (Hyderabad) Andhra Pradesh Technology Services Vishakhapatnam Export Processing Zone HITEC City Indian Institute of Information Technology
2.	Assam	Chief Minister : P K Mahanta . Phone No. : 0361 – 562222 Chief Secretary : P K Bora. Phone No. : 0361 – 561120 Minister – Industry : Gunin Hazarika. Phone No. : 0361 – 562628 I.T. Secretary, Finance Commissioner & Industry Commissioner: Mr S. C. Das	Government of Assam

S.No.	State	Key Contacts	Useful Links
3.	Chandigarh	Administrator: Lt. Gen. J.F.R Jacob, Phone: 0172-740740 Finance Secretary: Rakesh Singh, Phone No: 0172-741105 Director I.T.: Vivek Attray, Phone: 0172-741620	Chandigarh Administration
4.	Goa	Chief Minister: Mr Sardinha Francisco Phone: 0832-223970 Chief Secretary: Mr Ashok Nath Industry Minister: Mr Alexio Siquera, Phone: 0832-423983 I.T. Secretary: Dr Vijay Madan, Phone: 0832-222597	Governement of Goa Software Technology Park, Goa
5.	Gujarat	Chief Minister : Keshubhai Patel, Phone : 02712 - 32611 –19 Chief Secretary : L N S Mukundan, Phone : 02712 - 20372 I.T Minister : Bimal Shah, Phone : 02712-25920 I.T. Secretary : J S Rana, Phone No. : 02712 - 22107 Director STP, Gandhinagar : A. K. Sharma	Government of Gujarat Gujarat Informatics Limited
6.	Haryana	Chief Minister : Om Prakash Chautala, Phone No. : 0172 – 740356 I.T.Secretary : P K Chaudhary, Comm. Electronics, Comm. Indus. & Comm. Environment, Phone No. : 0172 – 740009	Government of Haryana Haryana State Electronics Development Corporation
7.	Kerala	Chief Minister : E K Nayanar, Phone No. : 0471 - 333812, 332148 Chief Secretary : M Mohankumar, Phone No. : 0471 – 327376, 327176 I.T. Secretary : Aruna Sunderrajan, Phone No. : 0471 - 333028, 327243 Director, STP, Thiruvananthapuram : Ramesh Kumar	Government of Kerala Technopark

S.No.	*State*	*Key Contact*	*Usefull Link*
8.	Madhya Pradesh	Chief Minister : Digvijay Singh, Phone : 0755 – 551581 Chief Secretary : K S Sharma, Phone : 0755 - 551370, 551848 Minister for Commerce & Industries: Narendra Nahata, Phone : 0755 – 550961 I.T. Secretary : Sunil Kumar, Phone No. : 0755 – 551462	Government of Madhya Pradesh http://www.mpgovt.nic.in Indian Institute of Information Technology and Management, Gwalior
9.	Orissa	Chief Minister : Naveen Patnaik, Phone : 0674 – 401100 Chief Secretary : S M Patnaik, Phone : 0674 – 400300 I.T. Secretary : S P Nanda, Phone : 0674 – 405652 Director, STP Bhubaneswar : Manas Patnaik	Orissa Government
10.	Pondicherry	Chief Minister : P Shangmugam, Phone : 0413 – 335530 Chief Secretary : T T Joseph, Phone : 0413 – 334145 I.T. Secretary : Dr. R Padmanabhan	Government of Pondicherry
11.	Punjab	Chief Minister : Prakash Singh Badal, Phone : 0172 – 740325 Chief Secretary : R S Mann, Phone : 0172 - 740156, 740860 I.T. Secretary : B R Bajaj Director, STP Mohali : Sanjay Tyagi	Punjab Government
12.	Rajasthan	Chief Minister : Ashok Ghelot, Phone : 0141 - 380351 Chief Secretary : Inderjeet Khanna, Phone : 0141 - 380254 I.T. Secretary : Arvind Mayaram Officer-in-charge STP, Jaipur : Sudhir Singh	Rajasthan Government Rajasthan State Agency for Computer Services Rajasthan State Industrial Development and Investment Corporation

S.No.	State	Key Contact	Usefull Link
13.	Tamil Nadu	Chief Minister : M Karunanidhi, Phone : 044 - 5362345 Chief Secretary : A P Muthuswamy IAS, Phone : 044 - 5361555 I.T Minister : M Karunanidhi, Phone : 044 - 5362345 I.T. Secretary : D Prakash Director STP, Chennai : Ms R. Rajlakshmi	Electronics Corporation of Tamil Nadu TIDEL Park National Informatics Centre
14.	Tripura	Chief Minister : Manik Sarkar, Phone : 0381 - 324000 Chief Secretary : V Thulasidas, Phone : 0381 - 323200 Industry Minister : Pabitra Kar, Phone : 0381 - 324929 I.T. Secretary : B K Chakraborty, Phone : 0381 - 324081	Government of Tripura
15.	Uttar Pradesh	Chief Minister : Ram Prakash Gupta, Phone : 0522 - 239296, 225757 Chief Secretary : Yogendra Narain, Phone : 0522 - 238212 Secretary I.T. & Electronics : Pankaj Agarwal Director STP, Noida : Dr. Sunil K. Agrawal	Government of Uttar Pradesh http://www.upindia.org
16.	West Bengal	Chief Minister : Jyoti Basu, Phone : 033 - 2214588 Chief Secretary : Manish Gupta I.T. Secretary : A K Deb, Phone : 033 - 2215533 Executive Director STP, Calcutta : Chiranjib Rudra, Phone : 91-33-3579663/65/67	Government of West Bengal West Bengal Electronics Industry Development Corporation Ltd

Source–Software Technology Park of India.

2.3 IT Laws and Regulations of India

The Government of India has announced IT as a thrust area. Accordingly, it is providing for more liberal policy framework for the sector. Major Laws and Regulations that affect the IT industry are listed in this section.

One of the major factors of excellent and consistent growth of Indian software industry can be attributed to continuous liberalisation of policies of the Government of India. Nasscom and the government have worked together in close cooperation over a long-time for forming and implementing these policies. During 1991, Nasscom lobbied with the Government and for the first time, secured income tax exemption from profits of software exports. Later, Government, systematically and gradually, reduced import duty on computer software from a high 114 per cent to nil. Copyright laws were also amended. We are enlisting here, some of the fiscal and non-fiscal incentives provided by the Government of India to IT software and services industry.

Intellectual Property Rights (IPR) Law in India

In India, the Intellectual Property Rights (IPR) of computer software is covered under the Copyright Law. Accordingly, the copyright of computer software is protected under the provisions of Indian Copyright Act 1957. Major changes to Indian Copyright Law were introduced in 1994 and came into effect from 10 May 1995. These changes or amendments made the Indian Copyright law, one of the toughest in the world.[58]

The amendments to the Copyright Act introduced in June 1994 were in themselves, a landmark in the India's copyright arena. For the first time in India, the Copyright Law clearly explained:

- The rights of a copyright holder.
- Position on rentals of software.
- The rights of the user to make backup copies.
- The most importantly the amendments imposed heavy punishment and fines for infringement of copyright of software.

Because most software is easy to duplicate and the copy is usually as good as original, the Copyright Act was greatly in demand. According to this Act, the infringer can be tried under both civil and criminal law.

According to section 14 of this Act, it is illegal to make or distribute copies of copyrighted software without proper or specific authorisation. The only exception is provided by section 52 of the Act, which allows a backup copy purely as a temporary protection against loss, distribution or damage to the original copy. The 1994 amendment to the Copyright Act also prohibits the sale or hiring, or any offer for sale or hire of any copy of the computer program without specific authorisation of the Copyright holder.

A civil and criminal action may be instituted for injunction, actual damages (including infringer's profits) or statutory damages per infringement etc. With these amendments, even the criminal penalties have substantially increased. Section 63 B, stipulates a minimum jail term of 7 days which can be extended up to 3 years. The Act further states the fine ranging from Rs. 50,000 to Rs. 2,00,000.

Government agencies have been very actively participating in protecting of the rights of the copyright holder. Both Ministry of Information Technology and Ministry of Human Resource Development have been active in incorporating amendments to the Indian Copyright Act. These agencies are now helping the law enforcing agencies e.g. the Police in enforcing the law. Today, Nasscom officers and those of these government agencies are committed to enforce copyright laws and eradicate the menace of software piracy.

The Anti-Piracy raids facilitated by Nasscom and Business Software Alliance (BSA) over the last few years in metros as well as smaller cities have already had salutary effect. The law enforcing authorities too supported these raids actively.[59]

Setting up IT Company in India

Setting up IT Software and Services operations in India has certain rules and regulations. And below we have listed brief guidelines for individuals / companies interested in doing this.[60]

General Indian Citizen / Company–An individual Indian citizen can set up IT software and services operations in India through the following:

- as an Individual / Proprietor
- as a Partnership / Firm / Trust
- as a Company registered under the Companies Act, 1956

No prior permission of Government of India is required to set up IT/Software units in India. Moreover, to encourage units in this sector, Government of India has announced many schemes:

- **Domestic Tariff Area**—When the primary focus is to sell in the domestic market in India. This unit can be set anywhere in India. All normal laws apply. No concession is available on import duties. Exports are permitted. A special Export Promotion Capital Goods (EPCG) scheme of Ministry of Commerce can be availed. This scheme allows zero duty import of capital goods against export obligations.

- **Special Economic Zones (SEZs)**—SEZ is a new scheme announced by the Government of India. SEZs are areas where export production can take place free from plethora of rules and regulations governing imports and exports. Units operating in these zones have full flexibility of operations and can import duty free capital goods and raw material. The movement of goods to and fro between ports and SEZ are unrestricted. The units in SEZ have to export the entire production. The first two SEZs are being set up at Positra in Gujarat and Nangunery in Tamil Nadu. At the same time, Santacruz Electronic Export Promotion Zone, Kandla Export Promotion Zone, Vizag Export Promotion Zone and Cochin Export Promotion Zones have been proposed to be converted in SEZs.
- **Export Processing Zones (EPZs)**—These zones are located at various places including Cochin, Falta (Near Calcutta), Kandla, Chennai, Noida, Santacruz (Mumbai), Vishakhapatnam and Surat. A unit can be set up in these zones subject to availability of space. 'Zero import duty' and a 'special 10 years income tax rebate' are some of the incentives provided. Also, there is no restriction on quantity of domestic sales.
- **100 Per cent Export Oriented Unit (EOU)**—This is similar to EPZ scheme. But in this scheme, there is no need to be physically located at EPZ. All other incentives are same as provided to EPZ units.
- **Software Technology Park (STP)**—This is a very special scheme under the Ministry of Information Technology. STPs are located at Noida, Navi Mumbai, Pune, Gandhinagar, Hyderabad, Bangalore, Chennai, Bhubaneswar, Jaipur, Mohali and Thiruvanathapuram. This scheme offers zero import duty on import of all capital goods, special 10 years income tax rebate, availability of infrastructure facilities like high-speed data communication links, etc.

Overseas Company

A foreign company or individual planning to set up business operations in India can do so as under:

- As a foreign company through a Liaison Office/Representative Office, Project or a Branch Office Owned Subsidiary
- As an Indian company through a Joint Venture or a Wholly Owned Subsidiary
- Foreign Company is one that has been incorporated outside India and conducts business in India. These companies are required to comply with the provisions of Companies Act, 1956.

Liaison Office / Representative Office[61]

A liaison office is not allowed to undertake any business activity in India and earn any income here. The role of such offices is limited to collecting information about possible market opportunities and providing information about the company and its products to the prospective Indian customers.

The Foreign Exchange Regulation Act (FERA) regulates the opening and operation of such offices. Also, approval of Reserve Bank of India (RBI) is required for opening of such offices. These offices have to ensure the following:

- Expenses of such offices are met entirely through inward remittances of foreign exchange from Head Office abroad.
- These offices do not undertake any trading or commercial activities. Commercial activities should be limited to collecting and transmitting information between overseas Head Office and potential Indian customers.
- Liaison offices should not charge any commission or receive other income from Indian customers for provisioning of liaison services.
- Permission for such offices is initially granted for a period of three years and may be extended from time to time.

Project Office

Foreign companies planning to execute specific projects in India can set up temporary project / site offices in India with the approval of RBI. Such approval is generally accorded in respect of Government approved projects.

Branch Office

Foreign companies engaged in manufacturing and trading activities abroad may set up Branch offices in India, with the permission of RBI, for the following purposes:

- To represent the parent company / other foreign companies in various matters in India e.g. acting as a buying / selling agents in India.
- To conduct research work in the area in which the parent company is engaged provided the results of the research work are made available to Indian companies.
- To undertake export and import trading activities.
- To promote possible technical and financial collaborations between the Indian companies and overseas companies. A branch office is not permitted to carry out manufacturing activities on its own but is permitted to sub-contract these to Indian manufacturers.

As an Indian Company

A foreign company can commence operations in India through incorporation of a company under the provisions of Indian Companies Act 1956. Foreign equity in such Indian companies can be up to 100 per cent depending upon the business plan of the foreign investor, prevailing investment policies of the Government and on receipt of requisite approvals.[62]

Joint Venture with an Indian Partner

Foreign companies can set up their operations in India by forming strategic alliances with Indian partners. Setting up of operations through Joint Venture may entail the following advantages to a foreign investor:

- Already established distribution / marketing set up of the Indian partner.
- Available financial resources of the Indian partner.
- Already established contacts of the Indian partner that help smoothen the process of setting up operations.

Foreign investments are approved through two routes as under:

- *Automatic Route*: Approvals for foreign equity up to 50 per cent, 51 per cent and 74 per cent are given on an automatic basis subject to fulfilment of prescribed parameters in certain industries as specified by the Government. RBI accords automatic approval to all such cases.
- *Government Approval:* Approval in all other cases where the proposed foreign equity exceeds 50 per cent, 51 per cent or 74 per cent in the specified industries or if the industry is not in the specified list, it requires prior specific approval from Foreign Investment Promotion Board (FIPB).

Wholly Owned Subsidiary

The foreign investor has the option of setting up a wholly owned subsidiary, wherein the foreign company owns 100 per cent share of the Indian company. All such cases are subject to prior approval from the FIPB. Some of the criteria for setting up wholly owned subsidiary include[63]:

- Only "holding" operation is involved and all subsequent/ downstream investments to be carried out need prior approval of the Government.
- Where proprietary technology is sought to be protected or sophisticated technology is proposed to be brought in.
- At least 50 per cent of the production is to be exported.
- Proposals for consultancy.
- Proposals for infrastructure like roads, industrial model towns, industrial parks or estates.

Cyber Laws in India

In May 2000, both the houses of the Indian Parliament passed the Information Technology Bill The Bill received the assent of the President in August 2000 and came to be known as the Information Technology Act, 2000. Cyber laws are contained in the IT Act, 2000.

This Act aims to provide the legal infrastructure for e-commerce in India. And the cyber laws have a major impact for e-businesses and the new economy in India. So, it is important to understand what are the various perspectives of the IT Act, 2000 and what it offers.[64]

The Information Technology Act, 2000 also aims to provide for the legal framework so that legal sanctity is accorded to all electronic records and other activities carried out by electronic means. The Act states that unless otherwise agreed, an acceptance of contract may be expressed by electronic means of communication and the same shall have legal validity and enforceability. Some highlights of the Act are listed below[65]:

1. Chapter-II of the Act specifically stipulates that any subscriber may authenticate an electronic record by affixing his digital signature. It further states that any person can verify an electronic record by use of a public key of the subscriber.
2. Chapter-III of the Act details about Electronic Governance and provides inter alia amongst others that where any law provides that information or any other matter shall be in writing or in the typewritten or printed form, then, notwithstanding anything contained in such law, such requirement shall be deemed to have been satisfied if such information or matter is
3. Rendered or made available in an electronic form; and
4. Accessible so as to be usable for a subsequent reference
5. The said chapter also details the legal recognition of Digital Signatures.
6. Chapter-IV of the said Act gives a scheme for Regulation of Certifying Authorities. The Act envisages a Controller of Certifying Authorities who shall perform the function of exercising supervision over the activities of the Certifying Authorities as also laying down standards and conditions governing the Certifying Authorities as also specifying the various forms and content of Digital Signature Certificates. The Act recognizes the need for recognizing foreign Certifying Authorities and it further details the various provisions for the issue of license to issue Digital Signature Certificates.
7. Chapter-VII of the Act details about the scheme of things relating to Digital Signature Certificates. The duties of subscribers are also enshrined in the said Act.
8. Chapter-IX of the said Act talks about penalties and adjudication for various offences. The penalties for damage to

computer, computer systems etc. has been fixed as damages by way of compensation not exceeding Rs. 1,00,00,000 to affected persons. The Act talks of appointment of any officers not below the rank of a Director to the Government of India or an equivalent officer of state government as an Adjudicating Officer who shall adjudicate whether any person has made a contravention of any of the provisions of the said Act or rules framed there under. The said Adjudicating Officer has been given the powers of a Civil Court.

9. Chapter-X of the Act talks of the establishment of the Cyber Regulations Appellate Tribunal, which shall be an appellate body where appeals against the orders passed by the Adjudicating Officers, shall be preferred.

10. Chapter-XI of the Act talks about various offences and the said offences shall be investigated only by a Police Officer not below the rank of the Deputy Superintendent of Police. These offences include tampering with computer source documents, publishing of information, which is obscene in electronic form and hacking.

11. The Act also provides for the constitution of the Cyber Regulations Advisory Committee, which shall advice the government as regards any rules, or for any other purpose connected with the said act. The said Act also proposes to amend the Indian Penal Code, 1860, the Indian Evidence Act, 1872, The Bankers' Books Evidence Act, 1891, The Reserve Bank of India Act, 1934 to make them in tune with the provisions of the IT Act.

Advantages of Cyber Laws

The IT Act 2000 attempts to change outdated laws and provides ways to deal with cyber crimes. We need such laws so that people can perform purchase transactions over the Net through credit cards without fear of misuse. The Act offers the much-needed legal framework so that information is not denied legal effect, validity or enforceability, solely on the ground that it is in the form of electronic records.

In view of the growth in transactions and communications carried out through electronic records, the Act seeks to empower government departments to accept filing, creating and retention of official documents in the digital format. The Act has also proposed a legal framework for the authentication and origin of electronic records / communications through digital signature.[66]

- From the perspective of e-commerce in India, the IT Act 2000 and its provisions contain many positive aspects. Firstly, the implications of these provisions for the e-businesses would be that email would now be a valid and legal form of communication in our country that can be duly produced and approved in a court of law.
- Companies shall now be able to carry out electronic commerce using the legal infrastructure provided by the Act.
- Digital signatures have been given legal validity and sanction in the Act.
- The Act throws open the doors for the entry of corporate companies in the business of being Certifying Authorities for issuing Digital Signatures Certificates.
- The Act now allows Government to issue notification on the web thus heralding e-governance.
- The Act enables the companies to file any form, application or any other document with any office, authority, body or agency owned or controlled by the appropriate Government in electronic form by means of such electronic form as may be prescribed by the appropriate Government.
- The IT Act[67] also addresses the important issues of security, which are so critical to the success of electronic transactions. The Act has given a legal definition to the concept of secure digital signatures that would be required to have been passed through a system of a security procedure, as stipulated by the Government at a later date.
- Under the IT Act, 2000, it shall now be possible for corporate to have a statutory remedy in case if anyone breaks into their computer systems or network and causes damages or copies data. The remedy provided by the Act is in the form of monetary damages, not exceeding Rs. 1 crore.

The IT law and regulation will go a long in facilitating and regulating IT industry and IT related service. New communication systems and digital technology has made dramatic changes in the way people transact business. Businessmen are increasingly using computers to create, transmit and store information in the electronic form instead of traditional paper documents. It is cheaper, easier to store and retrieve and speedier to communicate. Although people are aware of these advantages they are reluctant to conduct business in the electronic form due to lack of appropriate legal framework. The basis principal hurdles, which stand in the way of facilitating electronic commerce, electronic governance and other IT enable services, are the requirements as to writing and signature for legal recognition. At present many legal provisions assume the existence of traditional based records and documents, which should bear signatures. The law of evidence is traditionally based upon paper -based records and oral testimony. Electronic commerce eliminates the need for paper-based transactions. Hence, to facilitate IT enable services, proper legal framework has become an urgent necessity.

2.4 Location, Size and Units in India

Over the last couple of years some of the cities in India have come to be known as IT hotspots, similar to the Silicon Valley in United States. Bangalore, Karnataka has often been compared to Silicon Valley and is considered one of the most wired cities in Asia. Another city that is fast becoming the second most popular tech hot spot is Hyderabad, which is in the state of Andhra Pradesh. Although, the high growth in the IT industry has lead to the sprouting of many technology firms in several cities in India, Bangalore and Hyderabad have made a conscious effort to provide the infrastructure and a conducive enviroment for IT. In turn, vying several multinational technology companies to set up camp near these two cities.

1. Bangalore

Over the last decade Bangalore also known as Garden City has transformed from being a hot tourist spot to the 'Silicon Valley' of India. In 1999 there were over 300 software units in Bangalore. There has been a growth in IT exports from Rs.15 million in 91-92, to more than 320 million in 1999. This high tech hot spot accounts for more than 32 per cent of the country's IT software production with the IT sector here growing at a rate of about 58% per year. 13Main reasons that have lead to the creation of this IT ecosystem are the talent pool of highly trained professionals, the training infrastructure and progressive Government policies.[68]

Government Support

Bangalore is home to many IT companies such as Infosys, Wipro, Compaq, IBM and Lucent. The government of Karnataka where the city Bangalore is located has taken several steps to encourage the IT industry in Karnataka. Some of the incentives and the exemptions that the government offers to the IT companies are

- Sales Tax Exemption
- Entry Tax Exemption
- Power Tariff Concessions
- Quick Clearances from the Pollution Control Board
- Concessions on Company Registration Charges.

Technology Parks

In the 1980's and early 1990's, the advent of globalisation provided Multi-National Corporations (MNCs) in the manufacturing sector with access to low cost production centers in Asia. The story is being replayed in the IT industry today. There is huge wage gap between developed countries such as the US and developing countries such as India, with Indian workers demanding less than a quarter than their American counterparts. In that wage gap, lies a great potential for India, which is endowed with a pool of highly developed Information Technology park in India.

"Information Technology park" is a vague term by all accounts, used to describe a variety of efforts to stimulate the development of "entrepreneurial, knowledge-based small and medium-sized enterprises" (or SMEs) within a country. The term has at least 16 synonyms, with the most common being "science park," "research park," and "technopole." New terms are constantly arising as technology parks attempt to distinguish themselves from the considerable competition of at least 295 technology parks worldwide (Lalkaka[69] and Rustam[70]).

Technology parks have been in existence in the United States since at least the early 1950's and have since spread around the world, with new technology parks continually arising. Originally, the term "Information Technology park" had a very limited definition, focusing on the real estate aspect of the park concept, in which universities typically leased real estate, office space or research facilities to businesses. Sometimes these arrangements are referred to as "industrial estates" or "firm hotels.". (Löfsten[71], Hans[72] and Lindel öf Peter[73]).

Software Technology Parks, India

The Ministry of Information Technology (MIT) is setting up several Software Technology Parks (STPs) starting with Bangalore. The goal of the STPs is to promote and facilitate software development and exports through incentives and state of the art infrastructure.

Figure 2.2 Software Technology Park of India (STPI) Centres

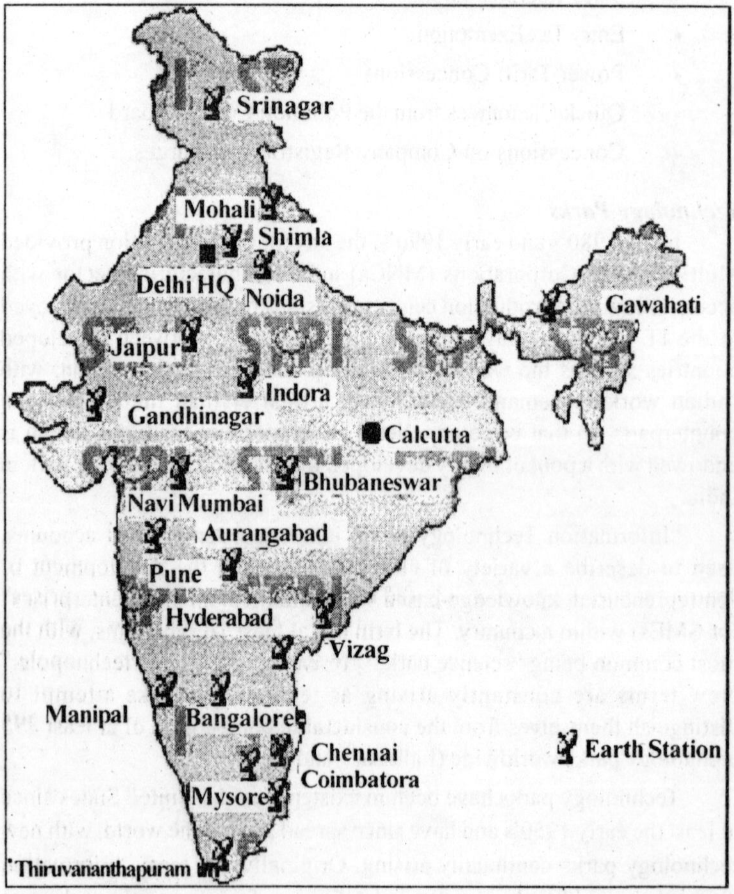

International Tech Park Limited— The International Tech Park is designed to appeal to the international technology companies. The park offers a one-stop shop providing commercial, residential and recreational needs in a single location.

Electronics City— Electronics City is a 330-acre industrial park that houses only electronic industries. This park currently houses over a hundred companies including Motorola and Siemens.

2. **Hyderabad**—Hyderabad can be compared to the 'Silicon Valley' in New York. After Bangalore , Hyderabad is the next city that has seen a rapid growth in the IT industry. One of the primary reasons for this cities success in attracting technology companies is -Manpower. Almost 23 per cent of software professionals in India are from Andhara Pradesh.The STPs in this city have maintained the highest growth rate in the IT sector. The area concentration has been in companies that specialize in offshore development, e-commerce, ERP solutions and IT training. A direct indicator of the growth that is happening today is the fact that while 29 new IT companies were registered with the STPH during 1997-98, that same number was achieved within the first six months of 1998-99. Today the city presents an assorted picture - global players like Microsoft and Intergraph and local blue chip companies like Satyam, InfoTech, Visual Soft etc. For more information on Hyderabad click on the link.[74]

Hi-Tec City—The Hyderabad Information Technology and Engineering Consultancy (Hi-Tec) city provides IT companies with un-interrupted power supply, high bandwidth communication facilities and other basic needs for software industry. Developed on 158 acres on the outskirts of the city, Hi-Tec city provides 550,000 sq ft of floor area of office space.

Government Support—The success of Hyderabad becoming an IT hotbed can greatly be credited to the state's chief minister Chandrababu Naidu, who has aggressively rallied to make Hydearbad the next 'Silicon Valley'. The numerous initiatives undertaken by the government include: offering concessions and incentives, taking an active part in promoting IT, creating a market for IT applications and enlarging the use of IT in all spheres of governance.

2.5 Growth of IT Industry

India's IT industry ranks among the fastest growing sectors within the country's economy. Driven primarily by software exports, the industry has been logging in extremely impressive year on year growth. The software industry in fact has been growing well over the 50 per cent mark and only in the last year, impacted by the worldwide economic downturn, has the momentum reduced marginally.

India's international-class manpower, that creates high quality software and services solutions is finding favour among overseas customers. The success story being played out by the IT industry at the global level is also being reflected on Indian soil, with more and more organisations embracing IT. The Government too is getting IT enabled and using state-of-the-art technology solutions to bring greater benefits to Indian citizens and improve its internal efficiencies.

The Indian software sector displays many unusual features from an Indian perspective. The most obvious one is its export orientation. Given India's size and history of inward development, most industries tend to be driven by the domestic market. However, exports account for 65 per cent of the total software revenue.[76] Not only that, software exports have grown somewhat faster than the domestic market, so that the share of exports has actually increased over time.

There are important qualitative differences between the export market and the domestic markets. The first relates to different types of software developed. Table 2.8, gives the composition of the domestic and export software development and services market. The domestic market has a higher proportion of revenues from the sale of software packages and products. Whereas products accounted for nearly 40 per cent of the domestic market, they account for a little under 10 per cent of exports. Over 80 per cent of exports are software services including custom software development, constancy and professional services. Even though the bulk of the product revenues in the domestic market are probably accounted for by imported software products, Indian firms have produced some moderately successful products, such as accounting packages and word processing packages in Indian languages, for the domestic markets. A number of medium-sized firms make products for the Indian and Middle East markets which are very specific to the business culture etc. In the area of ERP packages, a couple of firms are trying to compete with global giants like SAP, BAAN and People Soft in the domestic market.

The second difference between the domestic and export sectors relates to the stages of software development as described earlier. Indian firms usually provide low-level design, coding and some types of testing services for export. For domestic clients the industry provides a wider range of services that usually spans the entire lifecycle of software development. Some of the domestic projects are much larger and more challenging than export projects, with the screen based trading system for the Bombay Stock Exchange and the Reservation System for Railways, both by executed by CMC, an experienced public sector firm, being two recent examples.

Domestic Scenario of IT industry

In Table 2.8 we see that most of the firms operating in the domestic sector sell software products and packages. A large fraction of the domestic software industry consists of resale of software packages developed by foreign, principally US, firms, thus overstating the extent of software written for the domestic market. On the other hand, there is a great deal of in-house software written by users, especially large Indian firms that is not being captured by these figures.

A number of Indian software firms have also developed software packages aimed at the domestic market. However, with very few exceptions, these packages have not been very successful. A number of firms had targeted the domestic market for products and services in the late 1980s. Some produced packaged software products for the domestic market, including a word processing packages for Indian languages, while others focused on developing custom software for domestic clients. For the most part, these efforts were not very remunerative compared to the export market[77]. This points to the higher profitability of exports of software services compared to other types of software development and even firms that are product focused have added software services and consulting to fund product development (Udell[78] 1993).

Although it is tempting to point to weak intellectual property rights as a culprit for the failure of Indian firms to develop successful packages, our interviews suggest that at least as important, if not more, has been the lack of experience, especially design and marketing experience, necessary to produce a successful product. In many cases, firms simply overestimated the willingness to pay and underestimated the difficulties of developing and supporting products. The reluctance of Indian users to pay large sums for software products has undoubtedly been very important, as has the slow rate of computerization of the Indian economy. Consequently, most of the established firms have turned to providing services for the export market. Firms that have had domestic experience with consulting do not appear to derive any advantage from it in the export market. Given the simpler and more routine tasks involved in current software exports, the sophisticated capabilities and expertise that firms had developed from serving domestic customers have not been of great value to them in the export market. The CEO of a software subsidiary of a very large Indian engineering firm, explicitly noted that the considerable experience his firm had in executing large in-house software development projects was of limited use in exports.

"As far as functional skills are concerned, these differ from country to country and client to client and there is a learning curve there. Domestic expertise may be useful in gaining technical expertise such as in coding and project management. However, domestic and export projects are two different ball games."

The domestic IT market in 2000-01 touched a revenue of Rs. 25,750 crore (US$5.65 billion), an extremely healthy growth of nearly 40 per cent. In terms of a share of India's GDP, the domestic IT market accounted for 1.3 per cent of the total during 2000-01. The economic downturn sweeping across the globe and a slowdown in IT purchases, both at the international and domestic industry levels, has been the reason for the slower growth during 2001-02. See in figure 2.3 and figure 2.4.

Unlike the IT export market, which is completely dominated and driven by the software and service segment, the Indian IT domestic market has a strong hardware component. The hardware contribution (including hardware, peripherals, networking and hardware services) to the overall IT revenue totals during 2000-01 was pegged at Rs. 13,531 crore. This was up from Rs. 9692 crore logged in during the previous year.

The key growth spurs for the IT industry during 2000-01 were as follows:

- The PC segment pushed growth following a fall in prices of products, availability of easy financing schemes and improved channel infrastructure. Segments such as finance and banking beefed up PC purchases on account of the RBI directive to push computerization.
- The server and workstation segment witnessed 76 per cent growth in value terms driven by demand from ISPs and dot coms. In the second half of the year, key orders came from banks, insurance companies and Government institutions.
- On the peripherals side, printers accounted for nearly 33 per cent of the market. The share of impact printers declined while non-impact printers such as inkjets sold rapidly. The SOHO segment also spurred demand. Other hot growth sectors were the larger monitors market, hard disk drives, scanners and other peripherals such as web cameras, SCSI cards and graphic cards.
- In the area of packaged software, application software accounted for nearly 70 per cent of the market with office productivity software contributing to nearly 70 per cent of sales. Growth was driven by upgrades, focus on SMEs and on bundled software. System infrastructure software such as networking, operating systems, firewalls, security etc. also grew rapidly.
- In the area of networking, investments from banks and old economy sectors like manufacturing and insurance, pushed purchases. The growth in the areas of leased line modems and remote access servers was driven by ISPs.
- The training and education market witnessed consolidation. New courses were launched around C# and on-line education became pervasive. Large training institutes bagged courses for computerization of schools in key states.

Statistics of Indian IT industry

The Indian IT industry has grown from Rs. 5,450 crore (US$1.73 billion) in 1994-95 to Rs. 64,200 crore (US$13.5 billion) in 2001-02. In terms of a share of GDP, the IT industry figures have risen from 0.59 per cent in 1994-95 to 2.87 per cent in 2001-02.

A look at the composition of the IT market in India over the 1994-2002 period reiterates the IT industry's software export orientation. While revenues from hardware, peripherals and networking are estimated to touch Rs. 14,500 crore during 2001-02, India's software and services exports will account for a hefty Rs. 36,855 crore of revenues during the period (over half of the IT market projections of Rs. 64,200 crore for the year). See Figure 2.5.

Figure 2.3–Domestic Market (Figures in Rs. Crores)

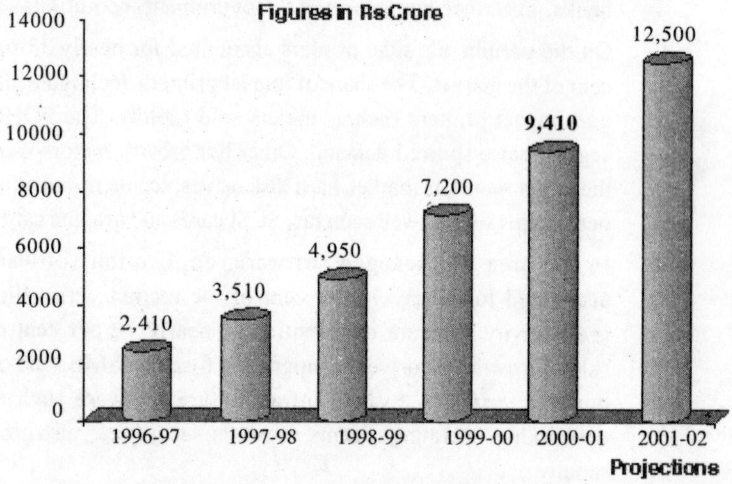

Source–NASSCOM

Figure 2.4–Domestic Market (figures in US $ Million)

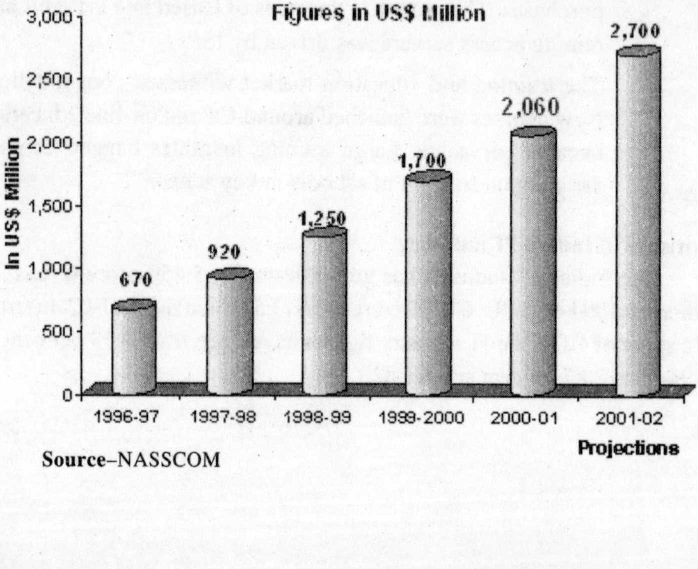

Source–NASSCOM

Figure 2.5– Indian Domestic IT Market

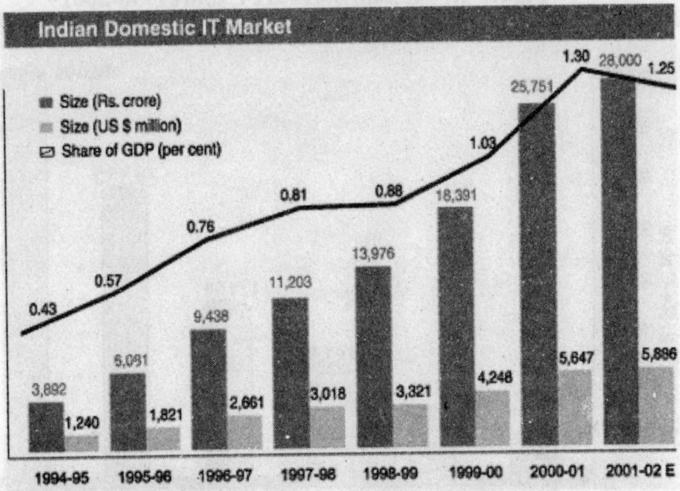

Source–NASSCOM

Figure 2.6– Indian IT Market (1994-2002)

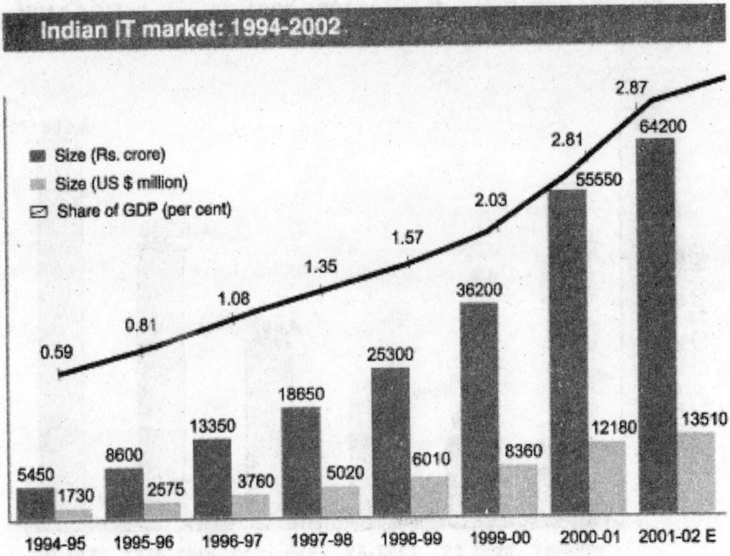

Source–NASSCOM

Figure 2.7– Indian Software Export 1996-2001 (Figures in Rs. Crore)

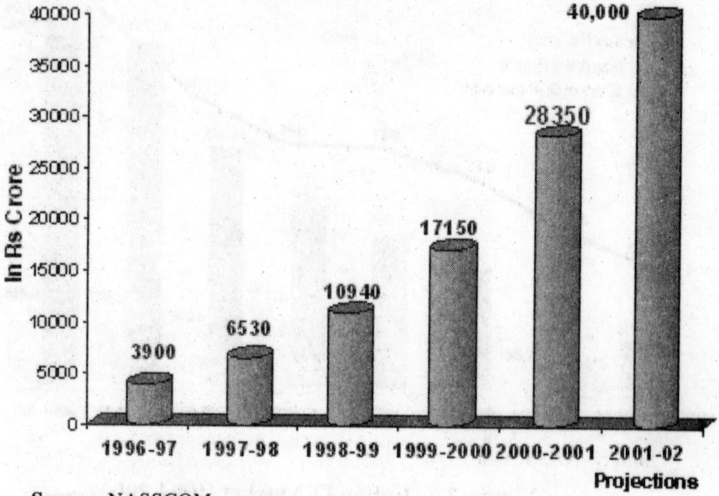

Source–NASSCOM

Figure 2.8–Software Exports 1996-2001 (Figures in US $ Million)

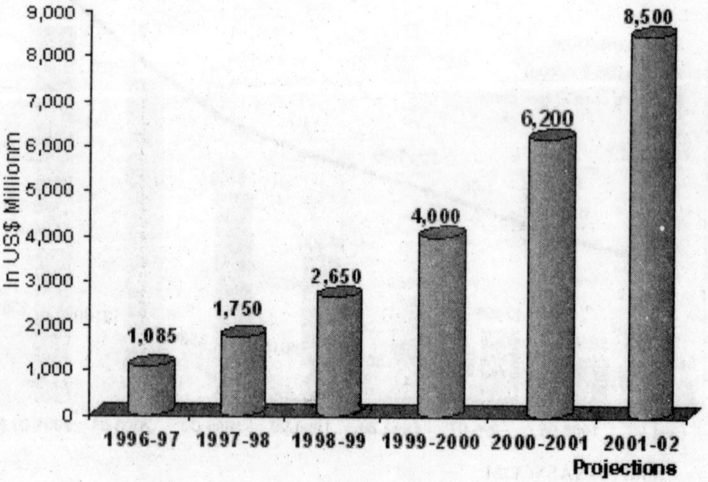

Source–NASSCOM

India's IT industry ranks among the fastest growing sectors within the country's economy. Driven primarily by software exports, the industry has been logging in extremely impressive year on year growth. The software industry in fact has been growing well over the 50 per cent mark and only in the last year, impacted by the worldwide economic downturn, has the momentum reduced marginally.

India's international-class manpower, that creates high quality software and services solutions is finding favor among overseas customers. The success story being played out by the IT industry at the global level is also being reflected on Indian soil, with more and more organisations embracing IT. The Government too is getting IT enabled and using state-of-the-art technology solutions to bring greater benefits to Indian citizens and improve its internal efficiencies.

The facts and figure related to the Indian IT Industry and the major trends in the IT marker are a reflection of immense growth the sector has witnessed in the last one-decade.

Software

India's software and services industry in India grossed an annual revenue of Rs. 37,760 crore (US$ 8.26 billion) during 2000-01, registering an overall growth of 55 per cent during the period. Of the total revenues in 2000-01, software exports grossed Rs. 28,350 crore (US$6.2 billion) while the domestic software market accounted for Rs. 9,410 crore (US$ 2.06 billion). See Figure 2.7 and 2.8.

The interesting highlight of 2000-01 was that one out of every four global giants, outsource their mission critical software requirements to India. The IT software and services sector accounted for almost 2 per cent of the country's GDP an this figure is expected to grow to 7.7 per cent by 2008.

India's Internet Market

The Internet market grew steadily in terms of subscribers, with the number of active subscribers projected to touch 1.5 million in March 2002. This represents an increase of 30 per cent over the 1.1 million figure in March 2001 (the figures however, exclude the users of free ISPs as well as inactive accounts). The slight slowdown in the growth of the Internet subscriber base is on account of the fact that nearly 80 per cent of PC owing households already have Net connections. The same is true of business establishments with Internet penetration reaching nearly 40 per cent.

PC Push

Personal Computers represent not only the largest component of the IT industry, they are also one of the fastest growing product categories. Although components shortage and currency devaluation kept the average sales value (ASV) of PCs on the higher side, it could not arrest the tremendous momentum that existed in the market.

According to IDC/Nasscom estimates, around 18.08 lakh PCs were sold during 2000-01. Of these, approximately one third found their way into homes. The home segment has been consistently growing above the overall average, which is pushing the share of this segment up.(Figure 2.13)

Apart from the home segment, the corporate marketplace also picked up PCs actively. Shipments of commercial desktops shot up by almost 58 per cent in first half of 2000-01 as compared to the same period in the previous year. Sales of notebook computers, which move primarily into the commercial segment, grew by 68 per cent in unit terms.

Servers and Workstations

While the total number of servers sold during 2000-01 touched 43,477 systems, around 11,857 workstations were sold during the year. While Standard Intel Architecture Servers (SIAS, earlier called PC Servers) contributed the maximum to the total server market and grew by over 30 per cent in value terms, the growth was driven by the non-SIAS segment, where the value jump was to the tune of 57 per cent. The Internet and ISPs emerged as the prime drivers for servers. The finance segment (including Banks, NBFCs and Stock Exchanges) meanwhile invested heavily on non-SIAS servers, especially in midrange and high-end during 2000-01.

Figure 2.9–Indian Software Industry as a Per centage of India's GDP

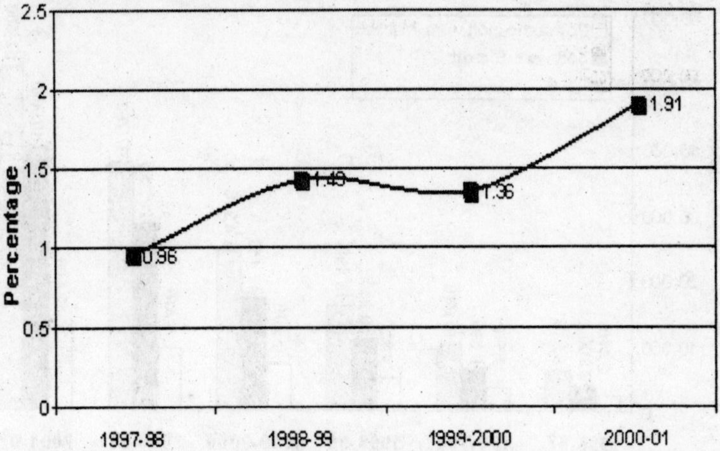

Source–NASSCOM

Figure 2.10–Indian Software Exports as a Per centage of Total Indian Exports

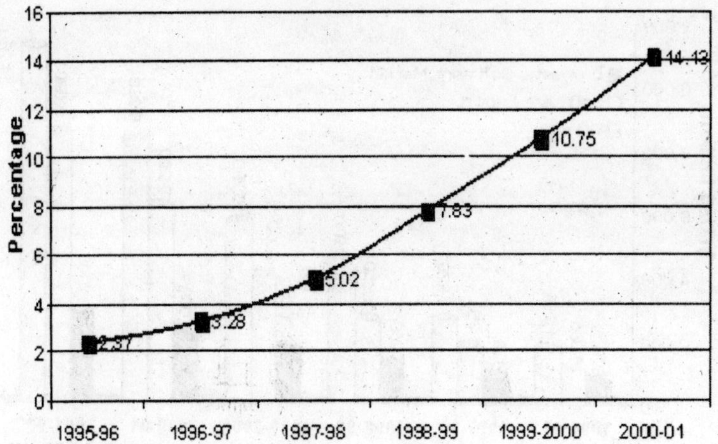

Source–NASSCOM

Figure 2.11– Indian Software Industry 1996-2001 (Figure in Rs. Crore)

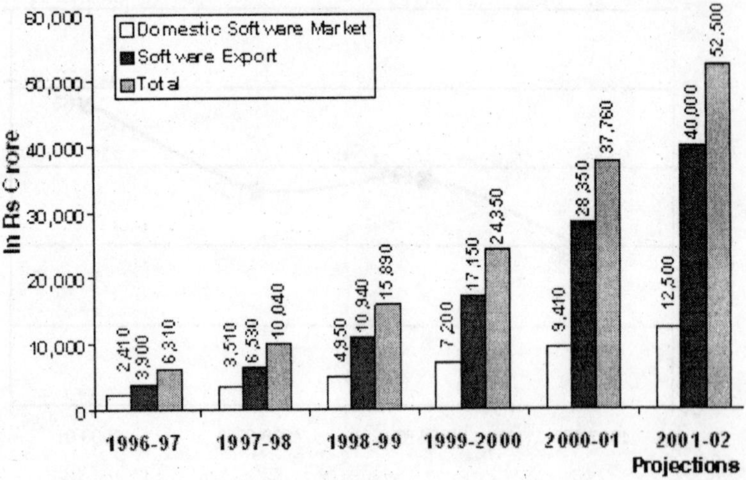

Source–NASSCOM

Figure 2.12–Indian Software Industry 1996-2001 (Figure in US $ Million)

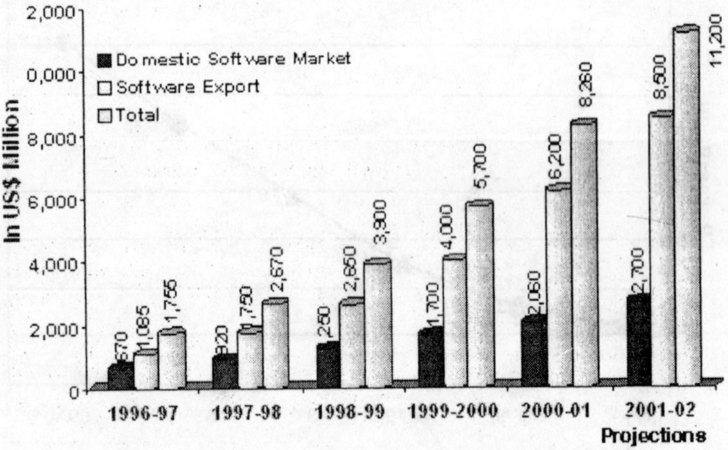

Source–NASSCOM

Figure 2.13–Indian Software and Hardware (IT) Market

Domestic Hardware Market	*1997-98*		*1998-999*		*1999-00*		*2001-02*	
	[Nos.]	*[Rs. Crore]*	*[Nos.]*	*[Rs. Corore]*	*[Nos]*	*[Rs. Crore]*	*[Nos.]*	*[Rs. Crore]*
Hardware System Service								
Large	6	26.95	7	45.25	4	30.00	14	81.00
Medium	571	361.81	338	160.39	635	284.00	691	482.00
Small	2,082	300.89	1,792	268.42	2,618	308.00	3,265	440.00
Total Non-PC Servers	2,659	689.65	2,137	474.06	3,257	622.00	3,970	1,003.00
PC Servers	14,991	360.73	20,885	478.46	26,623	401.00	39,507	801.00
Total Servers	17,650	1,050.38	22,822	952.52	29,880	1,023.00	43,477	1,804.00
Systems Work Stations								
Personal Wrokstations	3,030	56.65	3,093	60.03	3,500	58.00	7,073	92.00
Traditional Workstations	2,352	145.15	1,348	114.54	2,029	136.00	4,784	195.00
Total Work Stations	5,382	201.80	4,439	174.57	5,529	194.00	11,857	287.00
System Single User System								
Total Desktops	584,947	2,145.17	774,745	2,301.00	1,121,735	4,686.00	1,705.355	6588.00
Notebooks	25,546	258.00	28,545	291.05	25,768	331.00	42,864	446.00
Apple	10,000	80.00	855	11.43	9,000	81.00	12,000	105.00
Total PCs	620,493	2,482.68	803,290	2,592.05	1,147,503	5,017.00	1,748,219	7,011.00
Total Systems	643,525	3,735.35	830,551	3,719.14	1,182,913	6,234.00	1,808,553	9,102.00
Periphersls								
DMPs	235,898	226.36	256,746	249.57	308,000	370.00	257,685	301.00
Laser	42,000	162.52	56,695	199.46	102,000	235.00	68,882	196.00
Inkjet	135,487	108.00	225,535	150.50	319,000	215.00	472,165	326.00
Line Printers	1,597	33.77	2,507	57.35				
Total Printers	414,982	530.65	541,483	656.88	729,000	820.00	798,732	823.00
Other Peripherals		291.83		774.04		1,250.00		1,694.00
Total Peripherals	414,982	822.48	541,483	1,430.90	729,000	2,070.00	798,732	2,517.00
Networking		641.00		952.00		1,234.00		1,789.00
Total Hardware		5,198.83		6,102.04		9,538.00		13,408.00
Others		501.98		498.19		154.00		123.00
Grand Total		5,700.81		6,600.23		9,692.00		13,531.00

Source–NASSCOM

Networking

The networking market also did well during 2000-01, notching up revenues of Rs. 1,789 crore during the year. A strong growth in demand for switches and routers was the prime reason for this solid growth. Apart from a push from the ISP segment, large amounts of networking hardware was also bought by software exporters. The booming call center business in the country also spurred the growth of the networking market. (Figure 2.13)

Peripherals

Perhaps the largest beneficiary of the boom in the computing products market has been the peripherals industry. Apart from peripherals bundled with computing products, there was also a substantial after-market for peripherals like hard disk drives and monitors during 2000-01. The need to upgrade PCs in the installed base was the prime reason for higher growth rates for peripherals during the year.

In all, around 798,732 units of DMPs, laser, inkjet, line printers and other peripherals were sold during 2000-01, accounting for revenues of Rs. 2,517 crore. The growing demand for storage also led to an explosive growth in segments such as hard disk drives and higher capacity drives. In 2000-01 almost three fourths of all hard disks sold had capacities of 10GB or above, as compared to less than 1 per cent a year back, according to IDC. (Figure 2.13)

The printer market witnessed activity as competition intensified, especially in the rapidly growing inkjet category. Price and promotions were the main factors that differentiated the various players in the market.

Exports Scenario of IT industry in India

The Information Technology is so ubiquitous and applications are so pervasive that it could have implications on all spheres of human activity. More specifically, by the augmenting the process of information exchange and reducing transaction costs, IT offers enormous opportunities for productivity enhancement and growth in all sphere of the human activity. To reap the potential of Information Technology, a prerequisites, however is the diffusion of IT into different sectors of the economy and society. Unfortunately, there exists wide inter-country and intra-country variation in the diffusion of IT. On the one hand, we have developed countries like

US with a fairly high level of IT diffusion (with about 400 computers per1,000 people) wherein IT contributes significantly to GDP. At the other extreme are a number of developing countries wherein the extent of IT diffusion remain very low. In African countries, for example, it is estimate that the number of computers for every 1,000 people is 0.3. Even in India, the number of computers per 1,000 people is only about two and only in 10 is hooked up the internet. The resulting "digital divide" is best summarised by the statement made by Thabo Mbeke, president of Republic of South Africa: "more half of the humanity has never made a phone call."(Pohjola[79] 2000)

Therefore, it may appear paradoxical that in an era of 'digital divide' India enjoys enormous comparative advantage in the export of IT services (mainly software). Going by the available statistics, during the past decade IT services export from India recorded an annual compound growth rate of over 60 per cent in rupee terms (at current prices) and over 46 per cent in dollar terms. It goes without saying that Indian Software Industry has been able to establish credibility in the international market, which is unique compared with most other items in our export basket. In 1998-99, over 200 of 1,000 Fortune companies looked to India to meet their software requirements. Developed countries, in their efforts to solve IT-related problems, have come to forward even to relax visa restrictions for Indian software professionals.

State Initiatives in the IT Sector

There is a view, prevalent in some quarters, that the dynamism in the software sector is an outcome of 'benign neglect' rather that active strategic support (Kuttuman and Iyer 2001)[80]. To test the veracity of this argument and, more importantly, to place the forthcoming discussion in a proper perspective we being with an overview of the various state initiatives towards the development of IT in the country. These initiatives range from a series of policy formulations to active institutional interventions.

Though the genesis of software development in India can be traced back to the early 1970s, it received the direct attention of the police-makers only in mid-1970s, the share of software in the total case of a computer system was negligible compared with that of the hardware. Also, it was generally held that software and hardware are complementary and therefore separate initiatives are not necessarily called for. Hence, till the mid-1980s, while there were explicit policy announcements towards promoting the industry in general, there was hardly any specific policy towards software development. This also reflect the lack of the demand of the an account of the limited diffusion of computers. The use of computers was confined mostly to a few government departments, private sectors units and educational organisations, wherein software programmers were appointed to develop the required software. In general, software was not considered a product amenable for trade.[81]

The computer policy of 1984, probably for the first time, explicitly acknowledged the importance of software development and underlined the need for institutional and policy support. The policy called for setting up of a separate Software Development Promotion Agency (SDPA) under the Department of Electronics (DoE). Imports of inputs needed for software development,were made more liberal. The increase in the production and use of computers as a result of the liberal computer policy [Joseph[82] 1997] enhanced the domestic demand for various software products and services. However, the nascent industry could not meet this increasing demand. As a result, a sizeable proportion of domestic demand had to be meet through imports. At the same time, the rapid growth of global demand for software pointed to the increasing export potential. This is turn called for more concrete policies for the promotion of software development and export. Accordingly, in 1986, an explicit software policy was announced and software identified as one of the key sectors on India's agenda for export promotion. The policy underlined the importance integrated development of software for the domestic and export markets [GoI[83] 1986]. To facilitate the stated objectives, policy emphasised the need for simplifying procedures and tax holidays, tax exemption on income from software export, export subsidies and duty-free import of hardware and software.

With the initiation of economic reforms in the early 1990s, there have been a number of other policy initiatives that have facilitated the growth of IT. The new policy initiatives included the provision to finance software development through equity and venture capital, measures to make available faster and cheaper data communication facilities, removal of entry barriers for foreign companies and reduction and rationalisation of taxes, duties and tariffs[84] [Narayana Murthy[85] 2000].

In addition, the government also made certain institutional interventions. No less then four major national task forces have studies all aspects of IT in past four years and most of their recommendation have been acted up on by the government.[86] More significantly, chief executives of leading private sector IT companies have been fully involved in these task forces. A number of government agencies involved in different aspects of IT were brought together into an integrated ministry of IT. This was followed by an IT Act to deal with the wide variety of issues relating to the IT industry [Parthasarathi[87] 2001].

One notable institutional intervention has been the establishment of Software Technology Parks[88](STP) to provide the necessary infrastructure for software export. The fist ones to come into being were those at Pune, Bangalore and Bhubaneswar in Augest, October and December, 1990 respectively. In 1991, four more STPs were set up by the DoE at Noida, Ghandhinagar, Thiruvananthapuram and Hyderabad. As of now there are 18 software technology parks in the country and they play a significant role in the software export. The infrastructure facilities available in these STPs include, modern computer and communication networks which are beyond the reach of individual firms. The STPs also envisage a transparent policy environment and a package of concessions, which include: approvals under the single-window clearance mechanism and permission for 100 per cent foreign equity; STP authorities' approval for projects costing Rs. 30 Million or less with no foreign equity participation; Five-year tax holiday with no value addition norms; Imports completely duty free and domestic purchases eligible for benefit under deemed exports; Sub-contracting of software development activity by STP permitted and sales in DTA permissible up to 25 pre cent of the export [Oberoi[89] 1991].

In june 2000, an STP was set up in Silicon Valley comprising a business support centre and an India infotech centre, with a view to facilitate software export by small and medium firms to the US.[90] The centre also fosters business relationships by providing access to financial institutions in the US, venture capital funds and specialised trade bodies to promote partnerships and strategic alliances between US and Indian IT companies.

While the policy measures and the setting up of the STPs have led to a substantial increase in the investment for software exports[Venkatesh[91] 1995], the supply of technical manpower appeared to be a major constraint [Schware[92] 1987,Sen[93] 1995]. Software development is a skill-intensive activity although the intensity of skill requirement varies across different activities involved in software production. The development of the software involves broadly the following stages: requirement specification, prototyping designing, coding, testing and maintenance. While the first few stages call for highly skilled manpower, skill requirement is relatively low in the latter stages [Schware[94] 1987].

Traditionally, the main sources of software professionals have been the public sector education institutes such as the Indian Institutes (IITs), Industrial Training Institutes (ITIs) and the engineering colleges. To facilitate the entry of the private sector in the training of the personnel, the department of electronics started an accreditation scheme based on certain objective criteria.[95] As a result, a large number of private organisations were set up for providing training ranging form three weeks to one year or even more. These institutes primarily cater to the middle and lower level manpower requirements of the IT industry. Besides seven Indian Institutes of Information Technology(IIIT) were set up to train manpower on par with the academic standards of the IITs. Estimates show that in 1999 there were 1,832 formal educational institutions in India training more than 67,785 computer software professionals every year [NASSCOM[96] 2000].The structure of the current out-turn of technical manpower from these institutes indicates that three categories, namely, B.Techs, diploma holders and ITI certificate holder account for nearly 70 per cent of the total (Table 2.14), of which B.Techs account for as much as 24 per cent. The share of Ph.D. holders is only 0.14 per cent.

From the foregoing studies, it is evident that the international competitive-sector has been able to establish over the years have not fallen like a 'manna from the heaven' or the handiwork of the prophers of the market. Instead a series of state initiatives have played their due role. The form and content of state intervention however, has been different from the earlier regime. The role of the state has been that of a catalyst or facilitator and not as a direct participation. However, the focus of the state initiatives has been mainly on the promoting IT as a foreign exchange earner. What seems to have been missed in the whole process is a concerted effort to diffuse IT into various sectors of the economy for enhancing productivity, competitiveness and growth. More importantly, given the growing world demand and the on going processing of globalisation, the role of domestic market as a springboard for export seems to have not received adequate attention.

As we have seen, Indian software exports consist primarily of software services. Further, although some of the leading firms are beginning to differentiate themselves from the rest, Indian software export firms are remarkably similar in terms of their activities. Thus, the activities carried out by most firms in India are essentially maintenance tasks for applications on legacy systems such as IBM mainframe computers, development of small applications and enhancements for existing systems, migration to client-server systems, often referred to as porting or re-engineering. The Year 2000 (Y2K) problem has also opened a large market for firms that were traditionally doing mainframe based maintenance projects. Table 2.10, displaying results from our survey, shows that application solutions are the most common type of export, followed by reengineering (also called porting) and conversion projects, such as Y2K projects. Moreover, although Y2K projects were an important source of revenue, most of the leading Indian software firms have limited their dependence on such projects. Managers at most of the US firms agreed that the type of work outsourced was neither technologically very sophisticated nor critical to their business.[97] Requirement analysis and high-level design is typically done either in-house or by US based consultants. However, smaller firms may rely more heavily upon their Indian suppliers, as was the case of a small firm developing medical software. Not only is the work outsourced technologically undemanding, the projects are typically small. The mean number of man-months involved in the most important export project for firms that participated in our questionnaire survey is 510 man-months, whereas the median is only 150 man-months. Note that since the question related to the most important project, it implies that the typical export project is quite small, even for the large firms. Table 2.11 shows that the US accounts for over half of all export revenues (58 per cent in1997-98), compared with 21 per cent for Europe and 4 per cent for Japan. Many of the larger US firms we interviewed are knowledgeable about outsourcing software development and the strengths and weaknesses of Indian software services firms. Some of these firms have also outsourced software development to firms based in other countries like the Ireland, Philippines, Russia and South Africa.

The US is not only a major market; competition from US based service providers is a major source of competition. Although competition from other countries such as Philippines and China is typically cited in the press, as tables 2.12a and 2.12b show, most software exporters indicate that their main competitors are located either in the US or in India itself. However, with few exceptions, most of the US based competitors are themselves firms that extensively recruit Indian software professionals. Only the largest of Indian firms could hope to compete against established US firms.

Many Multi-National Corporations (MNCs) have set up liaison offices and subsidiaries as well. A number of them sought domestic partners. Initially, the partnerships were to sell the MNC products (both hardware and software packages). Increasingly, however, the objective is to use India as a place for software development as well, rather than merely as a place to sell. Some companies have established, or are in the process of doing so, software development centers in India and are exporting packages or components of systems to other countries from India. The work being done at these development centers is fairly sophisticated. For instance, the operating system for the "network computer" introduced by Oracle is said to have been designed entirely in India. Similarly, the Texas Instrument RandD center in India is capable of fairly sophisticated work, including analogue chip design. Other prominent MNCs operating in India include Motorola, Siemens, Hughes Network, Computer Associates, Microsoft and Cadence. As well, there are a number of US firms that have established large Indian operations. Firms such as Mastech, Information Management Resources (IMRs), Syntel, Cognizant (a subsidiary of Dunn and Bradstreet) and CBSL use their India operations much in the way that Indians software export firms do, to tap a large pool of relatively cheap but skilled workforce for providing software services to US based clients. These firms are similar in many respects to the Indian software firms. Virtually all are headed by entrepreneurs of Indian origin and started their existence, as did many of the leading Indian firms, by supplying software professionals such as programmers and analysts to clients in the US. As Indian software exporters establish overseas subsidiaries, the distinction between the two will tend to diminish.

Structure and Growth of IT Exports

Against the backdrop of policy reforms and institutional interventions, let us examine the structure and growth of software exports.

Conceptually, software export is, amenable to analysis in the framework of trade in goods, trade in services could be carried out in a different ways. In the literature on trade in services [Sampson[98] and Snape 1985], we find mainly four different modes of service export. These are (a) trade taking place with the movement of provider to the receiver; (b) trade wherein the receiver is mobile and not the provider; (c) movement of neither provider nor receiver is involved and (d) transactions wherein both provider and receiver move.

Trade in software, which is akin to service sector is carried out mainly through (a) onsite services;(b) offshore services and (c) offshore products and packages. The underlying distinction being the movement of provider and receiver involved. Let us now briefly deal with each of these in some detail for it is important in understanding India's software export performance. On-site services, popularly known in industry circles as 'body-shopping', are rendered the factors move to the site of receiver. In its extreme form this occurs when software manpower is exported to help solve the users' software-related problems. Here, the software firms actually export the manpower and need not necessarily have a complete understanding of user requirements. It could also take the form of undertaking the task of software development to solve specific problems. The development and execution of the software will be done on-site. Under this mode of export, it has been argued that the net export earning will be substantially less than the total export earning because a part of foreign exchange earned will have to be spent in the importing country itself [Heeks[99] 1996].

The second mode of software export is offshore services. This involves limited movement of both the factor and the receivers. The software is developed offshore according to the specified requirements and exported to the users. This method could be cost-effective because the software development process is carried out in the domestic country. At the same time, this calls for more investments in the form of hardware and communication network. The third mode of software export is offshore packages or software product development. Here, neither the factor nor the receiver of the service moves. This is also highly capital and labour intensive. Additionally, there is also the need for incurring substantial marketing cost. Nonetheless, the next export compared with others. On the whole, it appears that the extent of net export earning depends to a great extent on the structure of export. Hence, one of the major objectives of India's software policies has been to increase the offshore component.

The structure of exports in the early 1990s has been such that software services (developed mostly on-site) accounted for about 80 per cent of total software exports. As a result of the policy initiatives, the share of on-site services has come down to about 58 per cent. Thus, the comparative advantage of Indian firms has been in the export of services such as customised software development, with very few well known products of proprietary packages in the international market [Arora and Asundi 1999[100]]. Here again, the focus of the Indian firms is on the lower end of the value chain and carrying out low-level design, coding and maintenance [Kattuman and Iyer 2001[101]]. Thus, the Indian software industry competes primarily on cost advantage with very limited innovation capacity [Mahajan[102] 2000]. As a result, in 1999 revenue per employee in the Indian IT industry has been estimated to be of the order of $ 16,000. The comparable figures are almost 10 times higher for Israel ($150,000) and more than four times ($70,000) for Ireland![Arora[103] 1999].

Another aspect of India's software exports relates to the fact that India's presence in the fastest growing segment, namely, software packages (or software products) is negligible. Moreover, there is very high regional concentration in exports, with over 60 per cent of the total exports directed towards the US market. As per NASSCOM data the share of products has come down from about 9.5 per cent in 1995 to less than 8 per cent in 1999 (Table 2.15). This tends to indicate that technological changes in Indian Software are yet to reach a stage wherein the services splinter off from the factor. Software products are considered high value adding compared with services. It must also be noted that there are high entry barriers to the value-added software products market, which is dominated by large multinational companies spending 60-65 per cent of the price component of packages on marketing and distribution [Kumar[104] 2001]. The hesitation of the firms to go in for software products could also be seen in the context of the widespread software piracy in the domestic market. It has been said that software piracy has forced some companies out of the domestic packaged software market. The magnitude of the problem is illustrated by an estimate from Lotus Development Corporation, that of 1,50,000 copies of Lotus 1-2-3 in India, 1,40,000 have been pirated. Companies that developed microcomputer-based products for word processing, database management and accounting found selling their products in India practically impossible because of the piracy [Schware[105] 1992]. While software piracy would have played its role, a more systematic inquiry is called for to locate the factors that stand in way of firms upward movement in the value chain.

Given the present structure, let us now examine the trend in exports. It may not be an exaggeration to state that, paramount importance attached to software export and associated imports is difficult to obtain. There are three major data sources pertaining to software export. The first is the ministry of Information Technology, the second the National Association of Software and Service Companies (NASSCOM) and the third is the Reserve Bank of India. For unknown reasons, the first two sources deep silent about the imports associated with the export of software. Hence one cannot reach any definite conclusion about the net export earning (which is of relevance to the economy) from the first two sources. In the case of RBI, data on software export is included in the item on miscellaneous services. The import data is available only for the three years beginning 1997-98. The import of software, according to RBI, is $223 million, $348 million and $468 million respectively for financial years 1997,1998 and 1999[106]. Though the RBI provides the import data on both hardware and software, it is of not much use to reflect on the import intensity of software export. This is because the import of hardware and software as reported by RBI data. Here again, it may be noted that there could be a certain extent of underestimation because RBI data do not take into account import of software embodied in capital goods. Therefore, to arrive at the import intensity and net export earning, one has to make use of firm-level data.

For this work, we shall begin with on analysis of export trends based on NASSCOM data. The issue of net export earning is then taken up using firm-level data. Table 2.17 presents data on export earning. NASSCOM is an often quoted data source on exports. We have presented export earnings in both dollars and rupees, for the data is in current prices[107]. By comparing the export in rupee and dollar terms one could reflect on the possible effect of devaluation. From the data presented in Table 2.17, the following observations may be made. To begin with, the recorded rate of growth in exports (over 50 per cent in the sub periods as well as for the whole period), both in rupees and dollars, is almost unprecedented in any other sector of the Indian economy. Secondly, there is a wide margin between the recorded rate of growth in terms of rupees and dollars, which reflects the possible effect of devaluation of the Indian rupee via-a-via US dollar. Thirdly, the observed difference between the rate of growth in terms of Indian rupees and the US dollars (exchange rate effect) comes down as we move from the early part of the 1990s to the closing years of the decade. This, provably, points towards the reduced role of devaluation in sustaining export growth.

The phenomenal increase in export growth has to be viewed, inter alia, in terms of the growing world demand, comparative advantage that India has on account of the highly skilled, English-speaking manpower at relatively low cost (Table 2.18) and the time difference between India and the US, which still continues to be the major export market for India. While the cost of software manpower in India is much less than in developed economics, it is much higher compared with the prevailing wage rate in other sectors in India. More importantly, the salaries of software personnel have been growing at a rate of 25-30 per cent per annum [Kumar[108] 2001]. This has to be viewed against the backdrop of growing world demand on the one hand and a huge demand for software personnel on the other.

Let us now examine the trend in net export earnings as revealed by balance-sheet data of firms in the software industry. At the outset it needs to be noted that arguments with respect to net export earning may not be stretched too far, for our analysis is based on a sample of firms. Secondly, from a macroeconomics perspective, it is not necessary that each sector in an economy is a net export earner. We have obtained firm-level data from the computerised database of the Centre for Monitoring Indian Economy called 'Prowess'. Table 2.16 presents the details of the number of firms as well as their mean export and import. To begin with, it may be noted that the number of firms increased from 32 in 1993 to 79 in 1997. The share of these firms in total exports (as reported by NASSCOM) increased from 24.8 per cent in 1993 to 26.76 per cent in 1997. To the extent that our sample accounts for about 25 per cent of the total exports it may be considered as representative. From the table-2.16 it is also evident that the mean export earning has increased from about Rs. 8 crore in 1993 to over Rs 22 crore in 1997. At the same time, the import dept pace with exports, mean imports increasing from Rs. 4.5 crore in 1993 over Rs. 11 crore in 1997. What is important is that the ratio of imports to exports remained at over 57 per cent in the initial year, increased to over 64 per cent in 1995 and declined to 51 per cent in 1997. If the data presented in Table 2.16 is any indication, one could, one could safely conclude that the recent decline in import intensity notwithstanding, the net export earning from India's software exports is not more than 50 per sent.

From the study so far, it is evident that the software sector in India has been growing at a phenomenal rate in terms of gross exports. However, there have also been substantial imports associated with software exports. Hence, the net export earnings would be substantially less and not more than 50 per cent of gross exports. The higher imports intensity as well as lower earnings pr employee (compared with other competing countries) cannot be de-linked from the present structure of exports, wherein software services dominate and the share of software products is negligible, with a marginal decline in recent years. If the present structure of exports continues, net export earnings may not be more than $ 25 billion in 2008. To achieve the targeted $ 50 billion in exports it is important that the industry move away from the current strategy of competing on 'cost advantage' to one based on 'innovative capacity' so that the industry goes up in the value chain and progressively increases offshore development with focus on software products. Two issues arise against the backdrop of this discussion: the implications of the booming software export on other sectors of the economy especially those needing technical manpower. Secondly, as we have stated earlier, it is important that we inquire into the implications of relaxation in visa restrictions on Indian IT.

Table 2.9: Composition of Indian Software development and Service (Domestic and exports)

Software Activity	*Domestic Software(%)*	*Export Software (%)*
Turnkey Projects	28.6	31.5
Professional Services	4.1	48.4
Products and Packages	52.0	8.8
Training	6.1	1.5
Support and Maintenance	3.2	3.0
IT Enabled services	6.0	6.8

Source–NASSCOM

Table 2.10: Nature of Export Projects undertaken by Indian Firms

Service	*Number of Firms Providing Services for Export*	*Percentage*
Network designing and Engineering	19	20.4
Conversion project	25	26.9
System integration	22	23.7
Application solution software	71	76.3
System /Utility software	28	30.1
Application tools	22	23.7
Operation and network mgmt	7	7.5
Help desk operation	12	12.9
Datacentre management	12	12.9

Source–CWU Software dataset–CMU Survey of the Indian Software Industry

Table 2.11: Destination of Indian Software exports 1997-98

Destination Region	*% of Export Revenues*
USA	58
Europe	21
SE Asia	6
Japan	4
Australia & New Zealand	2
West Asia	2
Rest of the world	7

Source–NASSCOM

Table 2.12a: Location of Primary competitors of Indian Software firms

Location of Competitors	*Number of Firms*	*Percentage of firms*
India	75	82%
Israel	12	13%
Ireland	12	13%
USA	58	63%
Singapore	19	21%
Philippines	6	7%
Eastern Europe/ Russia	10	11%

Source–CMU Software dataset CMU Survey of Indian Software Industry, **N=92,**

Note–Firms were asked to list up to three countries

Table 2.12 b: Preceived location of Primary competitors

One of Top 3 locations	*Small*	*Medium*	*Large*	*%small*	*%medium*	*%large*
India	39	21	15	81	75	94
USA	27	17	14	56	61	88
Other countries	24	14	9	50	50	56
Total in category	48	28	16			

Source–CMU Software dataset CMU Survey of Indian Software Industry, **N=92,**

Table 2.13: Software Professional : Comparitive Salary

Designation	*United State ($ per annum)*	*India ($ per annum)*
Programmer	32000 – 39000	2200-2900
System Analyst	46000 - 57500	8200-10700
Programmer Analyst	39000 – 50000	5400-7000
Network Administrator	36000-55000	15700-19200
Database Administrator	54000-67000	15700-19200
Help-desk Support Technician	25000-35500	5400-7000
Software Developer	49000-67000	15700-19200

Note—1. Converted at exchange rate of Rs. 41.50/US$

2. Figures are starting salaries for large establishments employing more than 50 software professionals. These could be marginally lower for smaller organisations. Salaries for a particular designation would vary due to factors such as educational and experience profile of the professional; platform of operation; nature of assignment (contract/full-time); location of the employer; and additional technical/professional certification.

Source–INFAC, Mumbai

Table 2.14:Structure of the Out-turn of Software Manpower (in 1999)

Course	*Number*	*Per cent*
Ph.D	95	0.14
M.Tech	2130	3.14
B.Tech	16160	23.84
M.Sc	2800	4.13
B.Sc	3200	4.72
BCA/MCA	7700	11.36
PG Diplima	6000	7.38
Diploma	16700	24.64
ITI	14000	20.65
Total	67786	100

Table 2.15:Structure of IT Services Exports from India (per cent)

Type of IT Service	1995	1999
On-site services	61.00	58.18
Offshore services	29.50	33.92
Products and packages	9.50	7.90
Total	100.00	100.00

Source–NASSCOM (2000)

Table 2.16:Trend in Export, Import and Import, Export Ratio for a sample of Software Firms

Year	*Number of Firms*	*Mean Export(Rs Crore)*	*Mean Import(Rs Crore)*	*M/X per cent*
1993	32	7.915	4.570	56.73
1994	53	8.008	4.532	56.59
1995	57	11.651	7.568	64.95
1996	69	13.017	7.847	60.28
1997	79	22.125	11.387	51.47

Source–EPW Aug 25, 2001

Table 2.17: Trend in Software Exports from India

Year	*Rupees Million*	*Growth Rate*	*$ Million*	*Growth Rate*
1990-91	2500		128	
1991-92	4300	72.00	164	28.13
1992-93	6750	56.98	225	37.20
1993-94	10200	51.11	330	46.67
1994-95	15350	50.49	485	46.97
1995-96	25200	64.17	734	51.34
1996-97	39000	54.76	1085	47.82
1997-98	65300	67.44	1750	61.29
1998-99	109400	67.53	2650	51.43
1999-00	172000	57.22	3900	47.17
Annual average growth rate		60.19		46.45
Annual Compound growth rates				
1990-91 to 1995-96		76.18		54.74
1995-96 to 1999-00		61.63		51.82
1990-91 to 1999-00		60.02		46.10

Source–NASSCOM. Indian Software and Services Directory. deferent years.

Table 2.18: Comparison of Annual Wages in Software Industry (1994)

Country	*Computer Programmer US $*	*Index*	*Systems Analyst US $*	*Index*
India	4002	100	5444	100
USA	46600	1164	612001	1124
Japan	51731	1293	64519	1185
Germany	54075	1351	65407	1196
France	45431	1135	71163	1307
Britain	31247	781	51488	1287
Hong kong	34615	865	63462	1166
Maxico	26078	652	25851	658

Source–Gupta (2000).

Human Resources of Information Technology Industry in India

It is widely believed that the key to the success of the Indian software exports is the supply of trained, low cost software professionals. Table 2.13 shows that estimated wage costs in India were about 1/3rd to 1/5th of the corresponding US levels for comparable work. Other estimates suggest that the difference is smaller and that once all costs are factored in, the cost of software development is only of US levels. The size of the talent pool complements the cost advantage. In 1997, the total number of software professionals in India was estimated to be about 160,000 compared with 140,000 in the previous year, with a median age of 28.4 years (NASSCOM, 1998, p 69). Virtually all of these professionals have either engineering or computer science degree or a "Masters in Computer Applications (MCA)". India graduates about 155,000 engineers of various sorts and another 200,000 diploma holders per year. About 60,000 of these enter the IT sector. Most of the leading firms recruit either engineers or students with degrees in mathematics or science. Many also have in-house testing and training programs. Few of the firms we interviewed admitted to hiring graduates from private training institutes. However it would appear that some of the smaller and younger firms do hire graduates from these institutions, as do some domestic market focused firms. Responses to our questionnaire survey indicate that 80 per cent of the software professionals employed had engineering degrees, while 12 per cent had diplomas from private training institutes. Though the Indian software industry tends to recruit primarily engineering graduates, the bulk of the work is relatively non-technical and requires mostly logical and methodical work and a familiarity with software development tools and languages. However, a large number of engineering and science professionals also had diplomas or certificates in software development from private training institutes. Given the large number of science and arts graduates and the widespread availability of private training, the pool of potential software professionals is much larger than merely the engineering graduates. As one CEO we interviewed put it "Take somebody from a good college (any of the top 20 colleges in India), give him 3 months of orientation and they are ready to take up a programming assignment. I don't need all these engineers .... but. I don't want to be branded by my customers as a guy who hires NIIT graduates."

Table 2.19: Major Problems for Indian Software firms Number of Firms

Problems	*Exports*	*Domestic*	*Total*
Manpower shortage/skills	57	32	89
Employee attrition	44	27	71
Physical Infrastructure	12	12	24
Commercial infrastructure	24	17	41
Quality certification	11	6	17
Visas	33	NA	33
Finance/ Capital	20	14	34
Marketing access	42	17	59
Lack of domestic computerization	6	21	27
Lack of government Support	10	11	21
Tarrifs and other barriers	11	8	19

Note–The firms were asked to indicate their top three problems.

Source–CMU Software dataset–CMU Survey of Indian Software Industry, N=104

Table 2.20: Growth Rate of the Training Sector

Training	*1996-97 ($M)*	*1997-98 ($M)*	*Growth(%)*
Corporate	11.67	21.43	84
Individual	145.2	182.43	26
Total	156.81	203.86	30

Source– INFAC, Mumbai

However, software firms are reluctant to tap this pool because of the potential negative signals to their customers.[109]. This is a clear instance of a "race to the top" rather than a race to the bottom. With only limited market power, Indian software exporters, firms try to distinguish themselves from the competition by pointing to the quality of their processes and people and when possible, their experience. Firms also have quality concerns. Managers we interviewed believe that an engineering education imparts a set of problem solving skills, methods of thinking logically and learning tools that help quick adaptation to changes in technology, domains and tasks. Since Indian firms provide services across a range of platforms and domains, this is an important asset. The CEO of a small firm developing innovative products stated: "*Because things are changing so fast in this industry, knowledge of a particular operating system, a particular language, a particular technology is not as important as the ability to learn and adapt to change.*"

The problem thus appears to be that relying upon engineering graduates alone is not capable of meeting the demand while students trained by private training institutes are not seen as being appropriate for export services. Thus, despite the apparently large stock of human capital in India, NASSCOM claims that by year 2000, demand will outstrip supply. The NASSCOM study projects an annual demand of about 75,000 by the year 2000. The tight labour market conditions are reflected in the 20 per cent increase in wages and in attrition rates that are said to be nearly 20-25 per cent for the industry [110]. We believe that demand already exceeds supply for experienced project managers. Many of our interviewees mentioned their difficulty in recruiting professionals with 4-6 years experience, even though nearly 40 per cent of the workforce is reported to have 4-6 years experience. The loss, through immigration, of experienced software professionals to the U.S through the H-1B visa route is responsible for a substantial part of the shortfall.[111]. The entry of new firms exacerbates the demand for domain knowledge and managerial expertise. [Nidumolu and Goodman 1993][112].

Despite paying substantially above Indian standards, virtually all firms find it difficult to retain talented professionals. Virtually each of the over one hundred firms we surveyed mentions employee turnover and difficulty in attracting suitable employees as a major problem (Table 2.19). High rates of employee turnover constitute one of the most important challenges to the ability of Indian firms to progress beyond providing low-end software coding, development and maintenance services. Firms are responding to the problem of employee attrition in a number of ways. One popular way is by providing opportunities to work in the US. Many managers also stressed quality of life issues. Some firms stressed their ability to provide a career path for their employees, wherein they could move to being managers and would not have to remain programmers, apparently something valued by Indian professionals. Interestingly enough, few claimed to pay more than their competitors to attract and retain workers.

A number of firms were actively considering stock options for their employees, something that few firms in India do, with Infosys being an important exception. However they faced some legal restrictions on their ability to use stock options to compensate employees. However, these restrictions have been eased somewhat over the last couple of years.

Some of the firms expressed the need to make the organisation individual independent by addressing the loss of knowledge due to employee turnover. Thus one CEO told us that although, *"Our attrition is ... better than average.... It is difficult to retain segment [of the workforce with] 6-8 year's experience. We are tackling this by making organisation individual independent and stressing training and process methodologies."* Our sense, however, was that efforts at insulating the organisation from employee turnover are very much in their infancy and firms are still very vulnerable to this problem. The loss of employees is especially severe among consultants (programmers and analysts) sent overseas to work onsite in the US and our interviewees believe that a very substantial fraction quit within two years.[113] The other part of the solution is on the supply side. As noted earlier there are a large number of students trained by private, training firms such as NIIT and Aptech, which has resulted in high profits and growth for these firms. Indeed, as table 2.20 shows, the training sector industry has grown alongwith the software industry, with total revenues in 1997-98 estimated at Rs. 8.56 billion, about $225 million, up from Rs. 6.6 billion the year before. Although nearly 90 per cent of the revenues are from the individual training sector, corporate training is also growing rapidly.[114] While the general perception appears to be that such graduates are not well suited for software development, they appear to be well suited for tasks such as providing support and maintenance, for back office operations and for a variety of IT enabled services such as medical transcription and claims processing for the insurance industry.

Furthermore, we did find evidence that some large and reputable firms had tie-ups for professional practice with graduates from private training institutes and frequently ended up recruiting these graduates. The increase in certification courses such as the Microsoft Certified Software Engineer/Developer (MCSE/D), Certified Novell Engineer (CNE) and IBM Net Professional certification should also help enlarge the pool of potential employees. In addition, there are a number of public sector and industry initiatives to increase the supply of software professionals. The government has recently announced the establishment of Indian Institutes of Information Technology, along the lines of the well-known

Indian Institutes of Technology. A number of engineering colleges have increased their emphasis on Information Technology and, in some cases, have started IT management programmes. A number of private sector, for profit, institutes providing graduate level education, such as a joint venture between the Mahindra Group and British Telecom to teach methods and techniques for software development, are coming online.

A potentially serious constraint on the ability to rapidly increase the output of trained software and computer engineers is the shortage of engineering doctorates being awarded in India. Recent data show that the PhDs awarded in engineering disciplines have fallen from their high of 675 in 1987 to 375 in 1995. Concurrently, the number of engineers with postgraduate training has also risen only slowly, from a little over 12,000 in 1987-89 to a little over 17,000 in 1990-92. Surveys of the IITs shows that a very large fraction of postgraduates enters the IT sector, in some cases as many as 90 per cent! Although there are a substantial number of engineering doctorate holders of Indian origin working outside India, a long-run solution will require an increase in the postgraduate research and training infrastructure.

Information Technology has been recognized as the enabler of business in the 21st century. The rapid growth of IT within India bodes well for companies that plan to expand operations internationally and especially in India. This may not have been true a few years back but is definitely true of the present.

The overall success of the IT industry in India has to some extent managed to spill over to other industries in the country. The Indian economy has grown at the rate of 6.6 per cent a year for 1998 and 1999. In the last five years (1994-1999), the Indian IT Industry has recorded a C.A.G.R. (Compounded Annual Growth Rate) of more than 40.5 per cent which is almost double the growth rate of the IT industry in many of the developed countries. The business scenario within the country has gradually evolved and the credit goes to the government and the private sector. Business practices, infrastructure, knowledge base have all improved tremendously in the last decade. The Internet has wielded its magic as the great equalizer and in bringing distant places together, has brought India closer to the rest of the world, thereby boosting its development efforts.

Interestingly and fortunately for India, we are now witnessing a phenomena of "reverse brain drain". Indians who left the country in search for better and bigger opportunities, are coming back. They bring back with them diverse international experience, knowledge of latest technology, management skills and much more. This can only increase India's attraction to MNC's as a business location.

The last few years have witnessed increasing emphasis on management education alongwith technological input. Graduates from Management institutes are capable of managing large projects and the challenges within a global firm. What this translates into is that Global firms have a ready supply of local managers to manage their Indian operations. This not only drives down laboor costs but also improves business prospects for the local subsidiary. MNC's are required to recruit a minimum number of employees from the local market. In the 1980's, doing so would have adversely affected daily operations. Today, with the ready availability of an able work force, MNC's can win government favor by willingly recruiting local managers. With a large pool of trained IT professionals, India is a viable choice of new IT and non-IT ventures.

The Department of Information Technology and the Department of Telecom are pursuing very aggressive policies with regards to IT infrastructure. In view of their ambitious plans, the IT landscape within the country will change dramatically in the coming decade. Already, the advent of high speed lines, satellites, cyber parks, etc, is moving e-commerce and e-business ahead in leaps and bounds.

There is a distinct difference in the attitudes, buying behaviourr and outlook of the younger generation (ages 35 and below) when compared to the older generation (ages 35 and above). A well-educated and informed consumer base supplies the base for a competitive market scenario, which is essential for the development of any industry. Young Indian consumers are definitely tech savvy, well traveled, better informed and more sophisticated than their predecessors.. They present a challenging and attractive market for a diverse set of products ranging from consumer goods, to real estate, to electronics, home appliances, etc.

If an MNC was evaluating multiple locations across the globe for new business operations, India would definitely be within the consideration set. The present scenario and the expected future scenario within the country, supports its move into the choice set. Taking all factors into consideration, India is a good location for manufacturing activities and to a certain extent, sales activities. If development continues at the current pace, in a few years, infrastructure should be developed enough to support distribution activities also. But at the present, India's existing physical infrastructure comes a poor second to many other Asian countries.

The Future of Indian IT Enable Service

The McKinsey Quarterly reads, "Multinational companies already understand India's advantages as a platform for software development.

But increased bandwidth and universal networking standards are now giving them an opportunity to move many parts of their business systems. By 2008, global remote-service operations may undertake activities accounting for half a trillion dollars around the world and representing every element of the value chain: upstream activities such as research and design, manufacturing-related activities such as procurement and logistics, front-end activities such as marketing and sales and staff functions such as accounting, Information Technology and human-resources management. Such operations could generate cost and other savings of about US$ 400 billion, to be shared by the users and the providers as profits. Seizing the opportunity, one global financial services company has already achieved annual savings of more than US$ 250 million - according to its management, only a fraction of the total savings potential. "This view is shared by rapidly increasing number of Fortune 500 companies.

India's Irresistible and Sustainable Value Proposition

By outsourcing IT enabled services requirements to India, large overseas companies, including increasing number of Fortune 500 companies and existing overseas service providers, are not only achieving significant benefits in cost, quality and time but also creating platforms for building new businesses. Overall, these benefits are due to the advantages offered by relevant skill-surplus economies. India offers the case of best value proposition for all IT enabled services.

India's value proposition is already leading IT enabled services hubs such as Ireland and Singapore to back-end their operations in India, since skilled labour is becoming an increasingly scarce resource in these countries. To top it up, telecom infrastructure is increasingly becoming competitive in India. Coupled with active support of state, India is offering hard to beat proposition to emerge as a "Preferred Global Hub."

Seizing the opportunity, several companies in the financial service sector, for example, have saved at least 50-60 per cent of their process costs. The process redesign that comes with, out location also provides additional cost savings and consolidation of operations[115].

A comparison amongst some countries in Asia Pacific based on these factors highlights in the figure 2.14. (Ratings are on a scale of 1 to 3, with 1 being the lowest and 3 the highest.).

IT enabled service centres in India are able to deliver superior quality because of specialisation and scale benefits. India already has a large and rapidly growing number of IT enabled services' providers collectively covering a wide range of services with different levels of complexity and value adds. Yet another compelling rationale for IT enabled services is that it allows companies to capitalise on time zone differences and to provide round-the-clock services, every day of the week on (24 x 7) model. For example, doctors in the US can have transcribed records of their notes at the start of the next day by sending them to medical transcription services in India who will start work at the end of their working day in the US.

Finally, companies can discover new business opportunities in the skills they learn from operating IT enabled services. GE Capital, one of the largest IT enabled services' operation is now planning to extend its services beyond financial services to other GE group companies as well as to external customers. It aims to expand its IT enabled services' operations in India to over 10,000 employees. Also, there are already a large number of smaller Indian companies that provide services in many areas of the business system.

India and Ireland have emerged as particularly attractive locations for IT Enabled Services. These advantages are supported by the significant number of entrepreneurship opportunities dotting India's technology landscape as well as increasing value creation opportunities for venture capitalists through this sector[116]

Figure 2.14: India's Irresistible and Sustainable Value Proposition

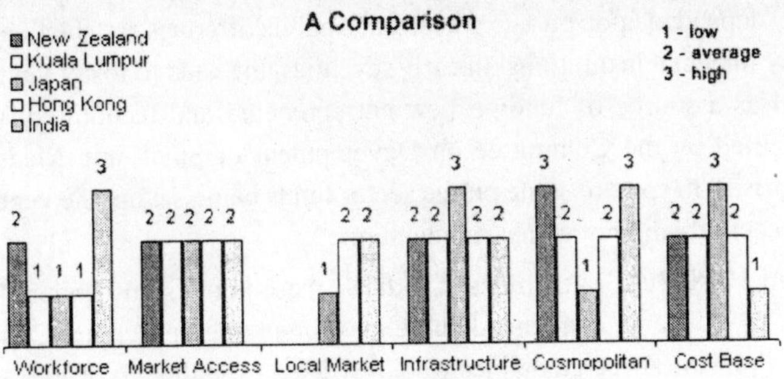

Source—NASSCOM

Figure 2.15: India and Ireland have emerges as particularly attractive locations for IT Enable Services.

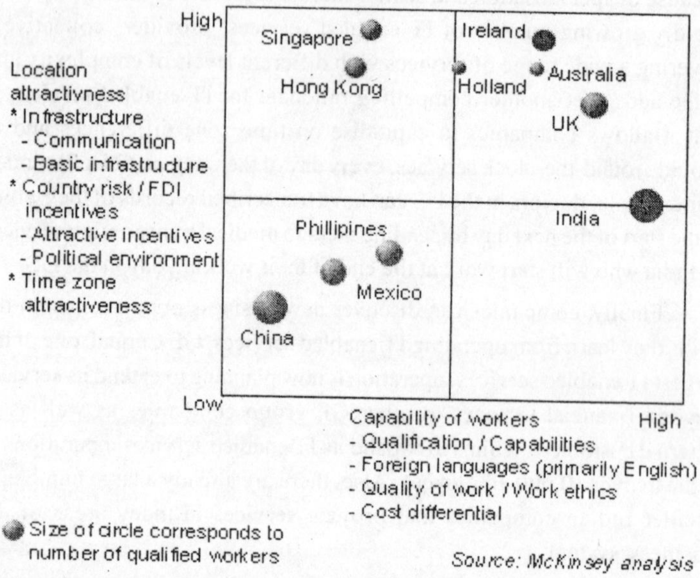

Source–Mc Kinsey analysis

Venture Capitalist Scenario in India

In the earlier years, individual investors and development financial institutions played the role of venture capitalists in India and entrepreneurs largely depended upon private placements, public offerings and the finance lend by financial institutions. In early seventies, the need to foster venture capital as a source of funding new entrepreneurs and technology was highlighted by the Committee on Development of Small and Medium Enterprises. In spite of some public sector funds being set up, the venture capital activity did not gather momentum.

In 1988, the Government of India[117], based on a study undertaken by the World Bank, announced guidelines for setting up Venture Capital Funds (VCFs). These guidelines were restricted to setting up of VCFs by banks or financial institutions only. Internationally, however, entrepreneurs who are willing to take higher risk, in anticipation of higher returns, usually set up venture capital funds. This is in contrast to banks and financial institutions, which are more averse to risk.

The Background

In September 1995, Government of India issued guidelines for overseas venture capital investment in India whereas the Central Board of Direct Taxes (CBDT) issued guidelines for tax exemption purposes. (The Reserve Bank of India governs the investment and flow of foreign currency in and out of India.) As a part of its mandate to regulate and to develop the Indian capital markets, Securities and Exchange Board of India (SEBI) framed the SEBI (Venture Capital Funds) Regulations, 1996.

Pursuant to the regulatory framework, some domestic VCFs were registered with SEBI. Some overseas investments also came through the Mauritius route. However, the venture capital industry, understood globally as 'independently managed, dedicated pools of capital that focus on equity or equity linked investments in privately held, high growth companies' (The Venture Capital Cycle, Gompers and Lerner, 1999) is still relatively in a nascent stage in India. Figures from the Indian Venture Capital Association (IVCA) reveal that, till 2000, around Rs. 2,200 crore (US$ 500 million) had been committed by the domestic VCFs and offshore funds which are members of IVCA. Figures available from private sources indicate that overall funds committed are around US$ 1.3 billion.[118]

Funds that can be invested were less than 50 per cent of the committed funds and actual investments were lower still. At the same time, due to economic liberalisation and increasing global outlook in India, an increased awareness and interest of domestic as well as foreign investors in venture capital was observed. While only 8 domestic VCFs were registered with SEBI during 1996-98, more than 30 additional funds have already been registered in 2000-01. Institutional interest is growing and foreign venture investments are also on the increase. Given the proper environment and policy support, there is a tremendous potential for venture capital activity in India.

The Finance Minister, in the Budget 2000 speech announced, "For boosting high tech sectors and supporting first generation entrepreneurs, there is an acute need for higher investments in venture capital activities." He also said that the guidelines for the registration of venture capital activity with the Central Board of Direct Taxes would be harmonised with those for registration with the Securities and Exchange Board of India.

SEBI decided to set up a committee on venture capital to identify the impediments and suggest suitable measures to facilitate the growth of venture capital activity in India. Keeping in view the need for global perspective, it was decided to associate Indian entrepreneur from Silicon Valley in the committee. The setting up of this committee was primarily motivated by the need to play a facilitating role in tune with the mandate of SEBI, to regulate as well as develop the market. The committee headed by K. B. Chandrasekhar, Chairman, Exodus Communications Inc., submitted its report on 8 January 2000[119].

In his Budget Proposals 2000-01, the Finance Minister announced new regime for venture capital funds. And proclaimed SEBI as the single point nodal agency for registration and regulation of both domestic and overseas venture capital funds. The new regime stipulated that no approval of venture capital funds by tax authorities would be required and that the principle of "pass through" would be applied in tax treatment of venture capital funds. Recently, the Government of India has also announced the "exit policy" for venture capitalists, (though a notification to this effect is awaited)[120].

Objective and Vision for Venture Capital in India

Venture Capital funding is different from traditional sources of financing. Finance innovation ideas have potential for high growth but with inherent uncertainties. This makes it a high-risk, high return investment for venture capitalists. Apart from finance, venture capitalists provide networking, management and marketing support as well. In the broadest sense, therefore, venture capital connotes risk finance as well as managerial support.[121]

In the global venture capital industry, investors and funded firms work closely together in an enabling environment that allows entrepreneurs to focus on value creating ideas and venture capitalists to drive the industry by the levers of control in return for the provision of capital, skills, information and complementary resources. This very blend of risk financing and hand holding of entrepreneurs by venture capitalists creates an environment particularly suitable for 200,000 and so engineer graduates from Government and private-run colleges in India.

Scientific, technological and knowledge-based ideas properly supported by venture capital can be propelled into a powerful engine of economic growth and wealth creation in a sustainable manner. In various developed and developing economies venture capital has played a significant developmental role.

India, along with Israel, Taiwan and the United States, is recognized for its globally competitive high technology and human capital. The success India has achieved particularly in software and Information Technology against several odds such as inadequate infrastructure, expensive hardware, restricted access to foreign resources and limited domestic demand, is a pointer to the hidden potential it has in the field of knowledge and technology based industry.[122]

India has the second largest English speaking scientific and technical manpower in the world. Some of the management (IIMs) and technology institutes (IITs) in India are globally known as centres of excellence. Every year thousands of young people specialize through diploma courses in computers and other technical areas. Management institutes produce 40,000 management graduates annually. Given this quality and magnitude of human capital India's potential to create enterprises is unlimited.

In Silicon Valley, these very Indians have proved their potential and have carved out a prominent place in terms of wealth creation as well as credibility. There are innumerable well-known success stories of successful Indians backed by a venture capital environment in Silicon Valley and elsewhere in US, supporting their innovation and invention. At least 30 per cent of the start-up enterprises in Silicon Valley are started / backed by Indians.

With the inherent skills and manpower that India has, it can be easily predicted that software exports will thrive with an estimated 50 per cent growth per annum. The market capitalization of the listed software companies comprises of approximately 25 per cent of the total market capitalization. Also greater visibility of the Indian companies globally is evident.

Given such vast potential, which is, not only confined to IT and software but also in other sectors like biotechnology, telecommunications, media and entertainment, medical and health etc., venture capital industry is playing and shall continue to play a catalyst's role in industrial development.

Thus, venture capital is valuable not only because it makes risk capital available at the early stages of a project but also because of the expertise of venture capitalist that leads to superior product development. And the big focus of venture capital worldwide is - technology.

VCs as a whole invested US$ 79.9 billion in the first three quarters of 2000, a 137 per cent increase over the corresponding period during 1999. Out of this, technology firms reportedly got around 75 per cent. Besides this huge supply from organised venture funds there is an even larger pool of "angel" funds provided by private investors. In 2000, it was expected that angel investment would be of the order of US$ 105 billion, thus making the total "at-risk" investment of US$ 185 billion in high-end technology ventures in a single year.[123] See figure 2.18.

Critical Factors for Success of Venture Capital Industry in India

In 1999, SEBI (Securities and Exchange Board of India) had set up a committee under the Chairmanship of Mr. K. B. Chandrasekhar to look into the issues of venture capital in India. The Report of the K. B. Chandrasekhar Committee on venture capital identified the following as critical factors for the success of VC industry in India:

- The regulatory, tax and legal environment should play an enabling role. This emphasizes the facilitating and promotional role of regulation. Internationally, venture funds have evolved in an atmosphere of structural flexibility, fiscal neutrality and operational adaptability. And we need to provide regulatory simplicity and structural flexibility on the same lines. There is also the need for a level playing field between domestic and offshore venture capital investors. This has already been done for the mutual fund industry in India.
- Investment, management and an exit option should provide flexibility to suit the business requirements and should also be driven by global trends. Venture capital investments have typically come from high net worth individuals who have risk taking capacity. Since high risk is involved in venture financing, venture investors globally seek investment and exit on very flexible terms, which provides them with certain levels of protection. Such exit should be possible through IPOs and

mergers / acquisitions on a global basis and not just within India.

- There is also the need for identifying and increasing the domestic pool of funds for venture capital investment. In US, apart from high net worth individuals and angel investors, pension funds, insurance funds, mutual funds etc. provide a very big source of money. The share of corporate funding is also increasing and it was as high as 25.9 per cent in the year 1998 as compared to 2 per cent in 1995. Corporations are also setting up their own venture capital funds. Similar avenues need to be identified in India also.
- With increasing global integration and mobility of capital it is important that Indian venture capital firms as well as venture financed enterprises be able to have opportunities for investment abroad. This would not only enhance their ability to generate better returns but also add to their experience and expertise to function successfully in a global environment. We need our enterprises to become global and create their own success stories. Therefore, automatic, transparent and flexible norms need to be created for such investments by domestic firms and enterprises.
- Venture capital should become an institutionalised industry financed and managed by successful entrepreneurs, professional and sophisticated investors. Globally, venture capitalists are not merely finance providers but are also closely involved with the invested enterprises and provide expertise by way of management and marketing support. This industry has developed its own ethos and culture. Venture capital has only one common aspect that cuts across geography, i.e., it is risk capital invested by experts in the field. It is important that venture capital in India be allowed to develop via professional and institutional management
- Infrastructure development also needs to be prioritised using government support and private management. This involves creation of technology as well as knowledge incubators for

supporting innovation and ideas. RandD also needs to be promoted by government as well as other organisations.

The above report was well received by the Government and few issues have already been resolved.

Venture Capital / Angel Investments for the IT Sector

In India, the venture capital creation process has started taking off with all four stages receiving attention:

1. Idea generation
2. Start up
3. Growth ramp up
4. Exit processes.

However, much more needs to be done yet. The following graph indicates the growth of venture capital and angel investments in India's IT software and services sector:

It must be noted that during 1999, approximately 80 per cent of the estimated US$ 30 billion worth of venture capital invested in United States, went to technology firms. India too, with its strengths in innovation and IT technology has attracted several Venture Capital firms.

In 2000 alone, 20 new venture capital funds have registered with SEBI, taking the total number to 30. In fact, VC or Angel investments in high tech firms in India have grown by over 5,000 per cent from Rs. 70 crore to projected Rs. 2,200 crore between 1996 and 2000. And this figure is expected to grow to Rs. 50,000 crore by 2008. An analysis of financing by investment stages indicate the figure 2.16. Further, the major contributors to the funds were:

National Venture Capital Fund for Software and Information Technology Small Industries Development Bank of India (SIDBI), in association with Ministry of Information Technology, Government of India, has set up a 10 year close ended venture capital fund called the "National Venture Fund for Software and IT industry" (NFSIT).

Prime Minister, Atal Behari Vajpayee launched this fund in December 1999. NFSIT has a corpus fund of Rs. 100 crore and is a dedicated IT Fund with a focus on small-scale sector. The objective of the fund, besides meeting total financial requirements of the units, is to enable these units to achieve rapid growth rates and develop and maintain global competitiveness. The fund endeavours to develop international networking and enable assisted units to attract co-investments from international venture capitalists. International linkages will help the assisted units to get a listing with foreign stock markets viz. NASDAQ; thereby achieving better valuations and offering alternate exit routes to the investors.

A portion of the Fund has been earmarked for incubation projects that involve high risks and might be used for development of software products. Software products require rigorous risk evaluation for which high degrees of expertise including international linkages are required. The fund managed to attract a number of high-class professionals as investment managers in the Asset Management Company.

Many state governments have already set up venture capital funds for the IT sector in partnership with local state financial institutions and SIDBI. These states include: Andhra Pradesh, Karnataka, Delhi, Kerala, Gujarat, Tamil Nadu among others.

Figure 2.16– Growth of VC and Angel Investment

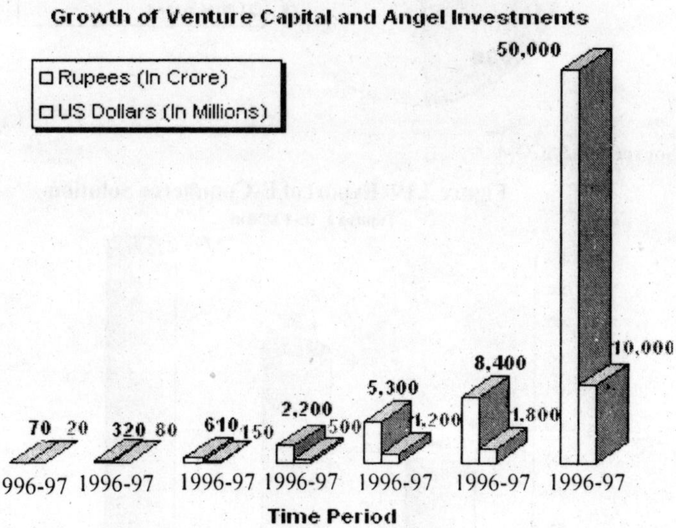

Figure 2.17– Analysis of Financing by Investment Stages

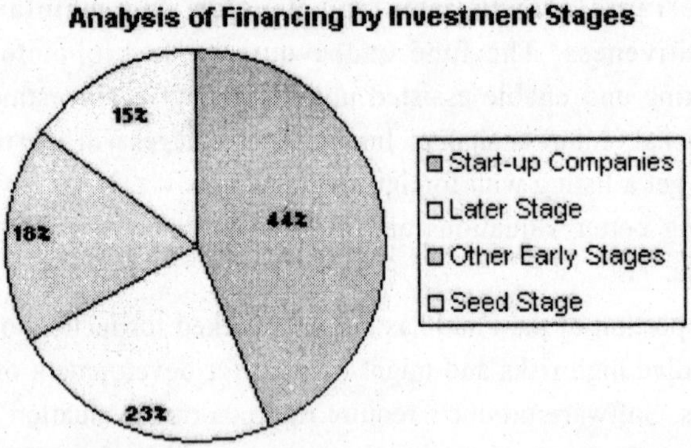

Source–NASSCOM

Figure 2.18– Growth of VC and Angel Investments

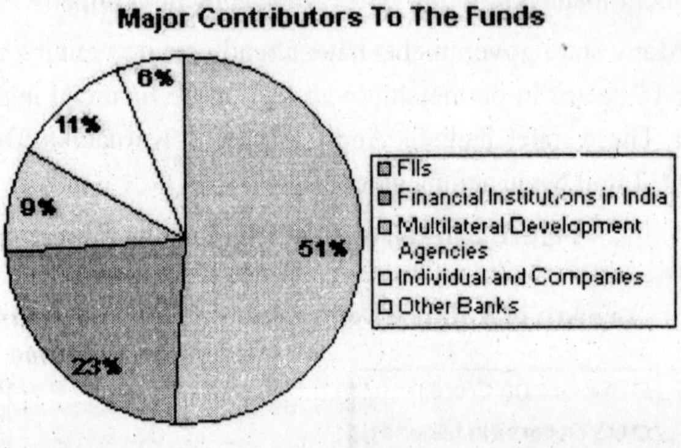

Source–NASSCOM

Figure 2.19–Export of E-Commerce Solution

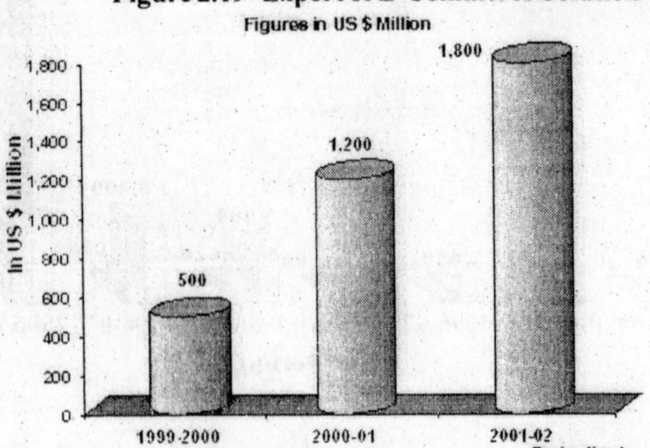

Figure 2.20–Growth in IT Enabled Services

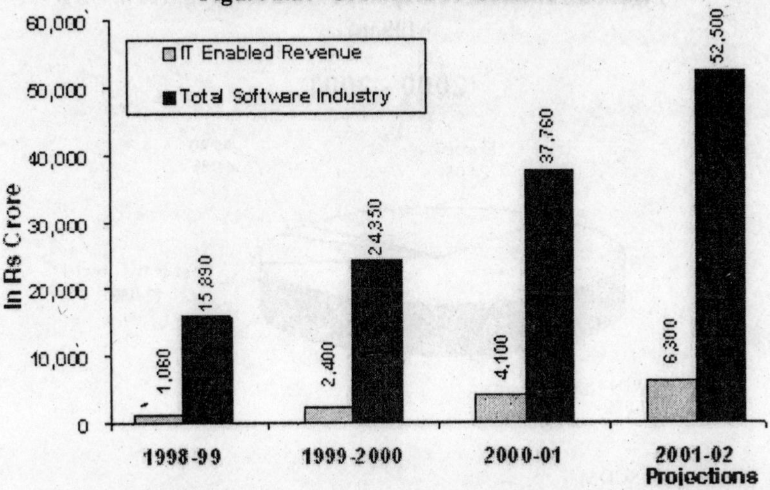

Source–NASSCOM

Figure 2.21–IT Enabled Services Revenue as a per centage of Total Software Industry Revenue

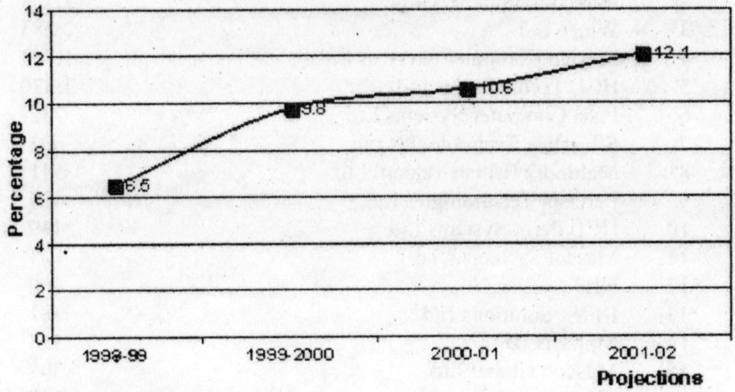

Source–NASSCOM

Figure 2.22:Software Exports 1996-2001 (Figures in US $ Million)

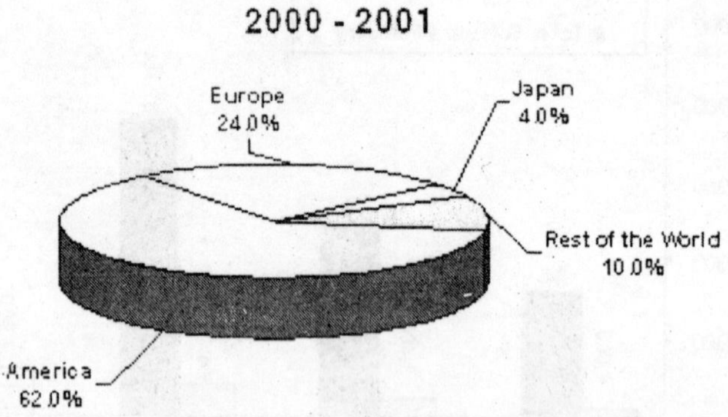

Source–NASSCOM

Table 2.23: Top 20 Indian Software Export Comapanies

1.	Tata Consultancy Services	3,882
2.	Infosys Technology Ltd.	2,553
3.	Wipro Ltd.	2,283
4.	Satyam Computer Services Ltd.	1,703
5.	HCL Technologies Ltd.	1,320
6	Patri Computer Systems Ltd.	732
7.	Silverline Technologies Ltd.	603
8.	Mahindra British Telcom Ltd.	541
9.	Pertasot Technologies Ltd.	460
10.	HCL Perot Systems Ltd.	449
11.	Mascot Systems LTd.	103
12.	NIIT	400
13.	I-Flex Solutions Ltd.	382
14.	Mphasis DFL	313
15.	Mascon Global Ltd.	307
16.	Masteck Ltd.	259
17.	Birlasoft LTd.	250
18.	Polaris Software Lab Ltd.	247
19.	Larson & Turbo Infotech Limited	245
20.	Hexamore Technologies Ltd.	241

Source– NASSCOM

Table 2.24– Top 10 MNC Software Exports

1.	IBM Global Services	3,100
2.	Cognizant Technolgoy Solutions	2,712
3.	Oracle India Pvt Ltd.	2,000
4.	Covansys (India) Pvt. Ltd.	1,595
5.	Syntel	1,580
6.	Hughes Software System Ltd.	1,500
7.	Hevlett-Packard (I) Software Operation Ltd.	1,489
8.	Digital Global Soft	1,480
9.	PwC	1,200
10.	OrbiTech Solutions	1,191

Table 2.25– Domestic IT Market

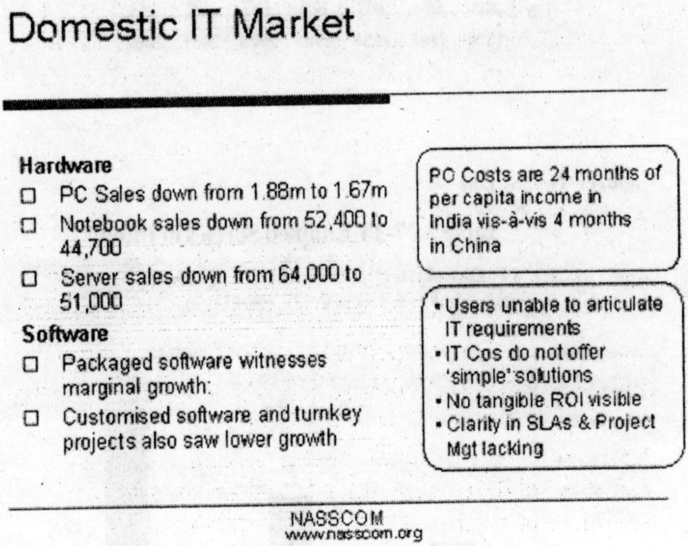

Source–NASSCOM

Table 2.26–Wealth creation by IT

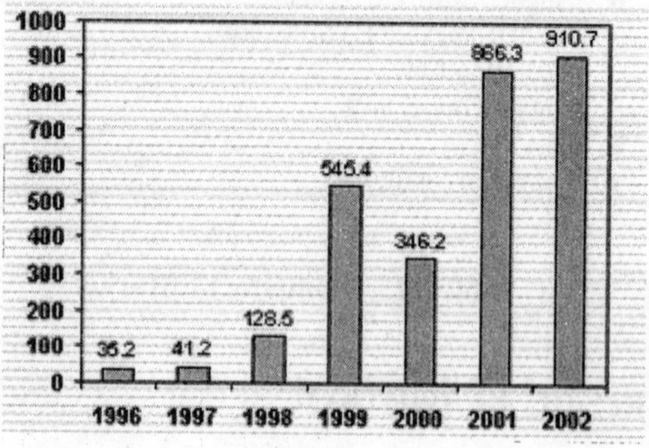

Source–NASSCOM

Table 2.27–IT Enabled Sercies in India

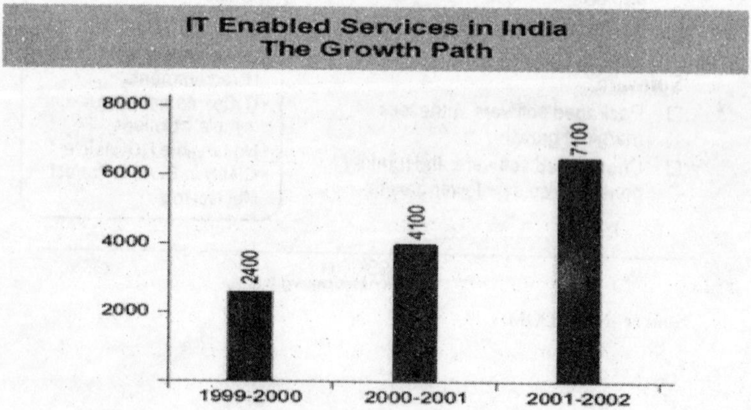

Table 2.28–IT Enable Services in Total Export

Increasing Contribution by IT Enabled Services in total exports

	IT Enbaled Services	IT Services
1999-2000	14%	86%
2000-2001	14.5%	85.5%
2001-2002	19%	81%
2002-2003	24%	76%

Table 2.2 *Source : NASSCOM*

Source–NASSCOM

Notes and References

1. Ministry of Information Technology, http://www.itfriend.mit.gov.in
2. India 1996, *Ministry of Informaiton and Boardcasting, GOI*
3. Ministry of Information Technology, http://www.itfriend.mit.gov.in
4. See in Website of Ministry of Information Technology, http:\\www.mit.gov.in\ smart sourcing.
5. *Ibid.*
6. *Ford to set up a global IT facility,* Economic Times, March 13, 2001.
7. see in planning commission of 8th and 9th plan http:\\www.nic.gov.in
8. Journal of Electronics Information Planning, M IT, New Delhi.
9. Arora, Ashish and Asundi, Jai, 1999, "Quality Certification and the Economics of Contract Software Development: A Study of the Indian Software Service Companies", NBER working paper 7260, Cambridge, MA.
10. Arora, Ashish and Asundi, Jai, 1999, "Indian Software Industry", Cambridge, MA.
11. Arora, Ashish and Asundi, Jai, 1999, "Quality Certification and the Economics of Contract Software Development: A Study of the Indian

Software Service Companies", NBER working paper 7260, Cambridge, MA.

12. An alternate model of software development is the Spiral Model (Boehm, 1981).

13. Royce, W. W., 1970, "Managing the development of large software systems: concepts and techniques", 1970 WESCON technical papers volume 14, p.723.

14. Heeks, R., (1996)"India's Software Industry: State policy, liberalisation and industrial development", Sage Publications.

15. Patni Computer Systems (PCSs), a privately held firm, was another early entrant. It started with a data conversion project because India was seen as a cheap supply source at the time. However, steep import duties on computer equipment imports (including keyboards and CRT screens), as well as union regulations, caused much of data conversion work to be shifted to China and Taiwan. PCS also formed an alliance with Data General, a mainframe computer firm, whose equipment PCS marketed and for whom PCS also provided some programming services. This hardware tie-up is apparently typical of other older SW firms (e.g., TCS-Burroughs, TUL-Unisys, Hinditron-DEC and Datamatics -Wang).

16. In addition to these firms that focused on software exports, there were others that served domestic users, most notable Computer Maintenance Corporation, or CMC. Responsible for maintaining computer systems after IBM left India, CMC has grown to over 2000 employees and developed the ability to develop and implement large and complex projects, especially for infrastructure systems. CMC has also proved to be a good training ground for managers that would later be employed by other, private sector firms.

17. India has around 40 engineers for every 10,000 people.

18. Economist, Feb 20, 1999, p 27.

19. A part of the explanation lies in the extremely low rates for domestic software services, of the order of $10,000 per person. By comparison, the rates for domestic work in Ireland are likely to be considerably higher. Tax considerations may also have caused some firms to book revenues in Ireland that were generated elsewhere in Europe. The importance of such accounting practices in accounting for the apparent differences in rates is unclear.

20. In related study, Arora and Asundi (1999) find that firms' efforts to differentiate themselves through ISO 9001 quality certification are rewarded

primarily through greater volume of sales rather than through higher price cost margins.

21. Annual Report Government of India, Ministry of Information Technology, 2001.
22. Vision in website of Ministry of Information Technology, http:\\www.mit.gov.in
23. Measure of policy measure in website of Ministry of Information Technology, http:\\www.mit.gov.in\advance_india.
24. Ibid.
25. http://itfriend.mit.gov.in
26. Advantage India, Ministry of Information Technology, New Delhi
27. http://venturefundindia.mit.gov.in
28. http://venturefundindia.mit.gov.in
29. Annual Report Government of India, Ministry of Information Technology, 2001.
30. Ibid.
31. Ibid.
32. Ibid.
33. Ibid.
34. Industrial policy approval in it_policies.asp at website www.nasscom.org.
35. New Industrial Policy 1991, GOI, New Delhi.
36. Action_ plan_1.pdf at website www.nasscom.org
37. Export-Import policy in exim_policies at website www.nasscom.org
38. Ibid.
39. Deemed export in http//www.mit.gov.in/itfriend/advanced_india/policy.htm
40. Electronic and IT sector in http//www.mit.gov.in/ itfriend/ advanced_india/ policy.htm
41. http//www.mit.gov.in/itfriend/advanced_india/policy.htm
42. ibid.
43. Customs Notification No.20/99 dated 28 February 1999
44. Customs Notification No. 70/98 dated 25 September 1998

45. Customs Notification No.47/98 dated 16 July 1998
46. Customs Notification No.18/99 dated 11 February 1999
47. Income tax inhttp//www.mit.gov.in/itfriend/advanced_india/policy.htm
48. Finance Bill (No.2) 1998
49. RBI Circular AD (MA Series) No.1 dated 8 January 1999
50. RBI Circular AD (MA Series) No.25 dated 7 August 1998
51. RBI Circular AD (MA Series) No.51 dated 15th December 1997
52. RBI Circular AD (MA Series) No.4 dated 10 March 1993
53. RBI Circular AD (MA Series) No.19 dated 8 September 1995
54. RBI Circular AD (MA Series) No.46 dated 10 November 1997
55. RBI Circular AD (MA Series) No.35 dated 28 August 1997, Ministry of Commerce Notification F.No.4/1/93-EP(01) dated 26 March 1997
56. Press Note dated 27 December 1999 and 23 March 2000 refers
57. RBI Circular AD (MA Series) No.27 dated 7 August 1998
58. Protecting_ipr.asp in website www.nasscom.org
59. Protecting_ipr.asp in website www.nasscom.org
60. Setting IT company in website www.nasscom.org\setting_itco.asp
61. Ibid.
62. Ibid.
63. Annual report of the Ministry of Information Technology Industry for the year 1999-2000.
64. http://www.nasscom.org/business_in_india/pdf/itbill2000.pdf
65. Ibid.
66. IT Act 2000 in website www.nasscom.org\setting_itco.asp
67. Ibid.
68. http://www.123bangalore.com
69. Lalkaka, *"Venture Creation and Growth through Business Incubators and Technology Parks,"* http://waitro.dti.dk/ Publications/ Seminars/ Best_Pra/ Lalkaka.htm, visited December 14, 2001.
70. Rustam, *"Venture Creation and Growth through Business Incubators and Technology Parks,"* http://waitro.dti.dk/ Publications/ Seminars/ Best_Pra/ Lalkaka.htm, visited December 14, 2001.

71. Löfsten, *"Science parks in Sweden - industrial renewal and development?,"* RandD Management, July 1, 2001, 313.
72. Hans, *"Science parks in Sweden - industrial renewal and development?,"* RandD Management, July 1, 2001, 313.
73. Lindelof Peter, *"Science parks in Sweden - industrial renewal and development?,"* RandD Management, July 1, 2001, 313.
74. http://www.hyderabad.com/index.htm
75. IT companies in website of www.stpi.soft.net
76. There are a couple of caveats to this observation. The domestic sector revenues include those from reselling imported software packages and therefore overstate the extent of software development in India for the domestic market. On the other hand, the figures exclude the possibly considerable amount of software developed in-house by users.
77. There are a few exceptions, possibly the most noteworthy being a subsidiary of Citicorp, which has successfully exported its banking products to a large number of developing countries. Other firms have also targeted other developing countries as outlets for specialized products for the financial, banking and hospitality industry. Firms like TCS and Infosys have their own banking packages, which they have exported, to other "commonwealth" countries with reasonable success.
78. Udell, Jon (1993) " India's Software Edge", Byte, pp. 55-60
79. Pohjola, M (2000), *Information Technology and Economic Development :An Introduction to Research Issues,* Paper No. 153, UNU/WIDER.
80. Kattuman, P and K Iyer (2001): *Human Capital in the Move up the Value Chain: The Case of Software and services Industry,* Department of Applied Economics, University of Cambridge.
81. A few firms, however, were engaged in the export of software but their mode of the export was mostly onshore.
82. Joseph, K J (1997): *Industry Under Economic Liberalisation: The Case of Indian Electronics,* Sage Publications, New Delhi, Thousand Oaks, London.
83. GoI (1986): *Policy on Computer Software Exports,* Software Development and Training, Department of Electronics, New Delhi.
84. Mention needs to be made of the substantial reduction in the duties and tariffs across the board for components and subassemblies, zero duty on software import and zero income tax on profits from software export.

85. Narayana, Murty N R (2000): *Making India a Significant IT Player in this Millennium,* Penguin Books, New Delhi.

86. The task forces include the national Task Force on IT, Task Force on HRD for IT, Task Force on Knowledge Society and the National Advisory Committee on IT comprising the chief executives of leading IT companies.

87. Parthasarathi, A (2001),*Tackling the Brain Drain from India's Information and communication Technology Sector: Need for a New Industrial and SandT Strategy,* Paper presented in the ACU conference, Cyprus, April 22-26

88. GoI (1995): *STP Info Database*, Department of Electronics, New Delhi.

89. Oberoi, S S (1991): *Software Technology Park: Concept, Procedure and Status,* Electronics Information and Planning, Vol. 19, No 3 PP 42-46.

90. STPI opens office at Silicon Valley, USA, *The Economic Times,* New Delhi, Special Supplement on Software Technology Park of India, June 11, 2000.

91. Venatesh, P (1995): *India's Software Export: A study with Reference to technology park,* M.Phil Dissertation, JNU.(Centre for Development Studies), Thiruvananthapuram.

92. Schware, R (1987): *Software Industry in Third world: Policy Guidelines, Institutional Options and Constraints*, World Development, Vol. 15 Nos. 10-11, pp 1249-67.

93. Sen, P(1995): *Indian software Exports: An Assessment,* EPW, Vol. 30, Nos 7 and 8, pp 2053-58.

94. Schware, R (1987): *Software Industry in Third world: Policy Guidelines, Institutional Options and Constraints*, World Development, Vol. 15 Nos. 10-11, pp 1249-67.

95. http://www.IT-Taskforce.nic.in (National Information Centre).

96. NASSCOM (2000), *Directory of Indian software and Service Companies,* New Delhi.

97. The managers at a leading electronics and telecom firm said they outsource work related to sophisticated but mature digital signal processing software to their Indian subsidiary. The telecom firms outsourced domain related software maintenance or tool development for the maintenance or enhancement of existing applications. The manager at a value added telecom services firm said that they were outsourcing testing of their existing software

and to some extent maintenance of their old UNIX based software. However, It is found one exception to the idea that the outsourced projects are not mission-critical: A leading computer manufacturer out sources critical device-driver software that is shipped directly from the Indian vendor for distribution.

98. Sampson, G and L Snape (1985), *Identifying Issues in Trade in Services,* World Economy, Vol. 8, No 2, June, pp 171-82.

99. Heeks, R (1996): *India's Software Industry: State Policy, Liberalisation and Industrial Development,* Sage Publication, New Delhi.

100. Arora , A and Jai Asundi (1999): *Quality Certification and Economics of Contract Software Development: A Study of Indian software Industry,* NBER, Paper No. 7260.

101. Kattuman, P and K Iyer (2001): *Human Capital in the Move up the Value Chain: The Case of Software and Services Industry,* Department of Applied Economics, University of Cambridge.

102. Mahajan, R (2000): *Moving India's Software Industry up the International Value Chain: The role of state in creating the institutional capacity for innovation,* Paper presented in the Third Triple Helix International Conference, Rio de Janeiro, April 26-29.

103. Arora , A and Jai Asundi (1999): *Quality Certification and Economics of Contract Software Development: A Study of Indian software Industry,* NBER, Paper No. 7260.

104. Kumar, N (2001): *Developing Countries in the International Labour in software and Service Industry: lessons from Indian Experience,* World employment report, 2001, Research and Information System for Developing Countries, New Delhi.

105. Schware, R (1992): *Software Entry Strategies for Developing Countries,* World Development, Vol. 20 Nos. 2, pp 143-64.

106. RBI Bulletin, April 2001

107. It would have been ideal to convert the export earnings into constant prices. In the absence of an appropriate deflator we are forced to carry out the analysis at current prices.

108. Kumar, N. (2001): *Developing Countries in the International Labour in software and Service Industry: lessons from Indian Experience,* World

employment report, 2001, Research and Information System for Developing Countries, New Delhi.

109. U.S. visa restrictions are another reason why firms prefer engineering graduates.

110. A report published by the Export-Import Bank of India (1996) estimates that in order for the industry to grow at the rate of 50 per cent annually, the number of software professionals involved in the software export sector has to grow at an annual rate of at least 30 per cent over the next five years.

111. Mr. Clyde Jones, Chief of Consular Services, U.S Consulate India estimates that around 30,000 H1-B visas were granted in 1999, mostly for software professionals (The Economic Times, 1999.) Chennai, (the only city in the south that has a U.S Consulate) reportedly accounted for 20,000 of these

112. Nidumolu S. R and S.E Goodman (1993). "Computing in India: An Asian Elephant Learning to Dance", in Communications of the ACM, Vol. 36, No. 4.

113. However, high turnover is also common in US software developers and in other service industries such as accountancy firms and as the CEO of the rapidly growing software services firm put it-"*Paying a premium price for talented people. This is a worldwide phenomenon. ... I am not worried*"

114. Many multinationals have started authorized training centers (ATC) that provide their own certified courses. These include IBM Global services, Oracle, Microsoft, Adobe, Cadence, Lotus and Sony.

115. www.nasscom.org/ites.indian-scenerio.asp

116. ibid.

117. http://www.nasscom.org/business_in_india/vc_scenario.asp

118. http://www.nasscom.org/business_in_india/vc_scenario.asp

119. SEBI Report, 2000, Mumbai.

120. http://www.nasscom.org/business_in_india/vc_scenario.asp

121. Vision for VC in http://www.nasscom.org/business_in_india/vc_scenario.asp

122. Ibid.

123. Ibid.

3

Structural Framework of Information Technology Industry in Madhya Pradesh

3.1 Geographical Framework of IT Industry in Madhya Pradesh

Madhya Pradesh lies in the geographical heart of India. Madhya Pradesh came into being in November 1956. State is surrounded by seven states. About 23.3 per cent of the total population of the state belong to scheduled tribes. The key feature of Madhya Pradesh are:[1]

Geographical Area—308 ('000 sq.km)

Capital—Bhopal

Number of Districts—45

Population (in 2001)—60,385,118

Principal Languages—Hindi

Other Languages—Hindi is the most widely spoken language though Marathi is also widespread. Urdu, Oriya, Gujarati and Punjabi are each spoken by sizeable numbers.

Sex Ratio—Females per 1000 males (2001) 920

Literacy Rate (2001)—64.11%

Male Literacy rate (2001)—76.80%

Female Literacy Rate (2001)—50.28%

Net Domestic Product (Rs. Million at current prices in 1992-93)—323,070

Per Capita Income (Rs. At current prices in 1992-93)—4,725

Information Technology Nodes—Bhopal, Gwalior, Indore and Jabalpur.

Adjoining States—Landlocked in the central part of the country, it is bounded by the states of Rajasthan to the northwest, Uttar Pradesh to the north, Chhattisgarh to the east and Maharashtra to the south and Gujarat to the west.

Major Rivers—Betwa, Chambal, Indravati, Narmada, Sindh, Sone, Tapti.

Climate—Madhya Pradesh has a topography that is crossed from north to south by plains separated by upland areas. The state has three main seasons: winter (November through February), summer (March through May) and the monsoon season (June through September). During the winter average temperatures range from 10° to 27° C (50° to 81° F). Summers are hot, with an average temperature of 29° C (85° F) and a high temperature that at times reaches 48° C (118° F). During the monsoon season temperatures average 19° to 30° C (66° to 86°). Madhya Pradesh receives as average annual rainfall of about 1200 mm (nearly 50 in), of which 90 per cent falls during the monsoon season.

Industrial Scenario—The Existing Industrial Structure in the State: Today 7 of India's top 10 Groups have a sizeable presence in MP, making it among the top 4 states in terms of industrial investment.

Madhya Pradesh has entered into an era of high-tech industries like electronics telecommunications. Petro-chemicals, food processing and automobiles. It is the first state of the country to start producing optical fibre for purposes of telecommunications. Very large number of automobile units are located in Pithampur. The state is leading in soyabean processing and manufacture of cement (producing more than 100 lakh tones).

Major public sector industries in the state are Bharat Heavy Electrical Limited at Bhopal, Security Paper Mill at Hoshangabad, Currency Printing Press at Dewas, Newsprint Mill at Nepanagar and the Alkaloid factory at Neemuch. More and more companies of all sizes seem to share the same opinion, invest in Madhya Pradesh. Hindustan Lever, TISCO, Raymond, Grasim, Ceat Tyres, Crompton Greaves, Cadbury , Hindustan Motors, Kinetic Honda, L and T, Tata Exports, Century Textiles, Procter and Gamble and Fujutsu Optel are just some of the big names already here.

Economy and Infrastructure[2]—Agriculture is the basis of Madhya Pradesh's economy. Less than half of the land area is cultivable, however and its distribution is quite uneven because of variations in topography, rainfall and soils. The main cultivated areas are found in the Chambal valley, the Malwa Plateau and the Rewa Plateau. The Narmada valley, covered with river-borne alluvium, is another fertile area.

Minerals—Madhya Pradesh is rich in minerals, though these resources have not yet been fully exploited. There are large reserves of coal and important deposits of iron ore, manganese ore, limestone, dolomite, copper, fire clay and china clay. Diamond reserves at Panna are of particular interest.

Power—The state is well endowed with potential hydroelectric power. Main hydroelectric projects (jointly developed with other states) are the Babanthadi with Maharashtra, the Ban Sagar with Bihar and Uttar Pradesh, the Chambal Valley with Rajasthan, the Narmada Sagar with Gujarat and Rajasthan and the Rajghat and Urmil with Uttar Pradesh. The Hasdeo Bango, Bargi and Birsinghapur thermal power projects are also within the state. The Narmada Sagar project has been a source of controversy because of its potential for damaging the environment.

Transport—The main railroads that pass through the state were originally laid down to connect the ports of Chennai, Mumbai and Kolkata with their hinterlands. Also connecting the state with other parts of India are airports at Bhopal, Gwalior, Indore, Jabalpur and Khajuraho, as well as several national highways.

Tourist—Khajuraho, once the capital of Chandella rulers is 595 km from Delhi. The embodiment of the great artistic activity of the 9th to the 12th centuries, only 22 temples temple out of 85 have survived. Ujjain where Kumbha Mela is held every 12th year, Sanchi with ancient Buddhist monuments, Bhopal the lake-side capital city, Jabalpur, famous for marble rocks and Gwalior with beautiful forts, Indore the largest city in the state, Panchmarhi, the hill station, Mandu the historical town. Kanha National Park near Jabalpur is one of the most beautiful wild life sanctuaries in India.

Temples—Among the temples known throughout the world for their erotic art are those at Khajuraho in the Chhatarpur district in the north of the state; dating from AD 1000, they were built by the Chandella kings. The temples at Gwalior and in its vicinity should also be mentioned. The palaces and mosque at Mandu (near Dhar), the majestic Bandhogarh fort built in the 14th century and the Gwalior fort—perhaps the most impressive of the residences of the former princes of Madhya Pradesh—represent other notable architectural achievements.

Cultural Events—The state has several well-known annual cultural events, such as Kalidas Samaroh (for performing and fine arts) in Ujjain, Tansen Samaroh (music) in Gwalior and a dance festival in Khajuraho, where artists from all over India participate. In Bhopal there is a unique multifaceted cultural complex, the Bharat Bhavan, which functions as a meeting ground for artists from various fields. Located along the Bhopal Lake, this sprawling complex houses a museum, a library, an open-air theatre and a number of conference halls. The state has important yearly religious melas (gatherings) in Mandasaur and Ujjain.

Information Technology Infrastructure[3]

Telephone Facility—The Department of Telecommunications (DoT) plays a vital role in establishing the communication infrastructure for the people of Madhya Pradesh. The Telecom Department is committed to provide modern telecommunication facilities of international standard to its customers in the state. It is engaged in setting up the most modern telecommunication infrastructure consisting of State-of-Art digital electronic telephone exchanges and digital transmission systems. Major industrial growth centres have electronic exchanges. In fact, anticipation of MP's industrial boom, the private sector is gearing itself to expand telecom facilities even further. M.P also has telephone services which are commercial / private - The Air Tel. All the district headquarters and sub-divisional headquarters have access to STD/ISD facilities.

Village Public Telephones (VPT)— MP Telecom Circle in this endeavour has provided a good number of village public telephone connections in the tribal and backward areas.

New Services: In its endeavour to provide latest telecommunication services MP Telecom Circle has launched a number of new services recently. Some of the popular services are:

Internet E-mail—Facilities are also available from all district headquarters.

ISDN—This facility has already been provided in Bhopal, Indore Jabalpur, Gwalior, Malanpur, Dewas, Ratlam and Mandideep. Using this facility on the same telephone line voice, data and video transmission is possible. Multi-media PCO centers have been opened where customers can use these facilities.

Cellular Services—RPG Cellular Services (Contact Mobile No : 98260 12345), Reliance Mobile Services (Contact Mobile No : 98270 12345)

Pager Services: Easy Call Paging Services.

Over the last five years some of the cities in Madhya Pradesh have come to be known as IT hotspots. Bhopal, Gwalior, Indore, Jabalpur has often been best IT cities in Madhya Pradesh and India. Indore city that is fast becoming the first most popular tech hot spot in the state of Madhya Pradesh. Although, the high growth in the IT industry has lead to the sprouting of many technology firms in several cities in India, Bhopal and Indore have made a conscious effort to provide the infrastructure and a conducive environment for IT.

Gwalior[4]

Centrally located between Delhi, the National capital and three State Capitals - Jaipur, Lucknow and Bhopal is the historical city of GWALIOR. The majestic fort built by Raja Man Singh Tomar provides a magnificent skyline to this bustling town of over 7 lakh population.

Connectivity—Gwalior is 317 kms south of Delhi and 400 kms north of Bhopal. The city is linked by air to Delhi, Indore, Mumbai and Bhopal and to all major cities in India by road and rail network. Shatabdi Express, the fastest train in India, provides convenient to Agra, Bhopal and Delhi. The Agra Bombay highway passes through Gwalior ensuring connectivity between Gwalior, Indore, Mumbai and Delhi.

Infrastructure— Ideally located in the centre of the Hindi heartland, Gwalior provides the potential to tap the markets in Rajasthan, U.P. and Bihar. The Indian Institute of Information Technology and 5 Engineering Colleges provide high quality trained manpower.

Rapidly expanding communication infrastructure, so essential for development of IT, is provided largely by DoT and now also by a private operate. DoT has planned to spend Rs.75 crore to upgrade the communication network in the region.

Malanpur, a growth centre in the suburbs of Gwalior offers industrial infrastructure and provides peaceful industrial relations. An EOU zone is also proposed at Ghirongi. Land availability, low levels of pollution and efficient administration also add to the potential of Gwalior.

Social Infrastructure—School of national renown, the famous jiwaji Rao University backed up by 5 engineering colleges, a medical college and 9 other science and arts colleges form one of the best educational infrastructure in the region.

Gwalior has a 700 bed hospital attached to the medical college. It also has 4 other large hospital including a specialized hospital for cancer treatment. A modern 500 bed hospital is under construction. It is the gateway to places of tourist interest like Shivpuri, Orchha, Khajuraho and Jhansi.

Indore[5]

Indore, the erstwhile capital of the Holkar, is now the undoubted trade and commerce capital of Madhya Pradesh. Located 180 kms south west of Bhopal, this is the largest city of Madhya Pradesh with a population of over 15 lakhs.

Connectivity— Indore is on the Agra Bombay highway and is only 600 kms from Bombay. Daily air flights and trains provide convenient connections to Bombay, Delhi and Bhopal.

Social Infrastructure—Devi Ahalia Bai University, Agriculture University, 10 linked Colleges with arts and science facilities, renowned public schools provide quality educational facilities.

Indore has two five star hotels and a whole array of restaurants and hotels to suit every budget. A large number of well known clubs with excellent infrastructure, stadium, water sports centre and cultural groups are responsible for Indore being a very lively city.

M.Y. Hospital, Choithram Hospital, upcoming Bombay Hospital alongwith a Medical College, Dental College and a number of modern private hospitals has meant to the availability of the best medical facilities in the state.

The climate remains moderate throughout the year. Peaceful law and order situation, peaceful industrial relations along with a stable political environment and efficient administration makes Indore an attractive investment destination.

Jabalpur[6]

Jabalpur is centrally located and is one of the oldest cities in Madhya Pradesh. Among the important establishment here are the High Court of Madhya Pradesh, Headquarters of M.P. Electricity Board and several defence establishments. Popularity known as the "Sanskar Dhami" (the cultural capital) one had its claim to be the capital of Madhya Pradesh in view of its size and the infrastructure that it continues to offer.

Jabalpur is on the main railway route between Mumbai and Kolkata. It also has direct train links with Delhi and major cities in South India connected by two National Highways. Jabalpur has an excellent road connection with Nagpur, Bhopal and several other important cities in the country. Jabalpur has an aerodrome also and its is hoped that soon it will be having regular flights. Jabalpur is situated in an area which is known for its mineral and forest wealth throughout India. It's rich limestone deposits have attracted in its surroundings making it an important business centre.

IT industry linkage—IT training institutes Number of IT training institutes : 100 (approximately) including 20 Franchisees. Number of students passing out yearly : 3000

Major Industries—1. Government undertakings - Vehicle Factory Jabalpur, Gun Carriage Factory Jabalpur, Telecom Factory Jabalpur, Grey Iron Foundry Jabalpur, Central Ordinance Depot., Ordinance Factory Khamriya (Jabalpur), Ordinance Factory Katni. 2. Private Ltd. Industries - Associated Cement Company Kyamore, Internet Everest Asbestos Ltd. Kyamore, ACC Refractories Katni, Madhya Pradesh Vidhuyut Yantra Ltd. Gosalpur, Burn Standard Company (refractories) Jabalpur, Burn Standard Company Katni, RPG Transmissions Pvt. Ltd. Panagar, Shaw Wallace Gellitiene Ltd. Jabalpur, Gas Filling Plant Shahpura - Bhitoni, Associated Cement Company Mahgaon.

Existing IT Infrastructure—PC penetration : 1 PCs/100

Telecom Infrastructure—

Digital Exchange Capacity—72,500

Widespread Access Network—Medium

TCP/IP Nodes Availability—Yes (DoT Node)

High capacity and fast connectivity to Gateway—ISDN, Intelligent Network Services (Proposed)

IT (Literacy)—Yes, growing exponentially.

Schools—Primary - 2433, Middle - 728, High Secondary - 200

Colleges—Total numbers are 65. The major colleges are: Govt. Engineering College, Government. Medical College, Agriculture College, College of Veterinary Science, Government Science College, Home Science College and several other colleges offering education and in almost all disciplines.

Hospital—The total number of hospital in Jabalpur are 150. The main health care centre in Jabalpur are: Government Hospitals - Medical College, Cancer Hospital, Victoria Hospital, Elgin Hospital and several large size private hospitals, clinies and pathological labs equipped with modern facilities.

3.2 Origin of IT Industry in Madhya Pradesh

The nineties have seen the emergence of a new Madhya Pradesh. The commitment to decentralization in the last five years involving communities and elected local authorities in decision-making has made the state, one of the most open societies in the country. Madhya Pradesh has adopted a new IT policy, which in keeping with state's other initiatives, is people oriented. The thrust of the policy is to effective the institutions and structures so that citizen services are improved. Use of Hindi in IT applications is critical to the success of the policy. Madhya Pradesh is centrally located and has a strong, modern and growing infrastructure. Stability of policies is a big plus. IT also has the best track record of public order. The alumni from the State's academic institutions captain several IT majors. The State assures availability of human resources at all skill levels. Madhya Pradesh has a strong industrial base. Industrial Growth Centres of Malanpur (Gwalior), Pithampur (Indore), Mandideep (Bhopal) have attracted large investments in a wide range of industries.[7]

Madhya Pradesh has an advantage few other States in the country have, in terms of the communications backbone provided by both public and private sectors. The optical fibers backbone available to the State is approx. 10,000 K.ms presently and is projected to grow even further bringing all tehsil and eventually development block head quarters in its fold. The Task Force recommends that software exports being the fastest growing segment of the IT industry, in order to attract software exporters to the State, the State must have 3 international gateway hubs. One such international gateway hub is being provided by VSNL at Indore. The State Government should move the Government of India to permit International Private Operators to create an international gateway hub each at Bhopal and Indore.

By end 1999, there would be further fillip to the telecom infrastructure in the State as the GOI has announced that the Inter-circle long distance network work would be privatized. A minimum of two backbone transmission networks connecting all the districts would be available from the private and public sectors. The Intra-district transmission network connecting all the tehsils/blocks would be in place, as the DoT is upgrading its network by year 2000.[8]

Madhya Pradesh is constrained by inadequate air links. The growth of the economy would justify efforts for setting up an international airport in the State. The State Government should move the Government of India for the purpose at the appropriate time and in the interim, better air traffic services should be provided (for e.g. round the clock flight landing facilities for private crafts in the existing air ports.). In attracting investments in the IT industry, the critical element is the ability of the investors to attract IT professionals from out side to the State. The State must create enabling conditions for this to happen, at least till such time as the IT industry in M.P. grows to a stage where there is local availability of trained manpower and also the forces of demand and supply take over. The profile of knowledge workers must be kept in mind while planning IT 'cities' and the necessary upgradation of facilities that contribute to enhancing the attraction of such 'cities' for the target population. The unique advantages of habitats in the State where these 'cities' are planned must be marketed along with the promotional package. Private sector should be encouraged to make all the necessary investments in the development of facilities such as housing, schools, amusement centres, etc. or in the upgradation of the existing facilities.[9]

Content industry and remote services will be pro-actively and vigorously promoted in the State to position M.P. as a lead State, in the country as well as generate large employment opportunities in IT and IT enabled services sector. Initially, as an incentive for setting up of IT units, land should be provided at industrial rates to IT industry and these transactions should be exempted from the levy of Stamp duties or other charges of registration. In the construction of buildings, the municipal bye laws should be appropriately amended to allow 50 per cent more FAR than the standard ratio.

Venture Capital availability should be given special focus by inviting Foreign Investors to be an integral part of State's IT vision. The M.P. Industrial Development Corporation or the MPFC should take the lead in setting up dedicated venture capital fund for IT. MPSIDC and MPFC should formulate special packages for providing financial assistance to the IT industry. The package should include equity contribution to small and medium enterprises, margin money assistance to promoters, interest subsidies and venture capital assistance in deserving cases. The packages should be marketed by MPSIDC, MPFC and also by MAPIT.[10]

The existing Software Technical Park at Indore should be further upgraded and expanded to bring it at par with the best in the country. State Government should establish STPs in the proximity of the cities of Bhopal, Gwalior and Jabalpur. These parks should be provided with comprehensive infrastructure facilities with regard to power, water and telecommunications in particular. Private entrepreneurs should be encouraged to set up IT parks, such parks can also be set up in partnership with private sector or industrial organisations.

Hardware technology parks for manufacturing units in computers, telecommunication equipment, entertainment electronics and related ancillaries should be promoted and established at Pithampur, Mandideep and Malanpur growth centres.

The existing schemes of self-employment generation such as the IRDP, TRYSEM, PMRY etc. should be utilized to provide assistance to youth for setting up of Information Kiosks or 'soochana gumtis' to provide email, internet and other value added services. The State has over 28000 STD PCOs at present. A phased strategy to upgrade these into information kiosks should be worked out in consultation with basic service providers, banks and industry department at no extra cost to the Government. Viability of these information retailers can be enhanced by utilizing them for the purposes of training of school teachers, school children, PRI functionaries and officials and in utilizing them for the storage and retrieval of information for the village level panchayats and as communication channels by the PRIs and other institutions in the rural areas.[11]

In the initial stages of development, the IT industry in the State must be treated with the care and concern that nascent industries deserve. This means that the State should create conditions whereby IT units being located in the State are insulated from irritants of a routine nature, particularly in dealing with a multiplicity of local and statutory authorities for clearances of various kinds. State Government should facilitate a single window clearance system and a universal over-riding permission that gives the right to enterprises to carry on with activities without barriers of any kind thereafter. Residential premises would be allowed to setup IT units, particularly related to content industry and remote services.

In order to promote IT industries in the very short run, IT industries requiring electrical power up to 15 KVA should be established without any location restrictions. Necessary amendment should also be made in pollution control act and the rules therein. IT industries should be treated as industrial (and not commercial) consumers for the purposes of electricity tariff and tariff applicable to the industrial consumers alone should be levied on IT units. IT industry should be given priority in sanction and servicing of power and should also be exempt from power-cuts in order to facilitate uninterrupted functioning. Installation of Captive power generation sets by the IT Industry should be encouraged through incentives by way of total exemption from payment of electricity tax without any time limit, as well as total exemption from payment of Sales Tax on fuel used for captive power generation.

Concessions to the IT industry should include exemptions from payment of Entry Tax, Commercial Tax on IT related capital goods. In addition, IT industries should be offered Sales Tax exemption for a reasonable period of time, irrespective of level of investment and location of the unit. These fiscal incentives would contribute to Madhya Pradesh being considered as an attractive location for new industries as well as those existing industries located elsewhere who look at expanding activities. The use of IT in trade and industry such as the banking and insurance sectors in the State and in the existing manufacturing and service sectors of the State's economy would be further accelerated through such concessions and incentives to the IT sector.[12]

Chief Minister Digvijay Singh's firm belief that in the era of knowledge economy, the might of Information Technology should be harnessed not just for creating a few individual dollar-billionaires and some more individual dollar-millionaires, but for the real empowerment and growth of the millions of our masses shapes the core vision for this sector in Madhya Pradesh. All the steps taken by the state government in the field of Information Technology have been oriented towards this goal. It is in consonance with this vision, that the state has chosen for itself the role of an enabling facilitator. Leaving the field wide open for the private sector enterprise, imagination and energy to tap the entire range of opportunities that have opened up as the nation moves on the global stage to occupy its rightful frontline position in an increasingly knowledge driven economy.

The origins of the state government's initiative in the Information Technology sector lie in the recommendations of a Task Force headed by the eminent scientist Professor Yashpal. The recommendations of this Task Force have been adopted as the State Policy on Information Technology. This policy also echoes the Chief Minister's concept of IT for millions:" There should be no islands of elitism or conclaves of wisdom in the information society of the future- where access to information and knowledge would be symmetric among all seekers and users."

That this vision is not merely a declaration of pious intent, but is an article of faith to be lived through in every day life has been amply demonstrated over the years. The international recognition in the form of the Stockholm Challenge Award for the year 2000- for the Gyandoot project of the tribal dominated Dhar district is a testimony to the initial success of this vision. Commending the project the Stockholm Jury observed: " Project "Gyandoot" is a unique government to citizen intranet project implemented in a tribal district, (Dhar) in Central India, with numerous benefits to the region, including a people-based self-reliant sustainable strategy." Gyandoot " is recognized as a breakthrough in a e-government, demonstrating a paradigm shift which gives marginalised tribal citizens their first ever chance to access knowledge, with minimum investment." [13]

It is this internationally recognised success of the vision of IT for millions that forms the bedrock of the growth of the range of business opportunities for everyone in Madhya Pradesh in the field of Information Technology. More significantly, the state has the infrastructure to propel this growth. It also has the right academic atmosphere to sustain its growing manpower needs. Above all, it has the forward-looking, modern attitude that is essential to nurture its growth.

IT Infrastructure in Madhya Pradesh

Madhya Pradesh is one of the first states in the country to experience the fruits of the transition from the stage of a public sector monopoly to a healthy competition between the public and the private sector in the field of basic telephony. Both, the Department of Telecom now in its corporatised form as the public sector Bharat Sanchar Nigam Limited (BSNL) and the private sector Bharati Tele Net Limited (BTNL) have been active in providing the basic telephony infrastructure for the Information Technology needs of the masses. These organisations have moved from strength to strength in the recent years and this has been a boon for IT sector.[14]

The state now has internet connectivity at all 45 districts and the remaining ones will be connected by March 2001. In most of the districts, the internet connectivity also extends to the tehsil places and it is always possible to browse the net even when you are holidaying in far off places like the exotic Khajuraho or the tribal Dhar. The reliability of this service is ensured through an optical fibre cable network that runs through a total of 18,000 route in the state. The BSNL has already placed 11,332 route kilometres of OFC in the state. BTNL has chipped in with 3,600 kilometres and Reliance Telecom will add another 4,400 kilometres by December 2001. Truly, an information super highway that would be the envy of any modern state. But then this is not all. According to current indicators, the total length of the optical fibre network to be put in place by these three majors -BSNL, BTNL and Reliance will be at least 28,000 route kilometers by December 2001. Given this extensive network, the urban as well as the rural areas of the state are well-connected when it comes to optical fibre cable network and basic telephony. All the major cities- Bhopal, Indore, Gwalior, Jabalpur and Ujjain have the optical fibre cable backbone. The BSNL's rural telephony projects cover 46901 villages so far and will extend to 5860 villages by March 2001. The remaining 19240 villages will be covered by the private sector BTNL. BSNL has plans to invest As. Rs. 715 crore in the year 2000-2001 and another as Rs. 723 crores in the financial year 2001-2002 in various development projects.[15]

BSNL has a subscriber base of 11.44 lakhs. But its installed capacity is for 15.16 lakh subscribers through a total of 2946 exchanges. It plans to offer at least 1.5 lakh new connections within the year. The private sector BTNL started its operations in June 1998 and currently services 27 towns and cities with a subscriber base of over 100,000. All its service locations are connected on its own optical fibre cable network that runs through 3600 kilometres. A major attraction for BTNL subscribers is free internet access through Mantra Online. Presently, 75,000 subscribers have this free internet access.

For the IT entrepreneur looking for faster means of communication for data, voice and text, both BSNL and BTNL offer ISDN connectivity at more than 20 locations-like Bhopal, Mandideep, Indore, Pithampur, Jaipur, Jabalpur, Gwalior, Malanpur, Dewas, Vidisha, Neemuch, Khajuraho,Satna, Chhattarpur, Sehore, Mandsaur, Datia, Sagar,Durg, Dhar, Aatlam- in the state. Access to leased lines is also available.Alongwith this widespread and reliable basic infrastructure, the state offers a compact location for the IT entrepreneurs at its Software Technology Park (STP) in Indore. It has been promoted by the Optel- Madhya Pradesh State Electronics Development Corporation. Located barely four kilometres away from the city centre, it is an ideal location for the software exporters in the field of Information Technology. Apart from proper built-up accommodation and other sites, it offers the entire package of incentives and concessions that have been earmarked for such parks by the government of India.[16]

Optel- the state sector enterprise for promoting the growth of IT - related activities is one of the pioneers in the field of the production of optical fibres. In collaboration with the Japanese giant Fujitsu, it had set-up a state of the art production unit at Mandideep in 1988. So far this unit has supplied 40,000 route kilometres of optical fibres to various clients. Besides, this it has supplied Rs.500 crore worth of opto-electronics systems. It harnesses the technical expertise it has acquired as a pioneer in the field of h:-tech electronics for the benefit of the investors in the STP at Indore. It also facilitates the clearance of the relevant projects from the STP at Noida. Shortly, Optel will also set-up similar STPs at Bhopal and Gwalior. The IT net is really spreading far and wide in Madhya Pradesh.[17]

Facilitators IT and IT Industry in Madhya Pradesh

This is an organisation that has been specially created for propelling the growth in the IT sector. It has a high-powered governing body with the Chief Minister as its chairperson and with the ministers for Higher

Education, School Education and Industry as its other functionaries. It is the nodal agency for the development of the IT sector and it has the following objectives:

To market the state as an attractive IT destination for investors

To coordinate and network with investors and industry, trade organisations, financial institutions in the public and private sector to promote the growth in IT sector

To coordinate and pursue the development of all support infrastructure including telecom in the state. The state's commitment to the IT sector is also underlined by the fact that it has appointed an IT professional of repute as the Chief Executive Officer of MAP-IT, with the rank of the secretary to the state government.

MPSIDC: Madhya Pradesh has always been an industry- friendly destination. It offers all the locational advantages that are the dream of a prospective investor and the result is that all the top ten industrial houses of the country have their manufacturing units based in the state. The Madhya Pradesh State Industries Development Corporation (MPSIDC) has always played the role of an efficient facilitator for the industry. It has enabled productive investments worth thousands of crore in diverse industrial activity. It is also playing the same enabling role in the field of Information Technology as well.[18]

Recently, it paved the way for a joint venture agreement with Reliance Industries Limited for the setting-up an e-governance project. This unique project will allow the state to set-up 7800 cyber kiosks all over the state with absolutely no cost for the state. The project is a part of the overall plans of the Reliance group in the field of IT -related activities and will help ordinary folks even ,in villages and small towns to e-interact with the government. The pricing of the services to be offered by these cyber kiosks will be decided in consultation with the government. This project could be a forerunner for several similar ventures. The state has more than 70,000 villages and this project to be completed by 2002 will cover only ten per cent of these villages. In tune with the needs of the changing times, the MPSIDC has several projects on the anvil for harnessing the potential of the IT -enabled services to propel the all round economic development of the state.[19]

Success Stories of IT in Madhya Pradesh

Within the quiet confines of everyday iife, Madhya Pradesh has seen the growth of several success stories that indicate the penetration of IT in the lives of millions of its people. All these success stories underline the basic commitment of the state-IT for millions. Just to recount a few[20]:

The Gyandoot project—This is a symbol of the drive, determination and the imagination of the people. It simply demonstrates the wide range of possibilities that lie in the realm of reality once the people are given the charge. In its essence, the Gyandoot project of the tribal district of Dhar is an intranet network of 26 soochanalayas (information centres) set-up at cost of just Rs. 25 lakhs, that benefit nearly half a million people at 311 Gram Panchayats in over 600 villages. The villagers are able to access any information like mandi prices of crops, copies of land records, grievance redressal, sending in emails in their language, apply for assistance under government schemes, get their health records accessed through the main hospital at Indore etc. The range is really wide. The government has only played the role of the facilitator in this project as well. In fact, even the sum of Rs. 25 lakhs that has been spent on the project was raised through the district's own resources. The centres are managed by "soochaks", who are locally folks and are not government employees. Each "soochak" is expected to earn at least Rs. 30,000 per annum and the maintenance of the network has also been handed over to a private entrepreneur.[21]

This is the kind of project that has been universally applauded. As the Times of India said in its editorial[22]: "The stereotypical image of the illiterate villager shuffling around the corridors of babudom in search o documents or records could well be in for a makeover. The Indian village is getting wired for empowerment." It is this change that makes Madhya Pradesh the right place for IT for millions. Obviously, the Gyandoot experience is being extended to other districts and the opportunities are opening up for the investors in the IT -related activities.

The NIC Successes: If the Gyandoot project is an example of the drive, determination and imagination of the people of a single district-Dhar, then the successes of the National Informatics Centre (NIC) in Madhya Pradesh are a symbol of the state government's unshakeable commitment to embrace the modern Information Technology in every possible sphere of activity. The NIC-GOMP partnership dates back to

1987, when an MOU was signed to extend the NICNET services to the state of Madhya Pradesh. Since then there has been no looking back. In the first place, this partnership has ensured that the state has a" Computer Culture" and has the mindset to harness the modern Information Technology.[23]

The result is that there is hardly any sphere of activity that has not witnessed the penetration of Information Technology. While all the 45 original districts of the state were wired up by NICNET in 1990, only six of the newly created 16 districts are out of the network. Besides, this network, there are a large number of sub-centres/cells that link the various government offices in the state. More than 6,000 persons have been trained at various levels and at least 300 other projects that relate to the use of the Information Technology in government departments, courts and other establishments have been implemented. The NIC-COMP partnership is ushering in the much need revolution. In the words of Dr. Amar Singh IAS, the secretary to chief minister, who has to process a load of documents on a daily basis: " Because of the computerisation (done by NIC), the CM office response to the various issues raised by the public representatives and general public has been of a very high order and public representatives in M .P. are highly satisfied today."

ITC's success stories: Come what may, we shall always remain a largely agrarian society. The farmer shall always be the main contributor to our economic wealth. So any concept revolving around the growth of the Information Technology has to bring the farmer in its purview. The corporate giant ITC Ltd. which has a strong presence in the agri-business as well has brought the farmer within the frame of the IT - related activities by setting-up a web portal in Hindi for the soyabean growers of the state- http://www.soyachaupal.com/ It is a pioneering effort that has gone done very well with the farmers as it helps them enhance their farm productivity by disseminating latest information on district level weather forecasts for short and medium terms, the best generic as well as specific farming practices and on farm field management support. Another vital area of the farmers interest is the information that is provided by the website regarding the mandi wise arrivals and prices, the Indian and international market prices of bean, oil and soyameal. Traditionally, the chaupal is the village center for activities and the ITC by providing a web chaupal has turned it into a virtual global reality. Though the site has been launched for the soya farmers, initially it shall be extended to other crops like to wheat, pulses and other states across the country. In terms of investment, ITC chairman Yog Deveshwar has made an initial commitment of Rs. 10 crore, For the masses, this is a boon from the Information Technology.There is yet another advantage. The chaupal sanchalaks-who are the local folks managing the "soyachaupals" in the villages will also be setting- up bulk silos and warehouses at the village itself, thus eliminating packaging costs. Once again it is the same mantra, it is IT for millions.[24]

The vision of Chief Minister Digvijay Singh. Its modern infrastructure. The industry friendly attitude of its facilitators. Its success stories. All drive home one simple fact. Madhya Pradesh is simply a land of endless opportunities-all waiting to be grabbed by those who have the ability to make the most of a challenge. There is a wide range of venues to choose from, when it comes to identifying a business location for your ventures in the field of Information Technology.

Software Technology Park Indore

Optel Software Technology Park provides the right environment and caring attitude for boundless creativity and ingenuity of human minds. The commercial capital of Madhya Pradesh, Indore is centrally located and offers the right mix of hi-quality industrial and social infrastructure comparable to that available in other metros, but at lower costs. Optel's caring attitude has been translated into modern infrastructure to cater to your needs at the software park.Situated approximately 4 kms from the city centre, the Optel Software Technology Park is the software developer's dream come true. The location, the facility and the support services provided are all of excellent standard, which will enable you to get on with your job.[25]

Software Technology Park , Bhopal [26]

Bhopal, once known for its nawabs and poets, has grown at an unpredictable pace over the last four decades. Its population has galloped from 6.5 lakhs in 1981 to 10.98 lakhs in 1991 and above 15 lakhs today. It is seat of the state government and offers the best of both the worlds-the traditional and the modern.

The proposed STP : The Corporation is creating the Park in sprawling campus of MACT and MP-STEP. It has signed a tripartite agreement with these parties. The Park will be equipped with all modern facilities, which are required for smoothly operating software export units, including high-speed data connectivity. The negotiations are on with STPI Ltd. in this regard. The park will provide ready space/modules, along the concept of plug-and-play, to software units. A/C as well as NON-A/C space will be available. Developed plots of required size will also be provided suiting the requirements of the units.

Advantage Bhopal: It offers facilities and climate, which are envy of everyone. Bhopal has none of the disadvantages of an over-crowded, bursting at seams metropolis and has all the advantages of a growing modern city. Some of these are listed below.

Feature: It is a clean and green city, with a lower population density as compared to other Metropolis in the country. Apart from the industrial township of the public sector giant BHEL, Bhopal has in its neighbourhood the thriving industrial area of Mandideep, which has attracted investments worth thousands of crore with some of big names in Indian industry operating their manufacturing units from this location. Strategically located-it has road, rail and air connections with all major business locations. IT. manpower is locally available from Maulana Azad College of Technology and a host of government/private technical institutions. Top quality manpower can also be sourced from Indian Institute of Management, Indore and Indian Institute of Information Technology, Gwalior, which are just few hours away. Bhopal has excellent social infrastructures, which includes presence of reputed hotel chains, housing facilities, health care, education, recreational avenues, etc.

Software Technology Park , Gwalior[27]

MPSEDC is actively working on a proposal to establish a hi-tech habitat at Gwalior near Indian Institute of Information Technology and Management, providing all necessary infrastructures for IT companies.

The Proposed STP: The park will be established on about 17 hectares of land situated near IIITM.The park will provide ready space/modules, along the concept of plug and Play, to software export units. A/C as well as Non-A/C space will be available.

Developed plots of required size will also be provided suiting the requirement of the unit. The park will be equipped with the necessary facilities, which are required for smooth operations of IT units like high speed data connectivity, uninterrupted power supply and support infrastructures such as canteen, postal/courier services, security services, banks, recreational, facilities, etc.

Advantage Gwalior—A major industrial town of MP, Gwalior has excellent potential to emerge as a leading infotech city. In addition to the existing industrial base base and infrastructures, Gwalior also has very good educational, social and recreational facilities.

Features—Well developed and thriving industrial base which includes companies like Godrej Soaps, Cadburry, Crompton Greaves, Grasim, Flex Industries, Surya Roshani, Jamuna Auto, Hotline CPT Ltd, Britania industries, etc. High quality well trained IT manpower locally available from the prestigious Indian Institute of Information Technology and Management, Jiwaji Rao University and several other institutions. The reputed Scindia School is also located here.

3.3 IT Policy of Government of Madhya Pradesh

1. Introduction

Individuals and communities are at the center of all developmental enterprises and policy priorities in Madhya Pradesh. The State acknowledges that it has the obligation to provide Simple, Moral, Accountable, Responsive, Transparent governance to its citizens. The State's policy environment is built around a staunch commitment to decentralization of administration and encouragement to community participation in decision making through Panchayat Raj Institutions and Urban Local bodies. The State believes that every citizen has a right (a) to information pertaining to his own welfare needs and opportunities for individual and social development; (b) to understand the processes of governance; (c) to know the rationale for decision making affecting citizen welfare and welfare of communities; and (d) to quick and effective delivery of citizen services. The State also believes that the use of technologies would enable information to bring about human development.[28]

The strength of the State lies in the strong telecom infrastructure available through both public and private basic service providers and the strategic location at the heart of India. Madhya Pradesh has some of the finest institutions in telecommunications, electronics and management, which not only have current and prospective utility, but also have a cadre of alumni many of whom are Non Resident and Resident entrepreneurs and IT professionals. The number of private institutions in the training sector as well as public institutions offer Madhya Pradesh as a source for low cost competent human resources. Political stability, high quality social infrastructure and quality of life, tranquil public order and a progressive and forward looking policy environment are strengths that few States in India can match. These strengths would be converted and exploited as opportunities.[29]

A State Task Force on Information Technology was constituted by the State Government under Prof. Yash Pal. in addition to giving a number of recommendations, about setting up infrastructure, encouraging industry and private initiative; the Task Force has also indicated measures to promote IT in Government and social sectors as well as measures for human resource development to utilize employment opportunities in the IT sector within and out side the state. The recommendations of the Task Force have been approved by the Government of Madhya Pradesh, as its State policy on Information Technology.[30]

2. Vision - Seamless Society with Global Opportunities

The vision statement for the State's IT Policy is the creation of a "Seamless Society with Global Opportunities". The Statement implies that there should be no islands of elitism or conclaves of wisdom in the information society of the future - where access to information and knowledge would be symmetric among all seekers and users. Every citizen must feel comfortable in accessing information through the facility of Technology - whether directly or where essential through public or private intermediaries. It is to create such a confident society of the future that human resources should be developed in the State.[31]

The State would aim for contributing 5 per cent to 10 per cent of the IT output of the country by the year 2008. This would translate into employment opportunities for between Four hundred Thousand to One Million persons in IT related activities.

To make Madhya Pradesh a lead IT State in India by the year 2003, the State aims to provide cost effective infrastructure and transparent and responsive governance based on a high level of stability in policies in the medium and long term.

The State has set a target of providing information access to all citizens at an affordable cost and for achieving IT literacy in all the High Schools and Colleges by the year 2003 and aims to do so in all the schools by the year 2008. IT penetration would be achieved through aiming for an optimistic average of one internet connection per 100 population and coverage of every habitat by 2003.

Computerization in Government departments and agencies must be the engine of growth of IT in Madhya Pradesh, in the initial period. An optimistic goal for computer penetration in the Government, its organisations including the Panchayat Raj Institutions and other local self Government institutions has been kept at one per ten employees by the year 2003, raised to one per five employees by the year 2005 and finally to one per two employees by the year 2008.

A targeted share of 10 per cent of the national IT output by the time frame indicated earlier, i.e. the year 2008 would be in the region of appx. Rs. 42000 crore and would require a direct private sector investment of the order of Rs. 4500 crore appx. Such a scale of economic activity is possible if the intermediate mile stones are in the region of appx. Rs. 200 crore or so in year 2001 and a four fold growth in investments by the year 2003, leading to output of approximately Rs. 1700 crore by 2001 and appx. Rs. 6500 crore by year 2003.[32]

The targeted share in national IT output would also be reflected in the aim for a share in the software exports in the region of Rs. 300 crore in year 2001 and Rs. 2900 crore or more by year 2003 and Rs. 28000 crore by year 2008.

The State Domestic Product (SDP) is currently growing at the rate of 5.50 per cent annually; and the share of IT in the Madhya Pradesh SDP is appx. 0.2 per cent or appx. Rs. 100 crore. Assuming pessimistically that the SDP in all other sectors would grow at the current rate, a goal of achieving a 10 per cent share in the national output would translate to roughly one-third of the SDP being contributed by IT.

The State aims to provide employment opportunities in the range of Four Hundred Thousand to One Million by the year 2008 engaged in the IT related activities. An estimated sixty per cent of the jobs could come from services, of which some 20 per cent would be low skilled data entry jobs and the balance from the growth of internet related services such as information kiosks in urban and rural areas. Software development could give employment to another 20 per cent, trade and commerce could contribute 10 per cent and the rest of the employment opportunities could be contributed by training related jobs and jobs relating to communications and hardware maintenance.[33]

3. Policy Initiatives

Creating an Enabling Environment and Niche Marketing

The nodal point and the prime mover for propelling IT growth and implementation of plan of action would be a registered society promoted by the Government- "Madhya Pradesh Agency for Promotion of Information Technology" ("MAP_IT"). The Agency's high powered governing body would be headed by the Chief Minister and would include the Ministers of Industry, Higher Education, School Education, Chief Secretary of the State Government, distinguished representatives from the IT industry, NIC, Science and Technology institutions, social sectors. The Chief Executive Officer of MAP_IT world be an IT professional of repute and would hold the rank of ex-officio Secretary to the State Government.

The objectives of MAP_IT would be the following[34] :

- To propel the growth of Information Technology (IT) in Madhya Pradesh and implementation of the State IT Action Plan for socio-economic development of the state.
- To coordinate with all the Government Departments/agencies for sectoral and cross-sectoral promotion and use of IT in Government and prescribe guidelines to enable smooth and widespread induction of IT.
- Coordinate and Network with investors and Industry, Trade organisations and financial institutions in public and private sector to promote growth in IT sector.
- To generate awareness amongst citizens and demystification of IT so as to promote its use as a comprehensive and cost effective means of disseminating information.
- Coordinate manpower needs and human resource development efforts for the above objectives.

- Coordinate and pursue development of all support infrastructure including telecom infrastructure in the State with the State Government and the Govt. of India and their agencies.
- Marketing the State as an attractive IT destination for investment.
- Identifying and developing opportunities for furthering innovative research of world standard on its own or in collaboration with one or more institutions and/or industry.
- Hindi is the medium of communication among governments and the population over the largest landmass of India. All the web pages of Government departments would also be in Hindi to increase their reach. The use of Hindi would also be promoted in all IT based databases and applications. Further, necessary action would be taken towards the following:
- To make Hindi E-mail as an important medium of communication between departments and field level offices.
- To ensure that in all public purchases of hardware/software, the systems being procured would have bilingual capabilities, e.g., all keyboards would be bilingual facilitating.
- Partnering the Hindi language news papers and other media organisations based in the state for popularisation, dissemination as well as access to Hindi formats.
- Collaboration with the other Hindi speaking states such as U.P., Bihar, Rajasthan, Delhi and H.P. for a joint programme of promoting Hindi's presence on the internet by uploading and enhancing Hindi resources. Easy availability of standardized fonts would be part of this exercise.
- Collaboration with C-DAC for the setting up of an institute and research center of world standing for addressing problems relating to use of IT in Hindi computing in these languages, promotion of software applications in the vernacular, etc.
- IT can not grow in isolation to the general pace and status of economic development of the State and so the IT policy will be dovetailed, giving it the pride of place in the Industrial Policy of the State. Commercial tax administration would provide

opportunities for such incentives by accepting computerized tax returns, encouragement to computerized billing, bar coding of inventory etc.

Promotion of Infrastructure, Industry and Investments

The State Government would move the Government of India to permit International Private Operators to create an international gateway hub each at Bhopal and Indore.

Sub-block level connectivity to the villages / Village Panchayats is a must for the introduction of IT for the social sectors including rural development. The Governement would enter into MOU's with private entrepreneurs to establish Information Kiosks and Community Facilitation centres in the rural areas.[35]

The MADHYA PRADESH Electricity Board (MPEB) would actively examine whether it can leverage the right of way its vast supply network by partnering with suitable private national or international communications companies with capital and technology in return for such right of way for connectivity.

Indore, Raipur, Gwalior and Bhopal would be developed as IT 'cities'. The required land will be identified and the norms for the allotment of the land so identified would be made to attract investments in the IT industry.

Content industry and remote services will be pro-actively and vigorously promoted in the State to position M.P. as a lead State, in the country, in this area as well as, generate large employment opportunities in IT and IT enabled services sector.

Venture Capital availability would be given special focus by inviting FIs to be an integral part of State's IT vision. The M.P. Industrial Development Corporation or the MPFC would work out a detailed proposal for dedicated venture capital fund for IT. MPSIDC and MPFC would formulate a special package for providing financial assistance to the IT industry.

Hardware technology parks for manufacturing units in computers, telecommunication equipment, entertainment electronics and related ancillaries would be promoted and established at Pithampur, Mandideep and Malanpur and other industrial growth centres.

The existing schemes of self employment generation such as the IRDP, TRYSEM, PMRY etc. would be utilized to provide assistance to youth for setting up of Information Kiosks or 'soochana gumtis' to provide email, internet and other value added services. The State has over 28000 STD PCOs at present. A phased strategy to upgrade these into information kiosks would be worked out in consultation with basic service providers, banks and industry department.[36]

State Government would facilitate a single window clearance system and a universal over-riding permission that gives the right to enterprises to carry on with activities with out barriers of any kind. Residential premises would be allowed to set-up IT units, particularly related to content industry and remote services.

IT industries requiring electrical power upto 15 KVA could be established without any locational restrictions. Necessary amendment would also be made in Pollution Control Act and the rules therein.[37]

Procedures in respect of some of the existing regulatory legislation relating to labour, factories, shops and establishments for the IT related units would be rationalised.

Promotion of IT in Government

IT Sub-plans: The annual plan of each department/sector in Government would have a detailed sub-plan for IT. Every department would be required to establish IT working group consisting of senior officers and representative of employees, a representative from MAP_IT and also co-opting IT professionals on voluntary or contractual basis from other departments or agencies. There would be a nodal officer or executive for IT related matters in every department.[38]

Budgetary Outlay: A distinct budgetary head of account for IT related activities would be introduced in the annual budget from this fiscal year. The State Government would impress upon the XI Central Finance Commission of the need to modernize administration at the level of State Government as well as at the level of the PRIs. Additionally, modernisation and computerisation of systems in the Panchayats, would be included in the list of priorities for grants given as per the recommendations of the State Finance Commission.

The financial resources for computer penetration for Gram Panchayats presently numbering 31,126 would be met out of the grants-in- aid for basic services and/ or by financing one educated unemployed Youth/Panchayat Karmi at each Gram Panchayat Headquarter to own/ operate a computer unit for various value added services including information retailing through kiosks.

An action plan would be prepared to ensure that all offices of the district Government including those at the sub-district levels are computerised and networked by the year 2003. In particular, the tehsil offices dealing with land records, revenue legislation, land acquisition information, collection and allocation of land revenue and cess to Panchayats, payments of compensation, planning an execution and expenditure on relief operations, information on listing of revenue court cases, monitoring of progress in disposal of revenue case work etc. would be taken up for computerisation by year 2003. Offices such as those of the district governments and the PRIs should be in a position to enable single window facilitation after computerisation.[39]

E-mail facility would be extended to all employees to encourage greater use of email facility for communication. The *'mantra'* for introduction of IT in Government departments would be Zero additional personnel costs, except costs on training and re-tooling of the serving employees. The present pace of training would be stepped up to match computer penetration goals.

A special scheme of incentives would be introduced to motivate all Government employees to become computer literate. To do so in the shortest possible time frame, there would be a strategy of contracting with public and private sector training institutes for specially designed short-term courses for different groups of users.

All hardware supplies would be contracted with a compulsory clause on familiarisation of employees in the operations. All bulk procurement of generic software as well as contracts on specialised application software development would be out-sourced on similar conditionalities for training.

Proposal to tie up with banks for hire purchase schemes for the employees and provide interest-subsidy for purchase of computers for personal use by employees would be worked out.

All departments will move towards electronic communication within the department. Necessary changes in the office manuals would be worked out for this purpose.

Networks : Every department would establish a LAN by the year 2003. The District Government offices, the Collectorate and the Zila Panchayats as well as all other large offices would also establish respective intra-office networks.

The state unit of NIC provides a wide range of IT services in Madhya Pradesh. The NICNET facility has enabled networking with the districts and creation of many information systems and databases in various departments/sectors. These systems/databases would be upscaled and/or augmented and made on-line seamlessly. Detailed plans would be prepared especially in respect of the following.[40]

(i) The Agriculture Market Information System on commodity arrivals and price movements in the major mandies.

(ii) The Treasury Accounting Information System.

(iii) The Commercial Taxes Information System.

(iv) The databases under the DISNIC-PLAN, Village Information System and Gram Sampark Abhiyan.

(v) The Transport Management System.

The schedule for implementation of IT based systems in Government departments would be in phases.

Promoting IT in the Social Sector

Role of NGOs: NGOs and non-government organisations would be encouraged to establish Janpad (block) level centres - 'samadhan kendras' for providing Hardware /Software or other support services.. NGOs volunteering to establish such centres would be encouraged to tie up with the mini ITIs, rural polytechnics and ITIs for manpower and skill development under TRYSEM and other schemes.[41]

Awareness Campaign— Using both formal and non formal channels, the State would disseminate information about the applications, advantages to communities of the use of IT .

For the widest possible involvement of people and communities in IT, benefits of computers and communication resources to be provided at the village Panchayat and sub-block or cluster levels must be utilised for rural development activities, agricultural and horticultural extension for farmers, career guidance for youth, technology guidance for rural enterprises, micro level planning etc. Communities and user groups or beneficiaries would be actively encouraged to participate, in all such activities, including in designing reporting formats and in deciding on control systems or entering data as it is an important way of demystifying the use of IT by and through communities.

All existing web sites relating to both Government and non-government agencies of Madhya Pradesh would be linked on a reciprocal basis.

The present public grievances redressal system of the State Government would be upgraded to facilitate access to citizens through any of the kiosks, Samadhan Kendras, public facilitation centers or Government offices. It would be made email based and strengthened to facilitate monitoring and on-line responses.[42]

The wired village's concept would be replicated with a pilot in each district. The State Government would stake its share of the claim in the various schemes, which form part of the recommendations of the National Task Force. Preparations for drawing up suitable proposals in order to leverage assistance as soon as GOI formally announces or launches these would be started straight away by the corresponding departments of the State Government.

The district Sainik Welfare Boards would list ex-service personnel with background in communications and computers. The services of IT hardware specialists from the Defence Forces can be beneficially exploited by local hardware/ancillary industry. Financial arrangements and schemes would be proposed in collaboration with the Defence Ministry, Banks/FIs for retired Defence personnel for setting up IT training/services enterprises and IT kiosks. The services of retired IT qualified Defence personnel would be utilized at school level for creating IT awareness in the villages/districts.

Creation of Intranet: Creation of Intranet among institutions in each social sub sector would qualitatively improve the services/training being provided by institutions with resource and faculty constraints. To begin with, all medical colleges in the State would be linked for leveraging each other's faculty strengths. Similarly, Tele or remote referral consultancy through linkages with medical colleges would be used to virtually upgrade the referral facilities at sub-district and district hospitals. The medical colleges would in turn tap institutions of excellence out side the state for consultations.

UGC is sponsoring the INFLIBNET which seeks to network all 176 Universities in the country. This would spur the use of Internet and Intranet resources by not only the campuses but even those local area networks that the University is able to create. Madhya Pradesh would take advantage of the INFLIBNET by promoting and developing LANs for every University in the State by working out a detailed strategy. Creation of virtual libraries in colleges would also be a priority.[43]

Creation of a Citizen Database: A unique social security ID number would be introduced for those availing various benefits such as social assistance, social security pension etc. The BPL household survey, survey conducted for electoral photo identity cards, etc. would form the database for such an exercise to improve delivery of services and eliminate leakage.

Manpower Development for IT

Training for Government Employees: Training efforts, which are at present confined to largely the NIC initiative, would be multiplied. The existing Training institutions for the training of employees of the various departments as well as the State Academy of Administration would be upgraded to meet the requirements. Training tie up with private institutes using a common modular training package would also be used for re-tooling of employees.[44]

Employees engaged in course studies in IT through distance education or other certification programmes would be allowed to use office computers after work hours. Recognition of computer time thus spent would be given due credit by the institutions awarding certificates.

Computer penetration in all the high schools in the next three years would be an effective way of spreading IT usage. All PRIs and urban local bodies would get at least one teacher or shiksha karmi in each high school, under their control, trained in IT usage or familiarity.

The National Task Force has recommended suitable floor space in Government buildings, which are not utilised during non-office hours, could be given to private educational institutions for IT training purpose in return for a proportionate number of free nominations of Government employees for IT training. This concept would be extended to permit commercial utilisation of schools/colleges/educational institutions after academic hours in return for free training of teachers, staff and students. Transparent norms to facilitate this arrangement would be evolved.[45]

Familiarization of PRI functionaries with benefits of IT uses would expedite introduction of IT based practices in these institutions. To begin with, Zila Panchayats and Janpad Panchayats would be introduced to IT during the training programmes to be conducted for the newly elected members in September 1999.

To meet the manpower needs of the State in IT, private sector training institutions and distance education format would also be encouraged along with other Government supported institutions. The courses of study in the ITIs and polytechnics would be upgraded and the training of teachers of these institutions would be taken up simultaneously where required. Action would be initiated for capacity enhancement of institutions imparting IT education in the State. The State would gear for leveraging its share of benefits from the GOI's decision to make computers and internet access available to schools, polytechnics and colleges by the year 2003. Proposals would be prepared for accepting these benefits in a phased manner each year.

The National Task Force has suggested setting up of IIITs. The State would propose to the Government of India setting up of at least one of the proposed IIITs in Madhya Pradesh fully funded by the Centre and in addition, promote private investment for setting up institutions of excellence in IT at par with IIITs by land grants. The Universities in the State would look at how IT course modules can be introduced in the existing degree programmes so that every student is exposed to concepts and rudiments of applications in his or her own area of study. The State would set-up a Virtual University as an enhancement of Open University model and also a Virtual School as an another dimension to the M.P. Open School. For Demystification of IT and computers, the State Council of Education Research and Training would develop and include course material of an elementary nature to arouse curiosity and satisfy young minds at the primary school level.[46]

Madhya Pradesh would aim at creating computer awareness among its masses of a magnitude far higher and not yet achieved or aimed by any other State. It would be universal in character. Only then can people benefit from the IT policy and drive up demand for IT in the State as also throw up the trained manpower. In the ultimate analysis people must feel comfortable in using technology

3.4. Location, Size and Units of IT Industry in Madhya Pradesh

Madhya Pradesh has an advantage few other States in the country have, in terms of the communications backbone provided by both public and private sectors.[47] The optical fibers backbone available to the State is apex. 10,000 K.Ms presently and is projected to grow even further bringing all tehsil and eventually development block head quarters in its fold. The Task Force recommends that software exports being the fastest growing segment of the IT industry, in order to attract software exporters to the State, the State must have 3 international gateway hubs. One such international gateway hub is being provided by VSNL at Indore. The State Government should move the Government of India to permit International Private Operators to create an international gateway hub each at Bhopal and Indore.

Location Issues of Information Technology Companies: Location can be a significant factor in an IT industry success. We look at the typical factors related to location and what factors a company is looking for when making a decision. A list of criteria is presented in order of preference.

By definition of an IT industry, a site must first be located near a university center engaged in research activities, which ensures an active research and development component to the park. The university presence results in a quality workforce that is engaged in cross learning via proximity to others with similar interests, which is critical to any research and development activity.

One location cannot offer the optimum situation in all of the factors, so clearly the goal should be to locate a IT industry in an area that can offer as many of the factors as possible or a pre-determined strategic mix.

An IT company may be strong in infrastructure and labor force, but it could also be located in an area that is costly to live in. This is the current case of Gwalior, Indore and Bhopal has become one of the most cost inflated regions in the Madhya Pradesh Land is at a premium and the cost

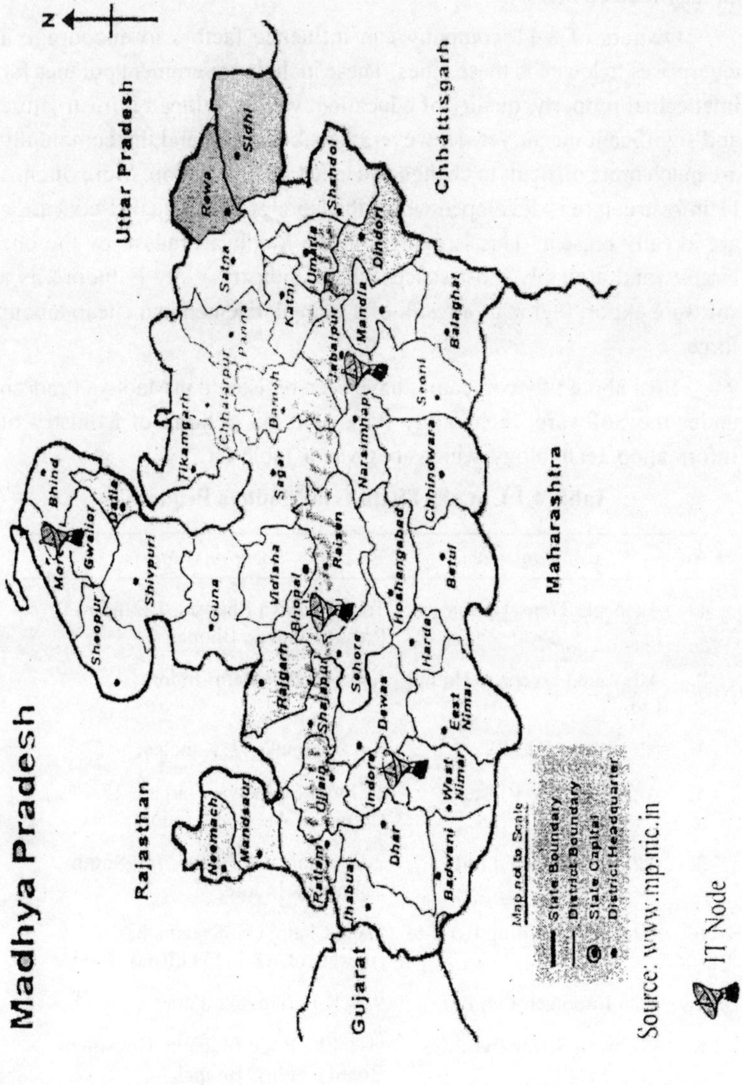
Madhya Pradesh
N
Uttar Pradesh
Rajasthan
Gujarat
Maharashtra
Chhattisgarh
Sheopur
Morena
Gwalior
Bhind
Datia
Shivpuri
Guna
Tikamgarh
Chhatarpur
Panna
Satna
Rewa
Sidhi
Shahdol
Umaria
Dindori
Katni
Damoh
Sagar
Vidisha
Bhopal
Raisen
Narsimhapur
Jabalpur
Mandla
Balaghat
Seoni
Chhindwara
Hoshangabad
Betul
Harda
Sehore
Rajgarh
Shajapur
Dewas
Ujjain
Indore
Ratlam
Neemach
Mandsaur
Jhabua
Dhar
Badwani
West Nimar
East Nimar
Map not to Scale
State Boundary
District Boundary
State Capital
District Headquarter
Source: www.mp.nic.in
IT Node

of living is very high. Government of Madhya Pradesh declared four nodes for promotion of IT and IT industry in state. These nodes are Bhopal, Indore, Jabalpur and Gwalior (shown in figure 4.1). However, these cities continues to benefit from the quality of higher education in the area and the synergies that are created by proximity among the high-tech industries already located there.

Owners of a IT company can influence factors to encourage a enterprises to locate in these cities. These include government policies for intellectual property, quality of education, well-developed infrastructure and significant incentives. However, the labour pool and the community are much more difficult to change and take time to develop. More often, a IT infrastructure is developed where the labor pool and quality education are already present. This is evident in the Madhya Pradesh by the one largest (and arguably most successful IT industry) city is Indore as a software export region as a result of a trained, talented and cheap labour force.

Near about fifty companies have been registered in Madhya Pradesh under the Software Technology Park of India, a body of Ministry of Information Technology, which are given in table 4.1.

Table 4.1 List of STP units in Madhya Pradesh

S.No.	*Company Name*	*Location Address*
1.	Aksheela Transcription Pvt. Ltd	Tarun Duniya Bhawan, 12, Indira Press Complex, Bhopal
2.	Alfavision Overseas (India) Ltd.	Janki Nagar (Main) Indore
3.	Alis Infotech Ltd.	Raj Complex, 42, Kanchan
4.	Alpin Infosys (P) Ltd.	1st Floor Shanowar Darpan, 27, Press Complex, AB Road, Indore.
5.	APL International Ltd.	203, Mahakosh House, 7/5, South Tukogunj, Indore.
6.	Athena Consulting Pvt. Ltd.	Dalal Chambers, Sagamatha Apartment, 18/7, M.G.Road, Indore
7.	Beta Infootech Pvt. Ltd.	9, R.K.Puram, Old Palasia, Indore.
8.	Bhilwara Scribe Pvt. Ltd.	H-2/496, Bagh Mugalia, Housing Board Colony, Bhopal.
9.	Celebrity Softech Pvt. Ltd.	58, Zone-1, M.P.Nagar, Bhopal

S.No.	*Company Name*	*Location Address*
10.	Data Care Prime Information Systems.	305, Manas Bhawan, 11, R.N.T. Marg Indore.
11.	EBusiness Datacom Ltd.	101, Kanchan Vihar, Kanchan Bagh, Indore.
12.	Ecubator Labs	136, Jaora Compound, Indore
13.	Futuerstic Softech India Pvt. Ltd.	101-A, Press House, 22, Press Complex, Indore
14.	CEI Human Industries Ltd.	26/A, Industrial Area, Govindpura Bhopal
15.	Impetus Computing (p) Ltd.	301-302, Aru Plaza, Kalyan Bhawan, 582, M.G.Road Indore
16.	Infoqesh Datacom Ltd.	3/5, New Palasia, Indore
17.	Infoquest Software Export Ltd.	3/5, New Palasia, Indore
18.	Innovation Computers (P) Ltd.	576, M.G.Road, Nemi Niwas, Indore
19.	Janki software & solution	199, Saket Nagar, Indore
20.	Logistics Technologies	441, Vishnupuri Extn, Indore
21.	Madhya Pradesh Glytchem Industries	201, Mahakosh House, 7/5, Tuku Nath Mandir Road, Indore
22.	Microlink Technologies	556, Khatiwala Tank, Indore
23.	Millenium Cybertech Ltd.	203, Princess Pride, 21/3, New Palasia, Indore
24.	Mirash Infotech Exports	B-307, Silvar Mall, 8/A, RNT Road, Indore
25.	Neeteam International	202, Amar Darshan, Saket, Indore
26.	NSIL Infotech Ltd.	26/3, Old Palasia, Indore
27.	Opel Infotech Pvt. Ltd.	157, First Floor, Zone-2, M.P.Nagar, Bhopal
28.	OSCO International	29/5, South Tukoganj, Street-1, Indore
29.	Oswal Data Processors	2nd Floor, Alankar Point, Geeta Bhawan Choraha, AB Road, Indore

S.No.	*Company Name*	*Location Address*
30.	Param Industries Ltd.	101, Mahakosh House. 7/5, South Tukoganj. Nath Mandir Road, Indore
31.	Patni Computer System Ltd.	110. Shalimar Trade Centre, Opp. Hotel Pallavi, RMT Marg, Indore
32.	Policy Management Systems India Pvt. Ltd.	Optel, STP, Near Perdeshipura, Elex. Complex, Indore
33.	Prem Sagar Impex (P) Ltd.	111, Apollo Bhawan, Chauraha AB Road, Indore
34.	Pumik Infotech Ltd.	Permaliu House, Hoshangabad Road, Bhopal
35.	Rising Sun Technologies	171, Saket Indore
36.	Ruchi Global Ltd.	504, Mahakosh House, 7/5 South Tukoganj, Indore
37.	Ruchi Infotech Ltd.	502, Mahakosh House, 7/5 South Tukoganj, Indore
38.	SAM Infotech Pvt. Ltd.	10/1 Manorma Ganj, 7/5, South Tukoganj, Nath Mandir Road, Indore
39.	Soft Vision Technologies India Pvt. Ltd.	13. Green Park, South Tukoganj, Indore.
40.	Sunrise Exports	170/10, RNT Marg, Film Colony, Indore
41.	Supar Scribe Pvt. Ltd.	Z-18, Zone-1, M.P.Nagar, Bhopal
42.	Suvi Information Systems (P) Ltd.	610, Chetak Center, 12/2, R.N.T. Marg, Indore
43.	Thyron Information (P) Ltd.	Thyron House, Kanchan sagar, 3rd Floor, 17/1, Old Palasia, AB Road, Indore
44.	Times Informatics Pvt. Ltd.	4th Floor, Kanchan Bagh, 181, Old Palasia, AB Road, Indore.
45.	Vertex Machineries Ltd.	509, Chetak Centre, RNT Marg, Indore
46.	Vigro Exports	188. Anoop Nagar, Indore
47.	VIS Transcription	Laxmi Tower, 576, MG Road, Suite 303, Indore
48.	Viscus Infotech Ltd.	31/2, New Palasia, Indore
49.	Apical E-Solution Ltd.	201, Silver Sachora Castle, 7, RNT Marg, Indore

Source–Software Technology Park of India, Electronic Complex, Pardeshipura, Indore.

Notes and References

1. Sharma K.K., *Population of India: 2001*, Upkar Prakashan, Agra 2001, P.41.
2. Economic infrastructure at web site www.mpindustry_nic.in. visited on December 30, 2001.
3. IT infrastructure at web site <http://www.dotindia.com/> - Department of Telecom, India. Visited on December 30, 2001
4. IT_gwalior.htm at web site http://www.mp.nic.in. visited on December 30, 2001
5. IT_indore.htm at web site http://www.mp.nic.in. visited on December 30, 2001
6. IT_jabalpur.htm at web site http://www.mp.nic.in. visited on December 30, 2001
7. Industry profile at web site www.mpindustry_nic.in. Visited on December 30, 2001.
8. <http://www.dotindia.com/> - Department of Telecom, India. Visited on December 30, 2001
9. Ibid.
10. IT_vision..htm in website http://www.mp.nic.in. visited on June 30, 2002
11. *Information Technology initiatives in Madhya-Pradesh,* Government of M.P., May 5, 1999.
12. IT_policy.htm # origin of IT industry: at www.mp.nic.in
13. Objective of gyandoot project at:www.gyandoot.com visited on July 12, 2002
14. Infrastructure.htm at www.bsnl.co.in visited on September 15, 2002
15. Ibid.
16. Software Park at www.optelmpsedc.com visited on September 15, 2002
17. Ibid.
18. Software Park at www.optelmpsedc.com visited on September 15, 2002
19. Ibid.
20. Itanddl.jsp at www.infochangeindia.org visited on August 23, 2002.
21. Profile at www.gyandoot.com visited on July 17, 2002.

22. *Times of India,* dated January 31, 2000
23. About NIC success stories at www.infochangeindia.org visited on August 23, 2002
24. Profile ITC at http://www.soyachaupal.com/ visited on August 23, 2002.
25. Indore_stp.htm at www.mpsedc.com visited on September 8, 2002.
26. Bhopal_stp.htm at www.mpsedc.com visited on September 8, 2002.
27. Gwalior_stp.htm at www.mpsedc.com visited on September 8, 2002.
28. IT_policy.htm # introduction at www.mp.nic.in visited on July 3, 2002.
29. Ibid.
30. Ibid.
31. IT_policy.htm # Vision - Seamless Society with Global Opportunities at www.mp.nic.in visited on July 3, 2002.
32. Ibid.
33. Ibid.
34. IT_policy.htm # Creating an enabling environment and niche marketing at www.mp.nic.in visited on July 3, 2002.
35. Ibid.
36. IT_policy.htm # Promotion of Infrastructure, Industry and Investments at www.mp.nic.in visited on July 3, 2002.
37. IT_policy.htm # Promotion of Infrastructure, Industry and Investments at www.mp.nic.in visited on July 3, 2002.
38. IT_policy.htm # Promotion of IT in Government at www.mp.nic.in visited on July 3, 2002.
39. Ibid.
40. Ibid.
41. IT_policy.htm # Promoting IT in the Social Sector at www.mp.nic.in visited on July 3, 2002.
42. IT_policy.htm # Promoting IT in the Social Sector at www.mp.nic.in visited on July 3, 2002.
43. IT_policy.htm # Promoting IT in the Social Sector at www.mp.nic.in visited on July 3, 2002
44. IT_policy.htm # Manpower Development for IT at www.mp.nic.in visited on July 3, 2002

45. IT_policy.htm # Manpower Development for IT at www.mp.nic.in visited on July 3, 2002

46. IT_policy.htm # Manpower Development for IT at www.mp.nic.in visited on July 3, 2002

47. *India 1999 A Reference Annual,* Ministry of Information and Broadcasting, Government of India, New Delhi.

4
Study of Information Technology in Madhya Pradesh

4.1 IT Companies of Madhya Pradesh

In the last few years, Indore has transformed itself from being a 'traditional industry's Paradise' to the 'Silicon Valley' of Madhya Pradesh. From a mere 13 software units in 1995-96, the units have increased to 50 as of 2001. The talent pool of highly trained professionals, the training infrastructure and progressive Government policies that have led to this amazing IT explosion in the city

Indore is home of the corporate giants in IT like Suvi, Impetus, PSM, Thyron, Horizon, Super Scribe etc. The functioning, management, business strategies, software and hardware specification and HandD of different IT companies are:

4.1.1. Suvi Information Sys Com. Indore

Suvi is a leading software development company focusing on providing robust business solutions. Suvi has a vertical focus on Health Care, Banking, e-Governance and Jewellry industries. Suvi has an excellent blend of expertise and experience, which ensures that the objectives are always realized. Suvi has strong set up in India with commendable delivery capabilities coupled with the global presence to help clients eliminate boundaries and join hands with the trustworthy company.

Suvi Profile

Established in 1988, Suvi has been providing software solution to the industrial and commercial sectors. A group experience of over 14 years in software design and development has paved the way for us to timely deliver cost-effective and high quality solutions to the dynamic industry requirements. Suvi has developed and implemented turnkey IT solutions for clients, some of which are the largest installations in the region and have also had the opportunity of working with some of the prestigious companies in the US and Europe[1].

Suvi's current business model addresses few specific sectors like Banking and Finance, Health care, Government apart from customized software development. With development center at India, company has expanded its marketing operations in New York, Delaware and San Jose through its affiliation with, Diaspark Inc. USA.

Over the years Suvi has gained tremendous experience working closely with domestic and international clients from varied industries. From consultancy and services to the addition of products for specific industries has been strategic move in the recent past. All along Suvi has been respected provider of customized software solutions and products.

Company Overview

Diaspark Inc. a affiliated to SUVI[2], is a premier e-business consulting and software engineering company provides state of the art IT consulting, customized solutions and products by creating an environment conducive to excellence in growth of knowledge.

Diaspark ranked at #196 in the Inc 500 list of the fastest growing private companies in America for 2001. Diaspark ranks in the fast 50 technology companies of New York and fast 500 companies of USA as ranked by Deloitte and Touche for the second year in a row - 2000 and 2001[3].

Profile: Skill Set

Suvi's core strength has been and is technical proficiency. A dynamic and young team of technical professionals put incessant efforts to provide the latest and best of technology to the clients. Significant effort has gone into developing the tools and framework to deliver the best in the stipulated project period and also to follow standard software development practices. Offshore development calls for better systems, communication, project execution methodology, quality assurance and constant support. Suvi has the requisite infrastructure and team to tackle the critical aspects of this area.[4]

Suvi currently working with following technologies—

Application Servers: IIS, IBM Web sphere, Oracle Application Server.

Web Technologies: VB.net and ASP.net, VB /ASP /COM/DCOM, Java/JSP/EJB, XML.

RDBMS: Oracle, MS-SQL Server, Sybase.

Client/Server Technologies: VB and VB.net, Power Builder, D2K.

Application Design Tools: Rational Rose, Power Designer.

Profile -Fact Sheet:

2001—Indian company gained strong foothold in vertical markets (Healthcare, Bank and Government). US Operations ranked as 196th Fastest growing private company in Inc. 500 (October 2001 issue).

2000—Expanded US Operations and opened new offices in Delaware and San Jose. During the year US Company was ranked as New York's 8th fastest and USA's 89th Fastest growing Technology Company. Indian operations excelled in offering web based solutions.

1999—Company moves to spacious 15,000 square feet office with world class Infrastructure. Launch of http://www.epatra.com/; First Free Indian languages mailing services. Launch of world's First Hindi Portal http://www.webdunia.com/ offering news, culture, shopping, infotainment, Indian language e-mail using http://www.epatra.com/ and Indian languages chat Facility using e-varta. [with the advance technology of embedded Fonts] (Both these are now a part and product of separately formed company Webdunia.com (India) Pvt. Ltd.). Excelled in offering Client Server Solutions, Multi-tier solutions, successful products in vertical segment.[5]

1995—Affiliated with Diaspark Inc. New York, USA.

1992-94—Apart from Overseas Contracts, strengthened standing in domestic market. Mostly Developing and implementing turnkey Unix based solutions for textile industries in the industrial belts of Madhya Preadesh.

1992—Entry to overseas market.

1990—Shifted the office to Indore (M. P.) industrial capital of Madhya Pradesh, India.

1988— Started Suvi Information System in Bhopal (M. P.).

Suvi Management :

- Vinay Chhajlani - Founder and Director
- Vinod Jain - Executive Director

Suvi-Verticales

Suvi's vast experience facilitated product offerings for certain vertical market segments. They are user-friendly, flexible, comprehensive and path breakers in their respective areas[6].

Healthcare [Suvi Hospital Management System (Suvi HMS)]

Suvi HMS is comprehensive single point management software covering all the functions in Administrative and Medication needs of the hospitals. The software is designed modularly for ease of implementation, integration and linkage for providing on-line information system to the different levels of Management in the hospital.

Accounting Solutions [For Medium to Large-sized Businesses]

Suvi Soft Assist is a complete business management solution that helps companies of every size manage not only the finance, but virtually every aspect of their businesses. The package is result of more than 12 years of efforts in designing, developing and implementing business applications under prevailing technology.

The modular design of Suvi Soft Assist allows businesses to customize the applications to precisely correspond their requirements. And the software uses the latest Microsoft. Net technology to deliver the best of both the Intranet and Internet environment.

Banking

Suvi's Core Retail Banking solution provides a complete relationship management solution for banks ranging from Cooperative Sector to mid-sized Commercial Banks. It helps in delivering services that are Customer-focused. A modular approach allows selective deployment of the system to meet specific customer needs.

Product and Services

Consulting: Finding the right IT professionals to supplement your staff requires time. Diaspark Inc. can simplify the process for you. With access to thousands of databases and its own worldwide pool of IT talent,

Diaspark can cost-effectively deliver exactly the skills you need, precisely when you need them. From a single position to an entire department, on short or long-term projects, Diaspark Inc. provides flexible contract, contract to hire and permanent personnel.[7]

All Diaspark consultants are prescreened and reference checked. Rigorous technical interviews conducted by the recruiting department ensure that the candidates meet all your requirements. The database of consultants includes domestic and international candidates with mid to senior-level IT skills. Skill sets range from cutting-edge web development and programming to system administrators and database administrators.

Products: Diaspark Jewel: This product is meant to automate a Jewellry manufacturer's need for management of style, contracting, gold, return and repair and stone inventory. It is an integrated mini ERP packaged software having 16 modules to address these needs of Jewellry Manufactures. The product has been fully developed in-house. Diaspark has been successful in marketing Diaspark Jewel in the US Market with installation base of 40 clients which includes two US$ 100 Mn. Companies having 50 users each.

Foreign Clients[8]:

- Sun Microsystems
- Marsh Inc.
- Novell
- Viacom
- Tangent Design
- American Standard
- Adelphia Communications
- Concentric Networks
- Zaplet

Client Indian[9]:

- DPIP
- PHQ Bhopal
- SGM Hospital, Riva
- MP SCRC
- Hind Syntex Ltd.
- SWebdunia.com

Suvi Expertises :

We are currently working with following technologies:

Application Servers—IIS, IBM Web sphere, Oracle Application Server,

Web Technologies—VB.net and ASP.net, VB /ASP /COM/DCOM, Java/JSP/EJB, XML

Client/Server Technologies—VB and VB.net, Power Builder, D2K

RDBMS—Oracle, MS-SQL Server, Sybase

Application Design Tools—Rational Rose, Power Designer

Language Enabling—SUVI-Diaspark expertise in technology has brought Hindi onto the web. Thus opening a door to information dissemination in multi-lingual India. This would revolutionize the lives of common people, as Hindi is the language in which knowledge, philosophy and spirituality created world standards. The world is going the e-way with Internet becoming a necessity in everyone's lives.

http://www.epatra.com/http://www.epatra.com/http://www.naidunia.com/http://www.naidunia.com/ http://www.webdunia.com/http://www.webdunia.com/

Apart from providing e-business solutions in English, SUVI-Diaspark has expertise in providing the front-end/browsing screen in Hindi as well. Its research and development into this line helps to provide combination of using English for the back-end systems and Hindi for the front-end systems/browser. SUVI-Diaspark welcomes any such requirements, as it is always easier to conduct the business in one's own language.

Offshore Overview

Suvi's real business experience of more than twelve years and excellent project management capability provides an option of cost effective offshore development services to prospective overseas clients. This service delivery model reduces investment by 30-40 per cent hence high returns on the IT investment. Suvi aims at meeting client's expectations in terms of quality standards and time estimates, at the same time, reducing development costs and cycle times. A team of technically proficient and dedicated people, state-of-the-art communication facilities and infrastructure backs up offshore development services. It provides a virtual extension of client's development environment and 24x7 service.

Advantages:-

- Cost Effectiveness
- Quality Competence
- Additional Team Strength
- Quick Turnaround Time

- Excellent Technical support, Debugging and Running night schedule.
- 24×7 hours Service

OFFSHORE SERVICE DELIVERY MODEL[10]

Suvi has many service delivery models. A client can choose any of them depending upon the nature of the project, cost-effectiveness and estimated project execution period.

Offsite: This delivery model is suitable for clients having systems department capable of designing the required systems and drawing systems specifications. These system specifications are offloaded to us for coding and testing. After thorough testing, the system is delivered to the client for implementation.

Onsite: This delivery model is suitable for clients desirous of getting the project done fast but which is typically of 1-2 year time. In this case getting right professionals to carry out projects is a tough task. Suvi can provide consultant onsite for such projects.

Offshore Development Center: This service delivery model provides client with Suvi's Technologies, facility and staff dedicated for client's IT project requirements. A team of dedicated and trained application specialists/ programmers is placed in India, which coordinates with another team (usually smaller in composition; 1-2 persons) at client's office on daily basis. The Offshore team connects to client's machines via dedicated leased line/ Internet connection. Under this model Suvi provides dedicated Space, Hardware, Software, Communication Resources, Technical Staff and Project Managers with requisite skills and experience.

Suvi suggest a combination of onsite and offshore project execution model to meet the client's expectations and offer best value for money. All the above service delivery models can be worked on Time and Material / Fixed Price Contracts.

Offshore-Methodology

Suvi's large team of diversified computer professionals allows to meet the varied technological and functional demands of customers in an efficient, cost-effective manner. Our Software Development Methodology realizes projects using both structured and object-oriented approaches. Suvi has used Rapid Application Development (RAD) as the primary software development technology. The software development process consists of the following steps

- **Initial Project Scope Estimate**— Following initial meetings with the customer, Suvi provides a rough estimate of the project type, scope, probable cost, etc.
- **Development of Specification**—On award of the contract, Suvi sends high-level analysts to the customer's site to gather requirements define business processes and develop a detailed Specification. In case of overseas clients, this activity is carried out by Diaspark Inc. USA, a Company affiliated with SUVI.
- **System Development**—Employing iterative prototyping the system is build. The development process remains under version and change management controls using tool like MS Visual Source Safe.
- **Testing**—Prior to delivery to the customer, the system is fully tested for both functional and load. Suvi develops additional testing procedures together with the customer to further test the developed software.
- **Implementation**—After thorough testing the software is implemented at client site. In case of overseas clients, this activity is carried out by Diaspark Inc. Diaspark Consultants keep in touch with Suvi's development team for any bug fixing during implementation. Suvi even uses remote access tools like PC anywhere to fix the bugs, if any.
- **Deployment / Maintenance**—When the system is fully deployed, we maintain the software under a separate contract with the customer.

Offshore Client

• Vitech Systems. • Rosi Blue. • Quebecor World.

Suvi Services

Suvi's highly qualified and experienced IT professionals constantly sweat out their brains to give your business a global perspective as well as profitability by delivering software solutions that support your business system needs.

The team has expertise in adapting new technologies to the work place realities. Thereby is able to offer solutions that are better, faster and effective. Suvi's principle services include :

Industry Specific Solutions : Suvi offers few vertical industry solutions that are closely aligned with the needs of those industries. This includes Hospital Management and Banking Software. This is possible because of the in-depth domain knowledge that the company has acquired in various industry segments over the years.

It also carries a General Purpose Business Accounting solution which not only caters to accounting needs of any company but virtually every aspect of business viz. Sales, Purchase, Inventory, HR and payroll.

Custom Application Development : Designing and developing innovative solutions is our forte. With 12 years of experience in application development, creative ideas, proven frameworks and experienced professionals, we lay the foundation with crystal clear understanding of systems requirement and build the software on that using around client/ server, web based or the combo of the two architectures.

Suvi also provides staff augmentation services to provide the consultants who meet requisite knowledge and experience levels of your company. These services can be offered from a single position to an entire department, on short-term or long-term projects to hire permanent personnel for your company.

4.1.2. Impetus Company

Company Overview

Impetus was founded in India in 1991 as a small software product company. Its initial products are still being used at several hundred installations. Impetus is headquartered in Silicon Valley with a wholly owned subsidiary in India. The company's mission is to excel and innovate using technology and provide value to its customers. This desire to innovate and contribute pervades throughout the company. Impetus' management is made up of individuals with immense experience in all facets of the software industry.

Impetus has successfully incubated a Supply Chain Software company called Servigistics. Impetus' CEO, Praveen Kankariya, is a founder board member of Servigistics.[11]

Impetus People

Impetus engineers are recruited from the best universities. Company look for people who are driven self-starters and team players. Company round out the engineers we hire in our Impetus University, which is an internal organisation focused on training and educational needs of Impetus engineers. Dr. Chandwani who was a computer science professor at the University of Indore, India heads the Impetus University. As a result, Company has a powerhouse engineering organisation and we are continually enhancing and growing it.[12]

Company Partners

Impetus has partnered with premier software companies whose software products provide the basic infrastructure for Impetus' solutions. These include:

- BEA
- IBM
- Sun
- Microsoft
- Servigistics
- Propel

Impetus Services

Application Engineering :

Impetus has been developing software application products and custom solutions in several verticals, including:

- Financial services and insurance
- Supply chain management
- Healthcare
- CRM

Impetus' engineering teams have designed and developed large mission critical applications in record time and at economical costs and we take pride in our ability to right-architect scalable, maintainable and robust applications.

Our architectures are based on one of the two popular technology platforms:

- J2EE (Java 2 Enterprise Edition), or
- Microsoft .NET

J2EE— We have successfully developed over 15 J2EE applications. We have used applications servers like BEA Weblogic, IBM Websphere, Orion, Jonas and ATG Dynamo. Our architects understand that nuances of creating components architectures using Enterprise Java Beans.

Microsoft NET—Impetus has been developing on the Windows platform for the last 8 years. We have extensive experience developing large distributed applications using COM/MTS, IIS and XML.

Company have strong processes to manage, design and develop using teams distributed between the US and India. We fully leverage our suite of components to give a head start to our projects.

QA and Performance Testing—Impetus provides cost-effective quality assurance and performance testing services to several clients from its offshore development center in India. Our QA offerings can be classified into—

- Browser compatibility testing and resolution.
- User Interface (UI) testing of web applications.
- Functionality testing of web application.
- Application stress testing.
- Code testing.

Impetus has a dedicated group that performs creates and executes Quality Assurance services on applications. We use industry standard tools like Win Runner, Silk Performer, WAST, Rational Suite Test Studio or use our home grown tool, the Peak Load Tester to create load testing scenarios based on the anticipated transaction mix as well as create large data sets that mirror real-life usage. Impetus has the hardware infrastructure with Sun and Windows 2000 multi-processor servers to execute the tests. We provide detailed analytical reports with suggestions for performance improvements.

Embedded Software

Impetus believes Parachutes work well when open so do Minds. Having a core group of dedicated Engineers and leaders of vast experience, the Embedded Systems Division strives to deliver on time using time-tested design methodology and the most optimal implementation.

Core Strengths

- Embedded Systems development for Home/Industrial Applications.
- Wireless communication protocols.
- Network Protocols— Embedded TCP/IP and related protocols.

- Device-Driver development.
- Proven design methodologies.
- System Algorithm design and development.

Services Provided

- Technology Evaluation.
- Product Design.
- Product Reliability Testing.
- Fixed-Bid Consulting.
- On-shore Consulting (at client's site).
- Offshore Consulting (in India).

Weblogic Upgrade

Weblogic Upgrade from 4.5 to 6.1—Impetus has established a Migration programme from older versions of WebLogic Server to WebLogic 6.1, as a rapid, safe and cost-effective way for you to move your strategic applications to the new environment. Impetus engineers have created a methodical process to handle several changes between WebLogic 6.1 and several older versions. They have captured the common problems encountered into a knowledge base and devised recommendations for making appropriate choices based on the unique set of requirements of each application.

Success Stories[13]

3M HIS

Clinical Management and Inference System

The objective was to build clinical documentation system software "ClinDoc" for Healthcare agencies that would help them record and process clinical information of Patients as per the government-mandated procedure. The software developed had to record and produce the health information and generate clinical reports in the standard formats specified by the government like the OASIS Assessment Report, Clinical Data Export to HCFA Format, 485/7 Forms, etc. The standardised report formats required information gathering at various levels and the task of validating the data for "well-formed ness" is quite involved because of the detailed and exhaustive specification laid out by the government agencies. The software to be developed had to be compatible and work harmoniously with an existing legacy application. A restricted mobile version of the software had to be developed, which would allow users (nurses) to work offline collecting Clinical information during their visits to patients. The sync process had to be fast enough to handle huge datasets. This group of extremely complex applications is used by large home healthcare agencies to manage and track patients and their progress as well as diagnose diseases using a rule- processing engine. The biggest challenge was to come up with a user-friendly way of representing and maintaining the rules in a format that could be dynamically loaded and compiled by the application. The system also contains a series of OCR components to intelligently process forms. We are using Visual C++ 6.0, Visual Basic 6.0, MDAC, Oracle 8i, Oracle Lite, MSDE.

Resource Manager Framework

Impetus designed and developed dynamic object interaction architecture for Java applications and applets based on Taligent's MVP (model-view-presenter) model. This framework enables GUI programmers to develop live user interfaces that are uncoupled from the business objects. The framework[14]:

- Exposes the business objects using a declarative API.
- Provides for dynamic validation. When a user tabs out of a control, the new value is automatically checked and vetoed if incorrect.
- Sends update events to a UI component if the corresponding attribute value has changed exogenously or another attribute it depends on has changed in the local session.
- Sends update events to other UI instances on the network for persistent changes.
- Manages transactions in the persistent store (Object Store in the current implementation).

We designed the patterns for the business objects. These complex patterns enable the business objects to plug behind the interaction layer and support dynamic notification of changes in dependent persistent and

·alculated attributes/properties. A collection of commonly used UI components was sub-classed from off the shelf components to make them interaction layer aware.

- 3M HIS
- 3M IT
- Wells Fargo
- PricewaterhouseCoopers
- Deloitte and Touche
- Vantive / PeopleSoft
- Servigistics
- Kudzu
- Info-One
- NCS
- ViServ
- Flexstor
- InsureZone
- ViLink

Tools and Framework

Getting a Head start: *Impetus has made significant investments in ensuring that the reinvention of the wheel is minimized on its projects. The advantages are*[15]*:*

- Faster development
- Minimal new code
- Team stays focused on business functionality and not the infrastructure.

Taking a top down solution-centric view, we have built the routinely needed pieces missing in the popular infrastructure platforms like application servers that we use.

Tools—Impetus has significant experience in operating system internals and network programming on both Unix variants and NT. We have developed several products in this category.

4.1.3 Infinity Software Solution Company- Indore (M.P.)

About Company[16]

Infinity Software Solutions is a software development company, set to carve out a niche for itself in the area of IT enabled services and product development. Company provide the state-of-the art services, ensuring adaptability to client needs and thus bringing out the most innovative solutions in every business and technology today. A people's driven company, Infinity believe in making its employees highly professional knowledge workers. An air of professionalism pervades everywhere in the company which helps in delivering mission critical business collations very quickly. Consistent training, best HR practices empower Infinity employees to take on any challenge.

Company mission is to deliver cost effective, quality IT solutions in scheduled time to out clients by leveraging the experience of our dedicated team of professionals in diverse technology and business areas, lead to customer's satisfaction, our ultimate motto. The Infinity assurance for quality software solutions ensures that we always exceed your expectations and provide solutions beyond.

Services[17]

Web Solutions: In the global business environment today, an organisation's operations extend beyond just physical and geographical boundaries and the reach of the "Virtual Organisation" goes to determine its competitiveness. For business, the World Wide Web can empower customers, partners and employees to access information directly in a new, self-service paradigm, while reducing cost in business operations and IT infrastructure support. The real power of internet today is to provide universal access to information round the clock.

Infinity provides state-of-the art internet and E-Commerce solutions by drawing upon its wide ranging expertise in developing business applications, systems development, database integration, networking and multimedia applications. It is precisely here that our competitive advantage lies.

Infinity provide the following web based solutions and services:

Internet Consulting— Website / Internet / Extranet options, Capacity Planning, Equipment selection, Vendor Selection, Implementation, Training and Support, Website strategy development.

E-Commerce Services— B2C, i.e., Business to Customer E-Commerce, B2B, i.e., Business to Business E-Commerce, Online Customer Support and Auto e-mail responses and other such E-Commerce applications.

Specialized Services—Data Transfer, Solutions for particular segment like Automobiles, Logistics, Consulting Organisations, Government Institutions, including System Study, cost effective solutions.

Information Systems Strategy Planning—The last four decades have witnessed an information revolution that has transformed the global business environment. The rapid advances in Information Technology (IT) in supporting the planning, controlling, organising and decision-making needs of an organisation view information as a strategic resource. In tomorrow's world, Organisations will have to depend on IT to shape strategies and structures to fit the new and emerging technologies.

However, in several organisations the use of IT is restricted to a portfolio of stand-alone application systems that support the operational activities of various departments. Very often, these systems are developed in an adhoc manner using incompatible technologies. Consequently, these organisations face problems in meeting the processing requirements of growing business and customer needs, a changing environment and competition.

It is therefore imperative that information systems and Information Technology need to be planned to ensure alignment of information strategies with the business strategies of the organisation. Such planning will result in the adoption of appropriate and compatible IT solutions that will improve the business operations of the organisations, as well as ensure maximum leverage for competitive advantage.

ISSP is a planning methodology to develop information system plans, for immediate and future requirements, which support the business strategies of the organisation, while taking account of various parameters like financial and technical constraints. The benefits of ISSP are:

Addressing the entire enterprise wide IS support requirements Supports enterprise-wide data sharing Enterprise-wide system integration Facilitates investment planning in IS/IT Build quality into solutions Reduce maintenance overheads Use of IT for competitive advantage

Customized Software Solutions—Every organisation is a density with unique requirements. Consequently, the IT processes and systems that a firm utilizes must be sensitive to these requirements. To fulfil this objective, IT services and solutions provider must be able to deliver customized software solutions that are optimized for client needs.

Infinity's customized software solutions involve system analysis, design, development and implementation of integrated software systems, for a number of areas, business and industry sectors and utilities. The execution and implementation process is carried out in accordance with a sophisticated development approach that takes into account the specificity of the task at hand. In providing customized solutions, we employ several lifecycle development models that, according to us, offer innovative ways of fulfilling client needs. Company has created the necessary infrastructure for the successful completion of large and complex projects, namely skilled manpower, training programme and hardware and software facilities. Quality Assurance and Testing procedures. Software Development methodologies and documentation standards are well defined, properly documented and well propagated throughout the organisation.

Packaged Software Implementation—Selecting a software package that meets the requirement of the client, customizing the package and implementing the solution across the department or organisation is one of the fastest ways to deploy Information Technology, Infinity has experience in analyzing customer needs, evaluate various software packages that meet the requirement, customizing the selected package using business and technology, expertise and implementing it. Apart from application systems like Manufacturing, Sales and Marketing, Inventory, Personal, Payroll and Finance in which Infinity has a lot of experience in, one of the major focus areas of Infinity is Enterprise-Wide deployment.

Enterprise Resource Planning (ERP) promotes a fully integrated systems approach, enables companies to cut costs, operate more efficiently, be more responsive to customer demand, reduce overheads and assist staff in reaching in peak performance in all the services and products they offer. To achieve this objective, a company that provides this solution has to have a complete understanding of business goals, IT developments, integration issues and enterprise transformation challenges.

Infinity brings together business and functional expertise to the enterprise transformation process. They understand specific industry issues and then apply their technical expertise to achieve client's business goals.

Migration, Re-engineering and Porting— New technologies and constantly evolving business scenarios necessitate the migration of legacy software systems to state-of-the art environments. The critical consideration while catering to such expansions is to preserve established business rules and practices that are already coded in the old system. This protects investments in the legacy system from being locked in proprietary and outdated technologies.

Re-engineering an application is the most preferred form of migrating and existing host based application into a client/server environment. Infinity possesses specific skills in re-engineering systems and using a variety of migration tools that uniquely qualify it to work on migration and re-engineering projects. Our expertise and experience enable us to follow a highly effective system, while undertaking such projects. The various steps, infinity follows are:

Understand the existing application Define the scope and objective of the task to be undertaken Analysis Design Development of filters Migration of data Construction Testing Integration Deployment.

Multimedia Solutions—Media plays a vital role in promoting your products and services. Interactive media presentation empowers you to express your concepts more effectively than any other conventional promotional practices.

With a unique blend of creativity and technical expertise, Infinity offers full service production from conceptualisation to completion. We specialize in computer generated and computer driven content, delivering results on time, on budget and on target. Infinity's creative department delivers best of world class interactive multimedia solutions for various needs including company's profile, product/services, educational/training programmes, business proposals and many other applications.

Infinity Provides Full Range of Multimedia Services Includes—Concept development and design Interactive media integration 2D and 3D Animation Walkthroughs.

Company Technologies—*Company team of certified professionals from various streams uses multi-tier architecture for building an application, we are using Microsoft and sun technologies.*

Following are a few of technology area:

Internet and Intranet Client-Server Databases Systems Administration and Management Object Oriented programming Network Management System Design and development.

Following are a few of platforms :

Web / Internet Technologies [18]

- SOAP
- XML
- HTML
- DHTML
- VB Script
- JavaScript
- ASP
- JSP
- Java Beans
- Visual Studio
- Active X
- COM / DCOM
- Enterprise Java Beans (EJB)
- CORBA

Programming Languages—C, C++, VC++, VB and Java

Application / Commerce Servers

- MS IIS WebLogic
- MS Site Server
- MS Transaction Server
- RandD
- Microsoft.net
- WAP
- XML Telecom / Networking
- HTTP
- TCP/IP
- ISDN
- Routing
- SNMP
- Network Management
- Database Platform
- Oracle 8/8I
- MS SQL Server 7.0 / 2000
- Sybase
- Informix
- DB2
- MS Access

Operating Systems :

- Linux
- Windows NT
- Windows 95/98
- Unix
- Sun Solaris

Multimedia / Graphics :

- Interactive Design
- 3-D Design
- 3-D Modelling
- 3-D Animation
- Flash Animation
- Interface Desigining
- Macro Media Products

Company Alliances

Partnerships are essential in today's economical and technological scenario. ISS is versatile and proficient in all spheres.[19]

ISS develops close relationships with selected alliance partners. These partners have developed their own industry-leading technologies and best practices that complement ISS's core suite of enterprise applications. Together, ISS and its partners can provide better solutions and greater choices for joint customers.

Infinity offers a wide gamut of IT services including System Strategy Planning, Customized Software Solutions, Web Solutions and Multimedia Presentation, in association with Quantum Business Solutions Inc. based in New Jersy, USA.

4.1.4. Webdunia.com (India) Pvt. Limited

Webdunia.com (India) Pvt. Ltd. is the result of a focused effort at towards delivering Indian language based solutions and services. It is born out of the belief that Internet is a mass medium and that Indian language will play a dominant role in deepening the penetration of Internet in the country. Keeping in line with this, it focuses on the Indian Language Internet Space and provides world class applications and components in 11 major Indian languages. It has several firsts to its credit. It has done fundamental work in creating the most user friendly transliteration engines and has applied for a patent on the same[20].

Webdunia.com (India) Pvt. Limited is the world's largest essential internet-based services company for Indian languages—

Launched the world's 1st Hindi portal	www.webdunia.com
Launched the world's 1st Tamil portal	www.webulagam.com
Launched the world's 1st Telugu portal	www.prapancham.com
Launched the world's 1st Malayalam portal	www.weblokam.com
Launched the world's 1st language e-mail service in 11 Indian language	www.epatra.com
Launched the world's 1st search engine in Hindi and Tamil	www.webdunia.com
Launched the world's 1st chat in 11 major Indian languages	www.evarta.com
Launched the world's 1st e-greeting service in 11 major Indian languages	www.kamna.webdunia.com

All these services do not require the downloading and installation of a separate font for use. To give a small insight into the preference of the most elite viewers of cable and satellite in the urban towns of top 8 most affluent states of India, as high as 80 per cent to 92 per cent viewers prefer and watch local language content. As we move from 0.5 per cent Internet penetration today to 6 per cent penetration by 2003, Internet will demonstrate the same trends as the other media. In fact, if Webdunia.com were to be taken as a proof of concept in favour of our Indian Language Internet theory, we did 45 million page views in May 2002 and have 11,00,000 + e-mail - epatra users growing at 2,500 new registrants per day. This, we believe is a sizeable number and speaks volumes for the acceptance of Indian languages in the net world.

Company Founder : It is rare that an individual with the highest of qualifications and a promising career in the US comes back to his native place and demonstrates entrepreneurial skill in sharing his rich experience and vision with the local Industry. Mr. Vinay Chhajlani, Chief Executive Officer - Webdunia.com (India) Pvt. Ltd., the Managing Director- SUVI Information Systems Pvt. Ltd., now the Director and Promoter- the President of Diaspark Inc. New York and Director Technical - Naidunia News and Networks Pvt. Ltd. is one such person.

The World's first multilingual portal company and language technology service providers Webunia.com (India) Pvt. Limited, is the brainchild of its founder and CEO Mr. Vinay Chhajlani. Under his leadership, webdunia.com pioneered in the language internet world by providing internet services in Indian languages (Hindi, Telegu, Tamil and Malayalam). His team today has made e-patra (World's first free Web based multilingual e-mail), evarta (the World's first multilingual chat), Webdunia khoj (the World's first Indian language Search Engine) and kamna (World's first multilingual e-Greetings) a reality for webdunia.com.

Current Clients[21]: WebDunia have an impressive array of clients. We are working with them in different capacities and have learnt quite a lot in the process of language enabling them. Some of them are as outlined below

Clients : Media/Content Services, Language Technology Services and Media/Content Services.

Webdunia.com provides original, researched and tailor-made content for existing portals. A dedicated team of writers and journalists provide in-depth content and has the expertise to handle diverse subjects. The service is in Hindi for - Sify, Apollolife, CIOL, Indya, Lycosasia, Prabhasakshi, Amul, Naidunia, Pioneer ITI, Tatanova, Amways, PF Department Of MP,

Mantra online, Chitralekha, Rajasthan Patrika, IIAIC and NIIT and in Hindi, Tamil, Malayalam and Telugu for E-city. Our tie-up with E-city also includes offline partnership.

- Sify.com
- Lycosasia
- Indya.com
- Fun-Republic
- Apollolife
- CIOL
- Chitralekha
- IIAIC
- Tatanova
- Mantraonline
- Amul
- Amway

And the service in other languages are for Narmada Control Authority (NCA) and Sample Reels and Malyalam manorama. The media service revenue group of Webdunia.com also provides services like translating the English portals, enabling them to reach out to a wider user base.

Yahoo.co.in : The language cards on Yahoo.co.in in Indian languages are powered by Webdunia.com. For Maha Kumbh Mela 2001 over 60 per cent of the news on Yahoo was syndicated by Webdunia.com, also the official nodal website for the event.

Indiatimes: Providing languages services

Cnet—Cnet India Hindi site is also the in-house expertise of Webdunia.com.

Indiatimes—At Webdunia.com, we believe that the language market has immense scope and no target group is untouched by it. In the education field we have an interesting tie-up with Britannica India. While we language enable their online and offline presence, our tie-up also allows us an exclusive license syndicate their content online in all Indian languages.

Britannica : Language Technology Sales—The Language Technology Services of Webdunia.com is geared to enable corporations, government bodies, Small and Medium Enterprises and media houses to enhance their current systems and processes in Indian Languages alongside English by utilizing Webdunia.com's applications.

Technology Services—The Language Technology Services of Webdunia.com is geared to enable corporations, government bodies, Small and Medium Enterprises and media houses to enhance their current systems and processes in Indian Languages alongside English by utilizing Webdunia.com's applications. These technologies have a patent pending status with the US Government. Some of the familiar applications, which convert Local Indian languages to English (and sometimes vice versa), are

- Email Solution
- Chat Solution
- Discussion Board
- Search Engine
- E-cards
- Personal Home Pages
- Messenger
- SMS / WAP Solution
- Applications for Mobile and Handheld devices.
- Multilingual Application Development Framework for Mobile and Handheld devices.
- Custom applications in Indian Languages to wire up the Government / Corporations, which run on traditional, networks (VPN or open)

Webdunia is providing the solutions for various platforms like Windows , Linux , Sun Solaris etc. Continuous developmental effort to increase suitability and usage by non-initiated users on both the technology and linguistics aspects has enabled Webdunia retain market leadership.

Company Products[22]**:** India is a large multilingual society with as many as eighteen constitutionally recognized languages. There are multiple scripts for these languages. With increase in trade and development across the country it becomes necessary for the people to communicate in more than one language. In such circumstances, Information Technology appears to be a promising tool, which aim at overcoming the language barrier. Webdunia addresses a variety of uses concerned with the use and implementation of Indian languages. Our in-house research team strives to make the use of Indian languages more efficient and a wide range of products have been developed. Know more about our products by clicking the following links.

Products

- Browser
- Composer
- Pad
- Data Converter
- Type-n-cast
- Component

4.1.5. Ruchi Infotech

Ruchi Group industries is well known medium sized industrial group situated in Indore (M.P.) India with exiting activities of: Manufacturing Soya Food Products and Vegetable Oils, Manufacturing Galvanized and

Automobile Steel, Financial Services and Information Technology enable services and software development. The Group turnover for 1997-98 was over US$ 780 Million and the Net Worth is around US$ 100 Million.[23]

A measure of Public confidence in the Group is demonstrated by the presence of over 1,25,000 investors in its various companies. Belonging to a well known business family, Ruchi Group is a medium-sized industrial group based in Indore, India. Its various manufacturing units are located dotting the industrial map of Central India, in the state of Madhya Pradesh. The group has its Corporate Headquarters in Indore, with offices in Mumbai, New Delhi, Kolkata, Chennai and other major business centers in the Country. Plans are afoot to open offices in the U.K., the Middle East and Far East to cover up global market, as special thrust is being given to International trade. The Group's business interests are wide. It has manufacturing and trading facilities of Soya-based products, agri-business, oils and fats, flat steel, galvanized steel, cold rolled steel etc. Though export activities were started few years back only, it has achieved an export turnover of over US$ 200 million during the same period. Exports consist of Soya based food products, DOC (Deoiled cake), oil, Cold Rolled Steel Coils and Galvanized Steel Sheets. To keep pace with the rapidly changing industrial scenario, the group plans to expand and diversify its activities into new areas closely linked to the existing business activities.

Services

RIL provides a wide array of quality services with astounding reliability in many areas. RIL provides the full spectrum of software consulting and development services, targeted at specific business sectors. This approach allows for planned growth. Our services are used in a judicious blend tailored to meet the client requirements[24].

- Software Development
- Software Training
- Internet / Intranet Services
- Facilities Management
- Networking Solutions
- Multimedia
- E-commerce
- R and D
- Client/server services
- System Conversion to Oracle
- Database system scaling /downsizing Training
- Data centre operations support
- Tele/visual Computing
- Quality Manpower Placements

Software Development[25]**:** The software industry is today one of India's largest foreign exchange earners with export turnover of US$ 1.75 billion in 1997-98. India ranks as the World's second largest exporter of software. According to a recent study undertaken by NASSCOM, the Indian software industry is poised to earn annul revenues of more than USD 6 billion by the year 2000.

Software Training[26]**:** Our training activities encompass orientation in software development methodologies, quality management and software technology. Their skills are honed to perfection through a series of extensive training programmes and exposure to the latest and futuristic technologies. Our training makes the professionals very ambitious and enthusiastic and we have tried to ensure that they stay that way. Our management style encourages a high degree of involvement, participation and personal responsibilities. The Unique work ambience, environment culture stretches the abilities of our people and dares them to new heights.

Networking Solutions[27]**:** Our networking professionals can help you to implement, manage and support complex communications networks and connectivity. We have undertaken various networking assignments and have successfully carried out. Our solutions keep the network up and running while avoiding problems that can cost you time and money.

Internet and Intranet Services[28]**:** The Internet has opened up a whole new world of commercial possibilities. The Internet has grown at tremendous pace rate than any other media and has emerged as an increasingly powerful medium for enhancing the competitiveness of businesses around the world.

R and D[29]— In IT world, where processes and technologies get obsolete by the day and information keep updating, research and development is the essential key for being ahead of the future IT world. We provide innovative, integrated, multi-vendor R and D solution services to our customers in order to keep their technologies updated in this IT world.

Facilities Management[30]—Facilities management enables organisations to focus on their core competence while giving them ability to handle diverse needs. Facilities management integrates the planning operations and day by day management of IT resources into the business needs of the organisations. We are providing these services in today's electronic marketplace. These services are the quality solutions to meet your availability and affordability needs. We develop an integrated systems solutions that keeps you to manage your It environment efficiently and effectively.

Client / Server Solutions[31]: We have been involved with client / server initiative over a long-period and have developed a technology. RIL consultants help the customers by providing this skilled technology through developed tools to cater to growing client requirements.

E-Commerce[32]: As customers, employees, suppliers and distributors are all connected to the business systems and information they need, e-commerce actually transforms key business processes.

Multimedia[33]: Our creative team with their inexhaustible skills, empowered by our state-of-the-art equipment will bring to light your crowning ideas by providing interactive multimedia solutions to meet the needs of the commercial and corporate organisations, design CBT's and program multimedia software's.

Support Centre Abroad[34]: We are shortly going to set up our marketing and technical support centre in USA. The centre will be responsible for marketing our services and solutions to the clients in the United States and Europe. This will be followed by our presence at other important global centres too.

4.2 Cost -Benefit Analysis of IT industry in M.P.

Cost-Benefit analysis is a procedure that gives a picture of the various costs, benefits and rules associated with the system[35]. In developing cost estimates for a system, we need to consider several cost elements. Among them are hardware, personnel, facility and operating and supply costs.

1. Hardware costs relate to the actual purchase or lease of the computer and peripherals (for example, printer, disk drive, tape unit etc). Determining the actual cost of hardware is generally more difficult when the system is shared by various users than for a dedicated stand-alone system. In some cases, the best way to control for this cost is to treat it as an operating cost.
2. Personnel costs include EDP staff salaries and benefits (health insurance, vacation time, sick pay, etc) as well as pay for those

involved in developing the system. Costs incurred during the development of a company are one-time costs and are labeled developmental costs. Once the system is installed, the costs of operating and maintaining the system become recurring costs.

3. Facility costs are expenses incurred in the preparation of the physical site where the application or the computer will be in operation. This includes wiring, flooring, acoustics, lighting and air conditioning. These costs are treated as one-time costs are incorporated into the overall cost estimate of the company.
4. Operating costs includes all costs associated with the day-to-day operation of the system; the amount depends on the number of shifts, the nature of the applications and the caliber of the operating staff. There are various overhead. Another approach is to charge each authorised user for the based on computer time, staff time and volume of the out put produced. In any case, some accounting is necessary to determine how operating costs should he handled.
5. Supply costs are variable costs that increase with increased use of paper, ribbon, disks and the like. They should be estimated and included in the overall cost of the IT Company.

An IT company is also expected to provide benefits[36]. The first task is to identify each benefit and then assign a monetary value to it for cost-benefit analysis. The two major benefits are improving performance and minimizing the cost of processing. The performance category emphasizes improvement in authorised users. Minimising costs through the efficient system- error control or reduction of staff- is a benefit that should be measured and included in cost-benefit analysis.

Certain costs and benefits are more easily identifiable than other. Direct cost such as the price of a hard, are easily identified form company invoice payments or canceled checks. Direct benefits often related one-to-one to direct costs, especially savings from reducing costs in the actively in question. Other direct costs and benefits, however, may not be well defined, since they represent estimated costs or benefits that have some uncertainty. A category of costs or benefits that is not easily discernible is opportunity costs and opportunity benefits. There are the costs or benefits forgone by selecting one alternative over another. They so not show in organisation's accounts and therefore are not easy to identify.

The formula we have used here for computing compound growth rate is :

C.G.R. = [Anti log{ (log n – log m)/n } – 1]

In the case of Policy Management System we have the financial data from 1997-98 to 2000-01. To find the estimated value of 2001-02 financial year according to need of our study we use following formula:

$$B_{2001\text{-}02} = B_0 (1 + r)^n$$

Where $B_{2001\text{-}02}$ is estimated value of 2001-02 financial year B_0 is value of starting year (1997-98)., r is compound growth rate from 1997-98 to 2000-01 financial year and n is total number of years. The cost-benefit analysis of six sample companies are:

1. Policy Management System Pvt. Ltd : Policy Management System Pvt. Ltd. is one of the leading IT Company in Madhya Pradesh. During the financial year 1997-98 company recorded total benefits of Rs. 391.1 lakhs comprising the income from exports and domestic income. The cost during this period recorded Rs. 311.27 lakhs and the B/C ratio is 1.25646. Further in next financial year 1998-99 company recorded total revenue or benefit of Rs. 1624.19 lakhs and total cost recorded Rs. 859.29 lakhs. The B/C ratio during 1998-99 financial year is 1.89015. The growth rate of benefit and net profit of company is 315.24 per cent and 858.16 per cent respectively. Financial year 1999-00 company recorded total revenue or benefit of Rs. 2305.7 lakhs and total cost recorded Rs. 1651.19 lakhs. The B/C ratio during 1999-00 financial year is 1.59781. The growth rate of revenue and net profit of company is 41.96 per cent and -14.43 per cent respectively. Financial year 2000-01 company recorded total revenue or benefit of Rs. 2154 lakhs and total cost recorded Rs. 1348.09 lakhs. The B/C ratio during 2000-01 financial year is 1.5978. The growth rate of net profit is 23.13 per cent. Benefit of company is decline by 6.58 per cent. See in table 4.1 and figure 4.1.

The compound growth rate of benefit and cost of Policy Management System from 1997-98 to 2001-02 is 67.109 per cent and 49.139 per cent respectively.

Table 4.1: Growth Rate of Policy Management System (Rs in Lakh)

Year	*Benefit (B)*	*Cost(C)*	*Net Profit*	*ΔB*	*ΔC*	*B/C*
1997-98	391.1	311.27	79.83			1.25646
1998-99	1624.19	859.29	764.9	1233.09	548.02	1.89015
1999-00	2154.00	1651.19	805.91	520.81	488.8	1.59781
2000-01	3034.00	1348.09	757.56	880.00	928.35	1.33278
2001-02*	5096.68*	2296.61*	2800.06	2062.68	20.17	2.21921
C.G.R	67.109%	49.139%				

Note—Estimated Value, C.G.R means Compound Growth Rate, ΔB means change in benefit and ΔC means change in cost.

Source: Based on Survey and www.stpi.net

2. Oswal Data Processor

Oswal Data Processor is one of the leading and oldest IT Company in Madhya Pradesh. During the financial year 1997-98 company recorded total revenues of Rs. 65.99 lakh comprising the income from exports and domestic income. The cost during this period recorded Rs.51.04 lakh and the B/C ratio is 1.29291. Further in next financial year 1998-99 company recorded total revenue or benefit of Rs. 39.82 lakh and total cost recorded Rs. 42.18 lakh. The B/C ratio during 1998-99 financial year is 0.94404. The revenue and net profit of company is declined by 39.66 per cent and 115.78 per cent respectively. Financial year 1999-00 company recorded total revenue or benefit of Rs. 85.88 lakh and total cost recorded Rs. 82.83 lakh. The B/C ratio during 1999-00 financial year is 1.03682. The growth rate of revenue and net profit of company is 115.67 per cent and 229.24 per cent respectively. Financial year 2000-01 company recorded total revenue or benefit of Rs. 64.12 lakh and total cost recorded Rs. 65.07 lakh. The B/C ratio during 2000-01 financial year is 0.98540. The benefit and net profit of company is decline by 25.34 per cent and 131.37 per cent respectively. Financial year 2001-02 company recorded total revenue or benefit of Rs. 74.40 lakh and total cost recorded Rs. 73.00 lakh. The B/C ratio during 2001-02 financial year is 1.01917. The growth rate of benefit and net profit of company is 16.03 per cent and 247.37 per cent respectively. See in table 4.2 and figure 4.2.

The compound growth rate of benefit and cost of Oswal Data Processor from 1997-98 to 2001-02 is 2.428 per cent and 7.321 per cent respectively.

Table 4.2: Growth Rate of Oswal Data Processor (Rs in Lakh)

Year	*Benefit (B)*	*Cost(C)*	*Net Profit*	*ΔB*	*ΔC*	*B/C*
1997-98	65.99	51.04	14.95			1.29291
1998-99	39.82	42.18	–2.36	–26.13	–8.86	0.94404
1999-00	85.88	82.83	3.05	46.06	40.65	1.03682
2000-01	64.12	65.07	–0.95	–21.76	–17.76	0.98540
2001-02	74.40	73.00	–1.4	10.28	7.93	1.01917
C.G.R	2.428 %	7.321%				

Note—C.G.R means Compound Growth Rate, ΔB means change in benefit and ΔC means change in cost.

Source: Based on Survey and www.stpi.net

3. Suvi Information System Ltd.

Suvi Infosystem Ltd. is one of the leading IT company in Madhya-Pradesh. During the financial year 1997-98 company recorded total revenues of Rs. 54.33 lakh comprising the income from exports and domestic income. The cost during this period recorded Rs.43.09 lakh and the B/C ratio is 1.26084. Further in next financial year 1998-99 company recorded total revenue or benefit of Rs. 102.5 lakh and total cost recorded Rs. 79.14 lakh. The B/C ratio during 1998-99 financial year is1.29517. The growth rate of revenue and net profit of company is 88.66 per cent and 107.74 per cent respectively. Financial year 1999-00 company recorded total revenue or benefit of Rs. 223.1 lakh and total cost recorded Rs. 183.27 lakh. The B/C ratio during 1999-00 financial year is 1.21732. The growth rate of benefit and net profit of company is 117.65 per cent and 70.50 per cent respectively. Financial year 2000-01 company recorded total revenue or benefit of Rs. 393 lakh and total cost recorded Rs. 354.53 lakh. The B/C ratio during 2000-01 financial year is 1.01096. The growth rate of revenue and net profit of company is 76.15 per cent and-3.41 per cent respectively. Financial year 2001-02 company recorded total revenue or benefit of Rs. 453.42 lakh and total cost recorded Rs. 448.50 lakh. The B/C ratio during 2001-02 financial year is 1.01917. The growth rate of benefit of company is 15.37 per cent and net profit of company is decline by and 87.21 per cent. See in table 4.3 and figure 4.3.

The compound growth rate of benefit and cost of Suvi Information System from 1997-98 to 2001-02 financial year is 2.428 per cent and 7.321 per cent respectively.

Table 4.3: Growth Rate of Suvi Information System Pvt. Ltd. (Rs in Lakh)

Year	*Benefit (B)*	*Cost (C)*	*Net Profit*	*ΔB*	*ΔC*	*B/C*
1997-98	54.33	43.09	11.24			1.26084
1998-99	102.5	79.14	23.36	48.17	36.05	1.29517
1999-00	223.1	183.27	39.83	120.6	104.13	1.21732
2000-01	393	354.53	38.47	169.9	171.26	1.10850
2001-02	453.42	448.50	4.92	60.42	93.97	1.01096
C.G.R	51.81%	25.67%				

Note—C.G.R means Compound Growth Rate, ΔB means change in benefit and ΔC means change in cost.

Source: Based on Survey and www.stpi.net

4. Horizon Infotech.

Horizon Infotech is one of the IT company in Madhya Pradesh. During the financial year 1997-98 company recorded total revenues of Rs. 16 lakh comprising the income from exports and domestic income. The cost during this period recorded Rs.17.5 lakh and the B/C ratio is 0.91428. Further in next financial year 1998-99 company recorded total revenue or benefit of Rs. 27.0 lakh and total cost recorded Rs. 23.0 lakh. The B/C ratio during 1998-99 financial year is 1.14893. The growth rate of benefit and net profit of company is 68.75 per cent and 266.66 per cent respectively. Financial year 1999-00 company recorded total revenue or benefit of Rs. 36.0 lakh and total cost recorded Rs. 33.0 lakh. The B/C ratio during 1999-00 financial year is 1.09090. The growth rate of revenue of company is 33.33 per cent and net profit is decline by 14.28 per cent . Financial year 2000-01 company recorded total revenue or benefit of Rs. 45.0 lakh and total cost recorded Rs. 40.0 lakh. The B/C ratio during 2000-01 financial year is 1.12500. The growth rate of revenue and net profit of company is 25.00 per cent and 66.66 per cent respectively. Financial year 2001-02 company recorded total revenue or benefit of Rs. 41.0 lakh and total cost recorded Rs. 32.0 lakh. The B/C ratio during 2001-02 financial year is 1.28125. The growth rate of revenue and net profit of company is 8.88 per cent and 80.00 per cent respectively. See table 4.4 and figure 4.4.

The compound growth rate of benefit and cost of Horizon Infotech from 1997-98 to 2001-02 financial year is 20.708 per cent and 12.829 per cent respectively.

Table 4.4: Growth Rate of Horizon Infotech Pvt. Ltd. (Rs in Lakh)

Year	*Benefit (B)*	*Cost (C)*	*Net Profit*	*ΔB*	*ΔC*	*B/C*
1997-98	16.0	17.5	–1.50			0.91428
1998-99	27.0	23.5	3.50	11.0	6.0	1.14893
1999-00	36.0	33.0	3.00	9.0	10.0	1.09090
2000-01	45.0	40.0	5.00	9.0	7.0	1.12500
2001-02	41.0	32.0	9.00	–4.0	–8.0	1.28125
C.G.R	20.708%	12.829%				

Note—C.G.R means Compound Growth Rate, ΔB means change in benefit and ΔC means change in cost.

Source: Based on Survey and www.stpi.net

5. Viscus Infotech

Viscus Infotech is one of the loss making and small sized IT company in Madhya Pradesh. Company came into existence on 2000. During the foundation financial year 2000-01 company recorded total revenues of Rs. 3.55 lakh comprising the income from exports and domestic income. The cost during this period recorded Rs. 2.59 lakh and the B/C ratio is 1.37065. Further in next financial year 2001-02 company recorded total revenue or benefit of Rs. 0.43 lakh and total cost recorded Rs. 1.42 lakh. The B/C ratio during 2001-02 financial year is 0.30281. The benefit and net profit of company is decline by 72.56 and 197.98 per cent respectively. See table 4.5 and figure 4.5.

Table 4.5: Growth Rate of Viscus Infotech Pvt. Ltd. (Rs in Lakh)

Year	*Benefit (B)*	*Cost (C)*	*Net Profit*	*ΔB*	*ΔC*	*B/C*
2000-01	3.55	2.59	0.96			1.37065
2001-02	0.43	1.42	–0.99	–3.12	–1.17	0.30281
C.G.R.	–72.56%	–45%				

Note—C.G.R means Compound Growth Rate. ΔB means change in benefit and ΔC means change in cost.

Source— Based on Survey and www.stpi.net

6. Impetus Infotech Ltd.

Impetus Infotech Ltd is one of the leading IT company in Madhya Pradesh. Company came into existence on 2000. During the foundation financial year 2000-01 company recorded total revenues of Rs. 50.84 lakh comprising the income from exports and domestic income. The cost during th s period recorded Rs. 51.90 lakh and the B/C ratio is 0.97957. Fu ther in next financial year 2001-02 company recorded total revenue or benefit of Rs. 375.17 lakh and total cost recorded Rs. 339.85 lakh. Th benefit-cost ratio during 2001-02 financial year is 1.10392. The growt rate of benefit and net profit of company is 637.94 per cent and 656.86 p r cent respectively. See table 4.6 and figure 4.6.

Table 4.6: Growth Rate of Impetus Infotech Pvt. Ltd. (Rs in Lakh)

Year	*Benefit (B)*	*Cost (C)*	*Net Profit*	*ΔB*	*ΔC*	*B/C*
2000-01	50.84	51.90	–1.06			0.97957
2001-02	375.17	339.85	35.32	324.33	287.95	1.10392
C.G.R.	637.94%	554.81%				

Note—C.G.R means Compound Growth Rate, ΔB means change in benefit and ΔC means change in cost.

Source—Based on Survey and www.stpi.net

Figure-4.1: Cost, Benefit and Net Profit of Policy Management System

(Rs. in Lakh)

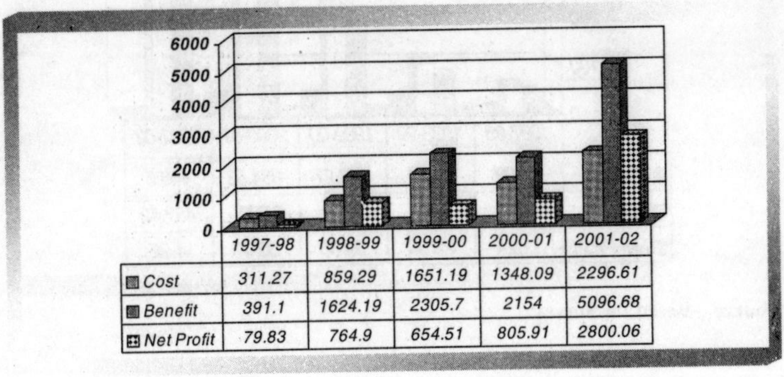

Source—Based on Survey

Figure-4.2: Cost, Benefit and Net Profit of Oswal Data Processor

(Rs. in Lakh)

	1997-98	1998-99	1999-00	2000-01	2001-02
Cost	51.04	42.18	82.83	65.07	73
Benefit	65.99	39.82	85.88	64.12	74.4
Net Profit	14.95	-2.36	3.05	-0.95	-1.4

Source: Based on Survey

Figure-4.3: Cost, Benefit and Net Profit of Suvi Information System

(Rs. in Lakh)

	1997-98	1998-99	1999-00	2000-01	2001-02
Cost	43.09	79.14	183.27	354.53	448.5
Benefit	54.33	102.5	223.1	393	453.42
Net Profit	11.24	23.36	39.83	38.47	4.92

Source—Based on Survey

Figure-4.4: Cost, Benefit and Net Profit of Horizon Infotech

(Rs. in Lakh)

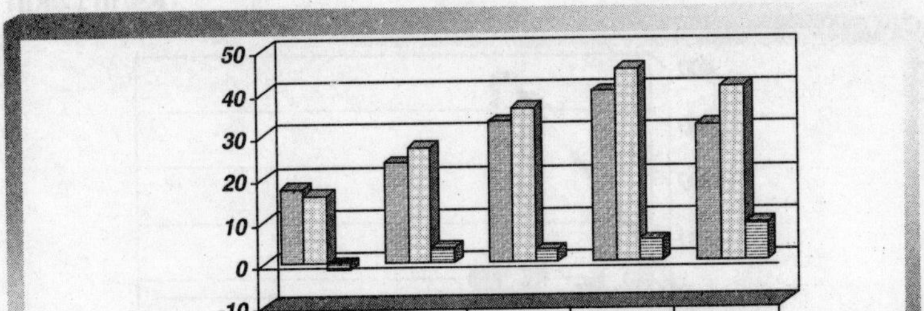

	1997-98	1998-99	1999-00	2000-01	2001-02
Cost	17.5	23.5	33	40	32
Benefit	16	27	36	45	41
Net Profit	-1.5	3.5	3	5	9

Source—Based on Survey

Figure-4.5: Cost, Benefit and Net Profit of Viscus Infotech

(Rs. in Lakh)

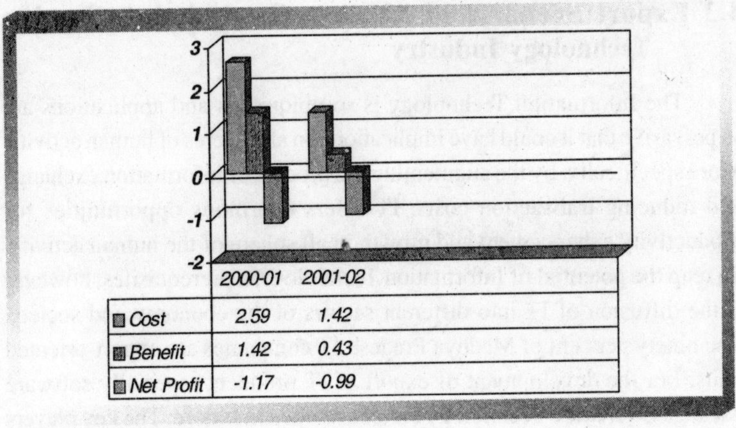

	2000-01	2001-02
Cost	2.59	1.42
Benefit	1.42	0.43
Net Profit	-1.17	-0.99

Source—Based on Survey

Figure-4.6: Cost, Benefit and Net Profit of Viscus Infotech

(Rs. in Lakh)

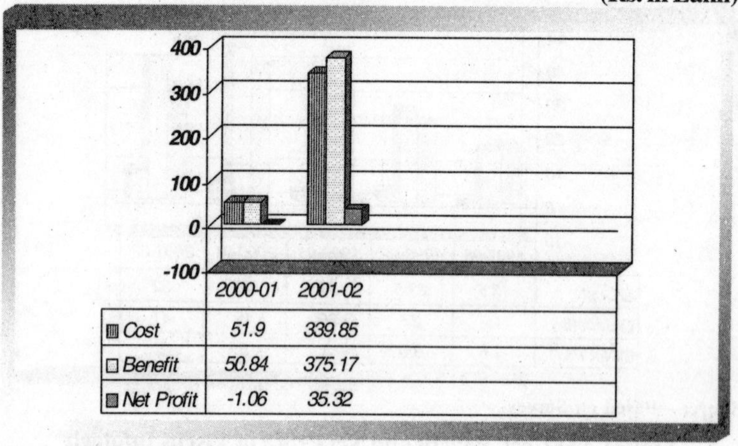

	2000-01	2001-02
Cost	51.9	339.85
Benefit	50.84	375.17
Net Profit	-1.06	35.32

Source—Based on Survey

4.3 Export Scenario of Madhya Pradesh Information Technology Industry

The Information Technology is so ubiquitous and applications are so pervasive that it could have implications on all spheres of human activity. More specifically, by the augmenting the process of information exchange and reducing transaction costs, IT offers enormous opportunities for productivity enhancement and growth in all sphere of the human activity. To reap the potential of Information Technology, a prerequisites, however is the diffusion of IT into different sectors of the economy and society. The ninety per cent of Madhya Pradesh IT companies are export-oriented units. For the development of export of IT products especially software packages, Software Technology Park developed in Indore. The key players of export of IT enable services and software developer are Policy Management System, Suvi Information System Pvt. Ltd., Impetus Infotech, etc. Financial year 1999-2000 total export of IT companies from Madhya Pradesh was Rupees 2722.37 lakh. Total export during 1999-2000 of Bhilwara Scribe Pvt. Ltd., Bhopal was Rs. 0.85 lakh. Total export during 1999-2000 of Impetus Computing Ltd. was Rs. 0.85 lakh. Total export during 1999-2000 of Impetus Computing (Unit II), Millenium cybertech Ltd., Policy

Management System, Pumik Infotech, Suvi Information System and Thyron Information Pvt. Ltd. were Rs. 339.2 lakh, Rs 10.05 lakh, Rs 18.50 lakh, Rs 2000.10 lakh, Rs 0.63 lakh, Rs. 112.43 lakh, Rs 240.61 lakh respectively[37]. During financial year 2000-2001 total export of Policy Management System, Impetus Computing, Suvi Information System, Oswal Data Processor and Thyron Information Pvt. Ltd. were Rs. 2800 lakh, Rs. 434 lakh, Rs. 400 lakh, Rs. 40 lakh and Rs. 186 lakh respectively[38]. The total export of Madhya Pradesh IT industry is shown in figure 4.7 during different financial years.

The US accounts for over half of all export revenues , compared with for Europe, Australia and for Japan. The share of export revenue from abroad is given in figure 4.8.

Figure 4.7: Export of Madhya Pradesh IT industry

(Rupees in Lakh)

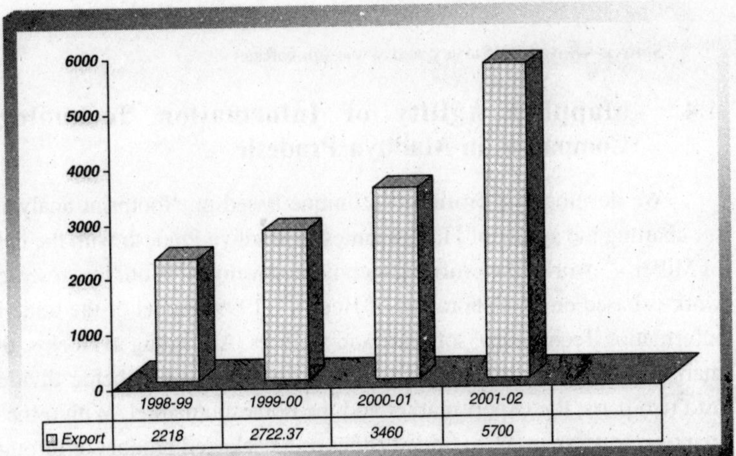

Source—Software Technology Park, Electronic complex, Indore and www.stpi.soft.net

Figure 4.8: Percentage of IT export in different countries

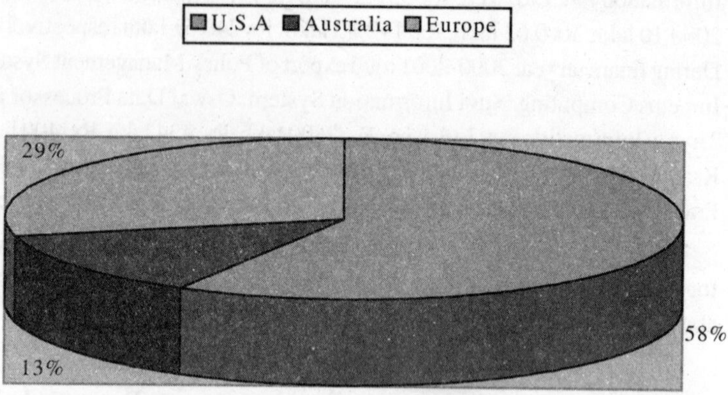

Source—Based on Survey and www.stpi.soft.net

4.4 Mapping Agility of Information Technology Companies in Madhya Pradesh

We developed a profiling technique based on 'footprint analysis' for charting the agility of IT companies in Madhya Pradesh with the help of Miller's[39] work. The profiling technique developed in our this research work is based on an elaboration of Heek's[40](1999) model of the trade in Information Technology, software and services. According to Heek's, the market for software and services can be characterised as being divided into two parts, the export market and the domestic market. Within these markets, software may be traded either as a packaged product or through purchase of services related activities of IT professionals (Figure-4.9).

Heeks argues that, when analyzed against this model of international IT trade, the participation of IT (software) producers in developing countries in general, particularly in India, is skewed in three main ways:

- **Output profile**—Most 'software stories' involves the export of services. Software packages represent only a small proportion of exports. Most companies can be located at portion A in the model.
- **Location Profile**—the majority of work takes place on-site at the client's premises. Teletrade and IT trade is limited.

- **Skill Profile**—With the exception of a small number of contracts performed by leading Indian and Madhya Pradesh IT companies, most work involves relatively low-skill, low value activities.

Firms in developing countries are typically prevented from entry to position B, export of software packages, or, C, sale of software packages in the domestic market, by the high cost and the risk of product development, high rates of piracy and preference for foreign software, even within domestic market. For most, a presence in position D, the commercial development of software packages for the local market, is not feasible because of the small size of the domestic market.

Position E, involving the provision of specialised services to niche markets is also a possibility for firms in developing countries. Niche markets can be sectored, such as the provision of software for banking, insurance or hotel management; linguistic, involving the production of software in Spanish or Chinese for instance; or application driven, for example Internet browser applications.

Heeks analysis implies that, in the absence of market dynamism, firms in position A in developing countries will be progressively excluded from participation in international software trade by price based competition for low-value work the 'winner' of this competition will be those firms that can cut their production costs to the bone. In sun, for firms in many developing countries, participation in international software trade will become unsustainable.

In order to identify whether active and market leading IT companies in Madhya Pradesh are demonstrating the agility in the IT market that is required in order to sustain and grow market share, the next section profiles a sample of IT companies against a two stage elaboration of Heeks (1999) modal. These elaboration are required in order to take into account two main variations that can be observed particularly among IT companies in Madhya Pradesh.

The first stage elaboration is necessary in order to take into account IT professionals activities that are not traded on the market (Figure-4.10). Untraded activities represent the majority of software development work worldwide and are estimated to be worth at least as much as the traded market.

Untraded software services (position F) includes the in-house development of software that is used to support internal business processes. For example, Policy Management System and Impetus Infotek use software that they have developed internally to support services. It also includes software that is supplied to parent company. This software may then be sold on by the parent company, acting as a marketing channel for locally produced goods.

Untraded software products (position G) also involve the in-house development of software that is used as an input to product innovation. Such software might be embedded in a complex system of different product technologies that is to be sold in a niche market; example include software produced in Impetus Infotech. This is represented by the extension of Heeks original position E to include untraded activities.

Figure 4.9 Strategic Positioning for Developing Country Software

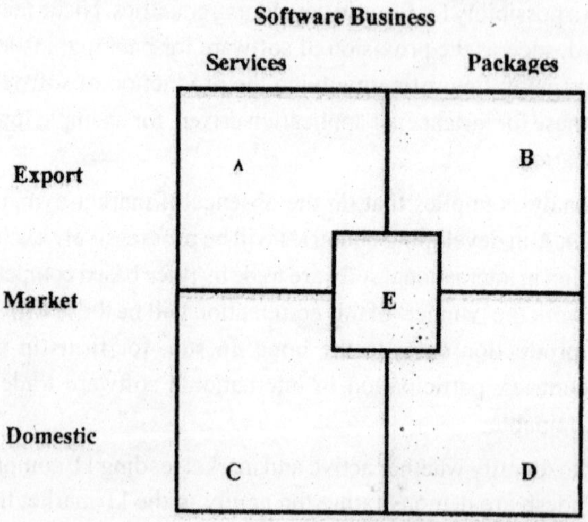

Source: Heeks 1999

The second stage extension (Figure-4.11) is required in order to take account of the historical linkages between software and hardware firms in the IT sector. Historical relationships are depicted, where the appropriate, by the addition of an extra dimension to the Elaboration (1) model within which a full range of professional software products and services (A^1-G^2) can be supplied.

Figure 4.10 Elaboration (7) of Heeks Model

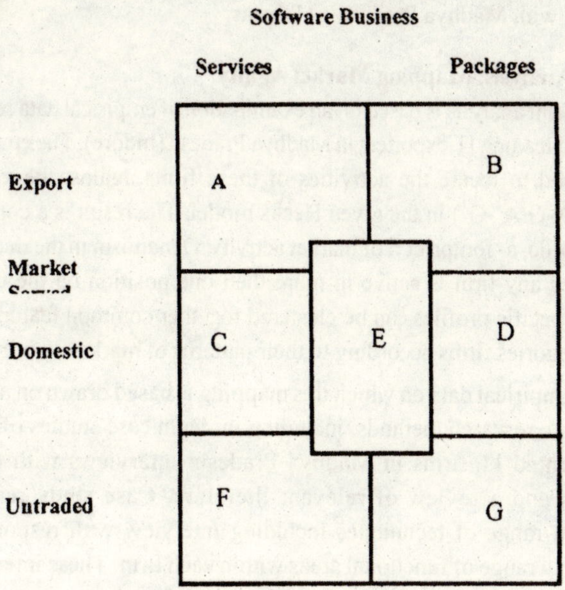

This second stage elaboration is considered necessary for two main reasons. First because, due to the interdependence between hardware and software, the distinction between the two can be considered arbitrary. Second because many IT companies of Madhya Pradesh have developed and grown through drawing on their synergistic relationships with hardware companies, for instance by using trade with hardware firms to sustain revenue during market repositioning. These firms include Policy Management System, a firm that encouraged from the software business, Suvi Infotech and Impetus Infotech where historical linkages with the US companies.

The relationships with hardware firms have been critically important to the market agility of a number of software providers. This is not just a characteristic of trade in the past; long-standing relationships were hardware companies can also be used strategically as a competitive weapon for the future. From our analysis we come to know that Policy Management System and other leading IT companies of Madhya Pradesh might gain the size that it requires in order to compete with leading US service providers by merging with Madhya Pradesh's IT firms.

Footprint Analysis: Mapping Market Agility

Footprint analysis is based on an examination of empirical data relating to active and leading IT exporters in Madhya Pradesh (Indore). The empirical data are used to locate the activities of these firms against the various positions ($A-G/A^1-G^1$) in the given Heeks model. The result is a company specific profile, a 'footprint ', of market activity. Dynamism in the market is shown when any firm is active in more then one position on the model. Company specific profiles can be clustered together common features and used to categories firms according to their patterns of market activity.

The empirical data on which this mapping is based drawn on a range of qualitative research methods, including in-depth case studies of seven export-oriented IT firms in Madhya Pradesh, interviews with expert informants and a review of relevant literature. Case study research employed a range of techniques including interview with respondents drawn from a range of functional areas within each firm. These interviews focused on key features of export trading relationships in order to identify instances of market agility and core characteristics of economic competence that are underlying them in our study.

Case-study firms were selected for research from among those that are active exporters of software and services in Madhya Pradesh. There was no intention that these firms should be some how representative of the total population of IT companies in Madhya Pradesh. Instead, the aim was to select to sample of firms that captured a range of characteristics that, taken together, could be said to be descriptive of advanced professional practice in the region. As result the study sample includes firms with different sizes and export revenues; different ownership structure such as Policy Management System; new entrants and established players in the market and firms that innovate products and those that concentrate on services such as Suvi Infortech Ltd.

Market Agility among Three Categories of Information Technology Firms

The market dynamism of case-study firms in the IT sector, cluster and categories firms according to shared patterns of market agility. Footprint analysis enable the identification of three main categories of IT companies amongst the sample of IT companies in Madhya Pradesh ; Diversifiers, Innovators and Dependents.

Diversifiers : The profiles the diversifiers companies display highly differentiated activity spanning the provision of marketed and untraded, niche as well as specialist, domestic and export, services and products. These firms have sustained growth through exploiting the competitive benefits of longevity, size and agility.

Long standing relationships with client firms (such as Impetus India relationship with Impetus Globle) have provide a constant source of revenue and information about international best practices and market dynamics. In addition and over time, extensive differentiation has allowed synergies to be built and exploited between different areas of core expertise (technological and business). These firms have enabled such firms to offer flexible and agile responses to the fluctuating demands of international clients.

Diversifiers include market leading firms such as Suvi Information System Ltd. Ruchi Globle Ltd. provide traded services for export, including export to hardware firms and the domestic market. The also supply untraded services, for instance to other firms in the Ruchi Group, including those that supply to the software business like Ruchi Infotech. Ruchi Globle has made some attempts to develop and export software packages but these have not met with much success. Sales of software to the domestic market, however, have proved more lucrative. Recent restructuring has enable to company to specialise and provide niche line-of-business and line-of-technology market offerings.

Suvi Information System Pvt. Ltd. has built on the initial untraded supply of software services to support the export and domestic market activities of its hardware division. It has used this as a platform for developing export trade in software services to select group of foreign clients.

Innovators : Profiles of Innovators, such as Policy Management System and Thyron Infotech, show that these have been able sustain and grow market share through exporting synergies from trading experiences in niche international markets for domain-specific applications and services.

There strategies for capability development have been central to innovative success. Policy Management System (Figure 4.12) originally focused on the provision of software exports services. The company has employed combined strategies of 'de-risking'[3] and 'learnability'[4] in order to develop deep strengths in niche, foreign, line-of-business and applications specific product and service market.

Thyron Infotech, a small company that has emerged from an historical relationship with the American Company, has integrated knowledge and experience from the provision of customer support and services to American firm users and other software development service-related activities. It has created a niche applications package to support the provision of on-line customer services.

Dependents : Of the three categories of IT companies profile here, Dependent firms that supply to foreign owned multinationals are potentially the most vulnerable. These are entirely dependent on the untraded exchange of software services, in target application domains, to foreign 'parent' firms. There are two main types to dependent firm; direct dependent specialists and indirect dependent generalists.

(1) Direct Dependent Specialists—Direct dependent specialist firms include, for example, Impetus Company. Impetus supplies advanced software product development and support services to Novell Inc in the US as input to product innovation to Novell Inc. Impetus India is a 100 per cent subsidiary of Impetus (USA) and provides the parent company with software inputs that are embedded in complex payment processing systems, involving hardware as well as software.

Both firm have migrated from their original position (F) involving the non-marketed supply of general software services to their foreign parent companies, to position E where they supply specialist and high value technical services as input to the development of niche products by the parent company.

They have made extensive use of technology to support professional performance on increasingly advanced, high value, software projects. In Impetus India, a large proportion of this work is carried out offshore; only Novell Software does not perform any software development work on its parent company site.

The professional work of both firms is supported by intense interaction with their parents. In effect, they have used their relationships with their foreign parent firms to move up the value chain to the extent where their activities might more appropriately be classified as specialist research and development. Their continued 'market' presence depends critically on these relationships and the high quality of the skills and capabilities that have been incubated and developed through them.

(2) Indirect Dependent Generalists— Indirect dependent generalists are more common- a dependent variant of those firms that form the basis of Heek's analysis. Their activities typically involve supplying general-purpose, low value-added, software services in target, often transient, market domains (such as Y2K and Euro conversion) to a foreign 'parent' company that acts as a marketing channel for their services. Their relationships with the market and therefore indirect, mediated by the 'parent' firm. Footprint analysis shows that the professional activities of indirect dependent generalists are predominantly located at position F, there is little indication of market dynamism and they appear vulnerable to cost based competition.

These firms include, to cite a more successful example, Information Management Resources (IMRs) India. In 1998, IMR India was ranked 32nd among the top 500 Indian firms. The company exports software services to its parent company, IMR global. IMR global in turn contracts these services out to its client base in the US internationally.

These innovative capabilities of such firms are directed towards cutting costs, for instance through the use of telematics technology to undertake work offshore and identifying opportunities for growth within their existing profile position. For example[41]:

Year 2000 compliance services have been used by IMR[India] as door openers to broaden our customer base. One of the first year 2000 projects was for a retail store chain. On completion of this project, IMR was entrusted with the maintenance of remediated applications. Subsequently when these applications were to be reengineered for an Open Systems environment, IMR was again awarded the project. The relationship has expanded over the years and we have done more complex and demanding work progressively.

With the contraction of the market for Y2K work, some of these firms have been attempting to hold on to and extend existing maintenance contracts with US companies and to leverage these into niche market line-of-business development contracts. Some have moved away from the market to specialise in software systems distribution and customer support.

This section has presented a competitive analysis of leading and active IT exporters in Madhya Pradesh. This has been achieved through the development and application of a technique to profile market agility, based on 'footprint analysis', to empirical, data relating to Madhya Pradesh (Indore)-based software providers. The result, a classification of market activity in the sector and an analysis of the sources of economic competence underlying it, has been employed to drive the identification of policy initiatives that might be required in order to foster the sustained growth of IT companies in the region.

From above study we recommends that the government should work together with industry in order to develop a coordinated approach to policy-making across a broad waterfront of political domains. These should include strategies for growth, skills and training, domestic and export trade, knowledge sharing and learning between firms and projects, remote and proximal work practices, social equity and protection from exploitation. In, addition, policy should encompass both proactive and reactive measures and reactive measures and these should be deployed appropriately and in context. For instance, leading edge IT companies and those that operate in uncertain and dynamic markets may benefit from reactive policy measures that offer targeted support in critical areas. Alternatively proactive policies might be best applied in domains that have general impact, such as infrastructure development, or where there may be mixed benefits from market success, for instance when competition is based on price and the advantages of competitiveness can be offset against the costs of labour exploitation.

The analysis makes clear that IT companies with different agility profiles have different competitive strategies and have developed distinct forms of economic competence. Policies to support the sustained growth of firms in the sector should be developed in recognition that they might only be appropriate to IT companies with profiles. Moreover, although similar policies might be recommended for IT companies with different profiles, for instance recommendations for specialist high-technology foreign-owned firms and Indian owned highly differentiated IT companies both include that policy should be responsive to the need of the industry, the reasoning underlying this recommendation is different in each case and the details of policy implementation are likely to vary.

The result of this study offer the potential for generalisation beyond the sample IT companies to companies with similar analytical profiles in the règion. However, attempts to generalise from the result of the research in Indore in Madhya Pradesh and Banglore to other region in Madhya Pradesh and India.

Figure 4.11– Elaboration (2) of Heeks' Model

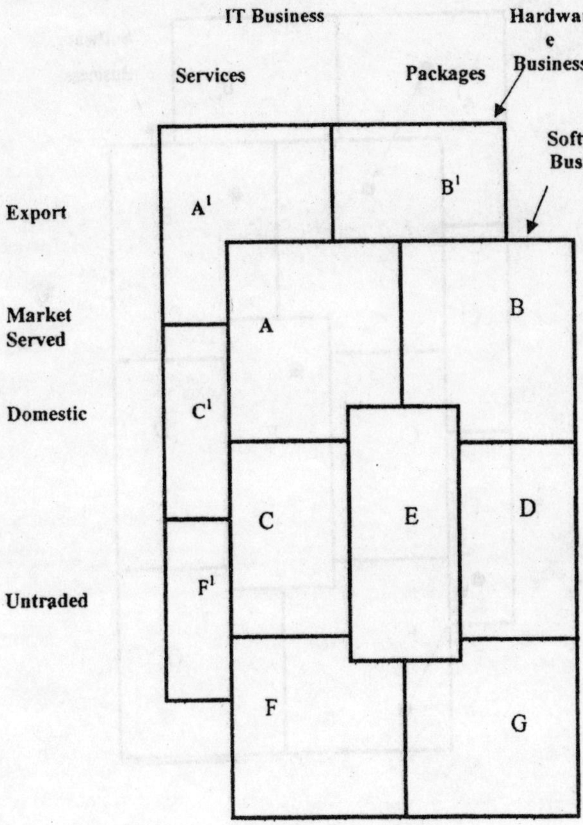

Figure 4.12: Example of a Diversifier: Footprint Analysis of Impetus India

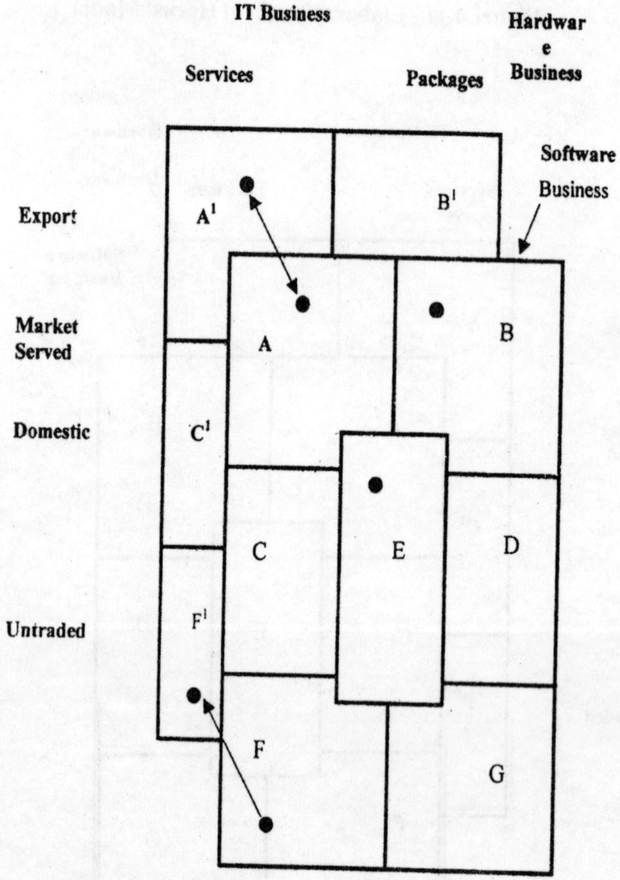

Figure 4.13– Policy Management System — Profile of an Innovator

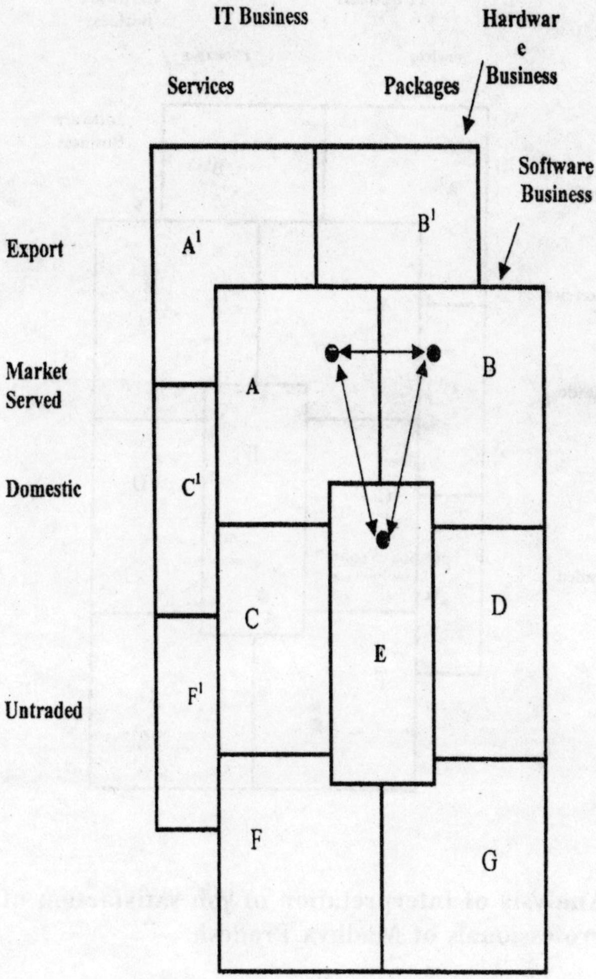

Figure 4.14— Direct Dependent Specialists

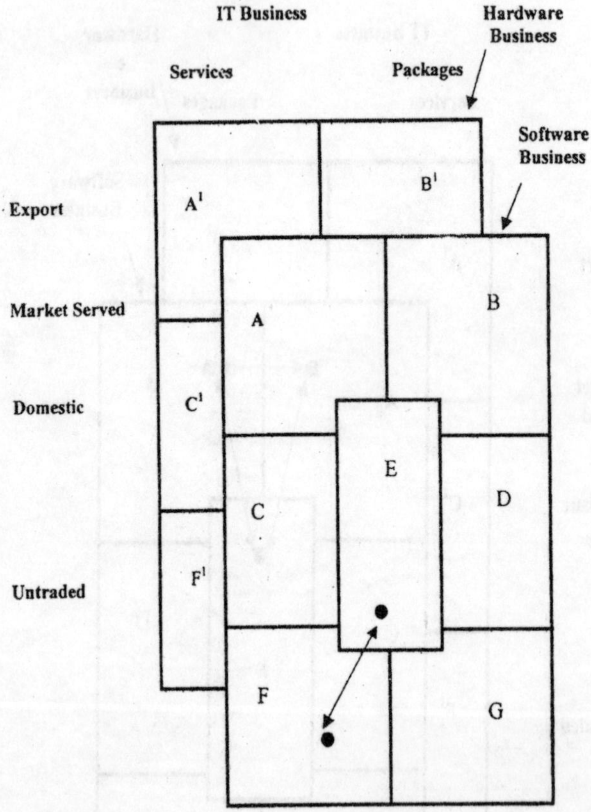

4.5 Analysis of interpretation of job satisfaction of IT professionals of Madhya Pradesh.

In order to evaluate the overall satisfaction level among the IT professionals of M.P., there is satisfaction level to each variable and also the satisfaction among the group of employee based on salary, sex, religion and experience, the data has been analysed and their effects have been shown in different tables.

Job satisfaction level among professional of IT companies based on job satisfaction scale to measure their job satisfaction. This scale consist of 14 statements of Lickert[42] type measuring job satisfaction in various aspects of IT professionals such as freedom in planning and execution of work, employer and employee relationship and working conditions. The range of score on this tool extends from 14 to 70 with mean of 42. Responses are made on a 5-point scale and the response categories are assigned weights from 1 to 5, Job satisfaction score of IT professionals was calculated by summation of his score on each statement of the scale. The data thus generated was then put to various statistical analyses.

IT professionals were divided into three groups i.e. satisfied, neutral and dissatisfied on the basis of their job satisfaction scores. Range of scores defining neutral is determined by adding +2 and –2 to 42, the mean job satisfaction scores on the job satisfaction scale. IT professionals with scores above and below this range were considered as satisfied and dissatisfied respectively.

A perusal of Table 4.8 shows that per centages of satisfied, neutral and dissatisfied IT professionals of the total sample were 54.62, 14.28 and 31.09 respectively. Further the result shows that the per centage in respect of male and female IT professionals were 51.35, 10.81 and 37.83 and 60, 20 and 20 respectively. Graphically it is shown in Figure 4.15. Thus it is evident from this analysis that majority of IT professionals are satisfied with their jobs. The results of the analysis also make it clear that more females IT professionals feel satisfied than their counterparts.

In general there exist a positive trend of job satisfaction among IT professionals irrespective of their qualifications, community, religion and sex but they differ in the degree of satisfaction. 54.62 per cent have a degree of job satisfaction scale more than the mean value 42 on the job satisfaction scale as compared to 31.09 per cent of professionals with scores lower than the mean, while the rest 14.28 per cent may be termed as neutral in terms of their level of satisfaction. The result obtain by our study is also supported by Morse (1953).

When the data was analysed to make a comparative study of the degree of job satisfaction of male and female IT professionals, the mean job satisfaction score and SD (Standard Deviation) were 58.24, 6.74 and 56.15, 6.33 respectively (Table 4.9). The calculated value of 't' for these two groups is 1.24, which is not significant at 5 per cent level with 63 degree of freedom (df). Since this difference is in the favour of female IT professionals, it can be said that female IT professionals have greater degree of job satisfaction than male professionals.

Analysis on the basis of sex shows that only 51.35 per cent male IT professionals feel satisfied as compared to 60.00 per cent female teachers. Consequently the per centage of female IT professionals with mean scores less than 42 on job satisfaction scale is less than the male professionals. Findings indicate that there is a significant difference between means job satisfaction scores of male and female IT professionals.

In the Indian society, the job satisfaction is believed to be different for male and female, while both may have the same social position and getting the same salary. A man's job is more closely tired up with his personal and family needs than the female's job. It is his sacred duty and social binding to earn and fulfil the requirement of family. Therefore, a job plays a more significant role in the lives of male than the female. The male is very often very sole source of income of the family. Females on the other hand, generally considered a job as of secondary importance, home and family being her prime interest. Females most often make it only to supplement the income of the family to spend time out of the home. On the other hand males are a more ambitious on their profession, so they have not high on satisfaction in females than their counterparts. Hence, it may be concluded that sex of the IT professional influences his/her job satisfaction. This gives credence to our findings.

For studying relationship of experience and job satisfaction, four groups of IT professionals having experience of 0-3, more than 3-6, more than 6-9 and more than 9 years were formed. The mean scores, SD, SE (Standard Error) and 't' values are given in Table 4.10. The mean scores on the job satisfaction of the above four defined groups are 47.5, 54.82, 52.74 and 54.20 respectively. From the trend it is quite clear that as experience increases job satisfaction decreases. When 't' test was applied to compare each mean with every job satisfaction score at 5 per cent level of significance, significant differences were obtained between the means of 1 and 2, 1 and 3, 1 and 4, groups. However there is no significant difference between the means of 2 and 3, 2 and 4, 3 and 4 groups.

In our study it is found that a perceptible and a significant difference exists in job satisfaction between groups of different level of experiences.

Dissatisfaction grows alongwith experience. The tendency becomes quite clear from the study of mean scores on the job satisfaction scale. In the first three years of service IT professionals are more satisfied towards their job and it continues to decline thereafter in the later parts of the service.

For studying the relationship between professional qualifications of IT professionals and their job satisfactions, the total sample of IT professionals was divided into two groups, i.e., trained and untrained. Trained IT professionals are highly qualified and have the degree of M.C.A, Ph.D., etc while untrained professionals have marginal qualification in the field of computer and software development, like diploma, certificate courses, etc. The details are given in Table 4.11. The means and SD of these groups were found to be 51.36, 6.328 and 55.26, 5.932 respectively. The obtained value of 't' is 4.8, which is significant at 5 per cent level. Since this difference is in favour of untrained IT professionals it can be said that untrained IT professionals have significantly more job satisfaction than the trained IT professionals.

For studying relationship of salary and job satisfaction, four groups of IT professionals drawing salaries of Rs. 3000-5000, more than Rs. 5000-10000, more than Rs. 10000-15000 and more than Rs.15000 per month. The mean scores, SD, SE (Standard Error) and 't' values are given in Table 4.12. The mean scores on the job satisfaction of the above four defined groups are 54.82, 54.20, 47.5 and 52.74 respectively. From the trend it is quite clear that as salaries increases job satisfaction also increase but when employee get highest salary then job satisfaction decreases because due to less future prospects in present company and their demand in other companies. When 't' test was applied to compare each mean with every job satisfaction score, significant differences were obtained between the means of 1 and 3, 2 and 3, 3 and 4 groups. However there is no significant difference between the means of 1 and 2, 1 and 4, 2 and 4. It is found that IT professionals drawing less salary are more satisfied than those drawing high salaries because during initial period fresher want experience and due to social security and cost some of the IT professional do not want to go other cities.

It is clear form Table 4.13 that the mean and SD of Hindu, Muslim and Christian IT professionals were 53.04 and 5.834, 52.25 and 5.76, 51.23 and 3.131 respectively. The obtained 't' value of Hindu and Muslim was 1.55, which is not significant at 5 per cent level. That means Hindu has higher level of job satisfaction than Muslim. Further the obtained 't' value of Hindu and Christian was 2.98, which is significant at 5 per cent level. Lastly the 't' value of Muslim and Christian was 1.22, which is not significant at 5 per cent level.

Lastly from above discussion the overall satisfaction, which is an aggregate towards in all variables, is high. This is based on aggregate scores 3729.17, which can be measures on the parameter as earlier in methodology. The overall score class 3729.17 falls to score class 3333-4998, which indicates marginal satisfaction.

Figure 4.15: Per centage of Satisfied, Neutral and Dissatisfied IT professionals (Total and Sex-wise)

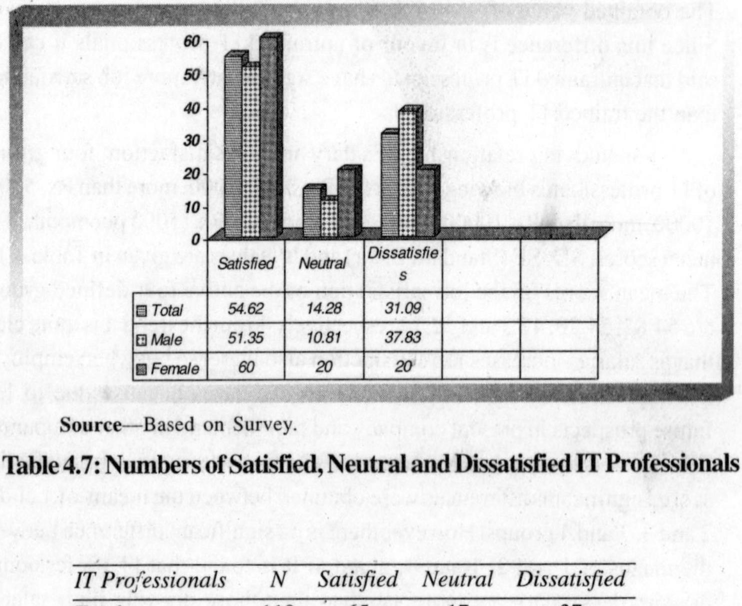

Source—Based on Survey.

Table 4.7: Numbers of Satisfied, Neutral and Dissatisfied IT Professionals

IT Professionals	*N*	*Satisfied*	*Neutral*	*Dissatisfied*
Total	119	65	17	37
Male	74	38	10	26
Female	45	27	7	11

Source—Based on Survey.

Table 4.8: Per centage of Satisfied, Neutral and Dissatisfied IT Professionals

IT Professionals	*N*	*Satisfied*	*Neutral*	*Dissatisfied*
Total	119	54.621	14.285	31.092
Male	74	51.351	10.810	37.837
Female	45	60.000	20.000	20.000

Source—Based on Survey.

Table 4.9: Comparison of Mean Job Satisfaction Score of Male and Female IT Professionals

Sex of the Group	*N*	*Mean Scores*	*SD*	*SE*	*t-test*	*df*
Male	38	58.24	6.73	1.09	1.24 is not sig.	
Female	27	56.15	6.33	1.22	At level of 0.05	63

Source— Based on Survey.

Table 4.10: 't' Value Obtained from Comparison of Mean Job Satisfaction Scores of Four Groups of IT Professionals Formed on the Basis of Experience

Group	*Experience in years*	*N*	*Mean Scores*	*SD*	*SE*	*Experience in years* 0-3	3-6	6-9
1	0-3	12	47.5	4.113	1.19			
2	3-6	23	54.82	6.53	1.36	3.447		
3	6-9	19	52.74	5.93	1.36	2.596	0.728	
4	9-Above	11	54.2	6.67	2.01	4.346	0.2515	0.221

Source—Based on Survey.

Table 4.11: 't' Value Obtained from Comparison of Mean Job Satisfaction Scores of Trained and Untrained IT Professionals

Qualifications	*N*	*Mean Scores*	*SD*	*SE*	*t-test*	*df*
Trained	39	51.36	6.328	1.01	Sig. 4.8 at	
Untrained	26	55.26	5.932	1.16	0.05 level	63

Source—Based on Survey.

Table 4.12: 't' Value Between Mean Scores of IT Professionals Drawing different Salaries Group per Month

Group	Salaries (in Rs.)	N	Mean Scores	SD	SE	t-test Salaries (in Rs. Thousand) 3-5	5-10	10-15
1	3000-5000	24	54.82	6.53	1.36			
2	5000-10000	11	54.2	6.67	2.01	0.251		
3	10000-15000	12	47.5	4.113	1.19	3.447	4.346	
4	15000-Above	19	52.74	5.93	1.36	0.727	0.221	2.593

Source—Based on Survey.

Table 4.13: 't' Value Obtained from Comparison of Mean Job Satisfaction Scores of Hindu, Muslim and Christian IT Professionals

Group	Community	N	Mean Scores	SD	SE	t-test Hindu	Muslim
1	Hindu	47	53.04	5.834	0.85		
2	Muslim	12	52.25	5.76	1.66	1.5117	
3	Christian	6	51.83	3.131	1.27	2.98	1.122

Source—Based on Survey.

4.6 Cobb-Douglas Production Function Model for IT Industry in Madhya Pradesh

In a general conversation production is considered to be the formation of a new commodity or a service. But we know that a commodity or goods can neither be created nor can it be destroyed. Creation and destruction are the function of the nature and not that of Man. Therefore a man through his effort tries to bring about such change are large number of goods so that they may become more useful than before.

In the traditional theory of production, the resources required to produce a commodity are called the factor of production. The commodity that is production is done is termed as the inputs. The relationship between the inputs and outputs of a firm is called the production function. Production function shows how can a producer, with the help of a given technical knowledge and managerial ability, obtain maximum amount of output through various combinations of inputs. In the words of Prof. Scitovsky- "The production of a given firm is the function of factors of production. It will be called production function, if expressed in mathematical form".[43] in the words of Prof. Samulson, "the production function is the technical relationship telling the amount of output capable of being produced by each and every set of specific inputs. It is defined for a given state of technical knowledge".[44]

Our study makes it clear that production function is very helpful in understanding the theories of production. Production function tells us that what result will be obtained if the variable inputs are increased, holding one factor as constant. What amount for physical output is obtained by ratio determination of labour and capital? Or to what extent does the output change through a variation in all the inputs? Production function exhibits the industrial relations between physical inputs and outputs. Therefore, it is said to be related with the field of services based sector. But Prof. Stigler[45] does not agree with view. It is the function of an industrialist to choose an appropriate factor combination for the desired quantity of output. For this enterprise has to have a knowledge about the price's of the technique being in the production of definite output through inputs in a particular period of time. All these technical possibilities are obtained through behavioural sciences, which cannot be solved only by the skilled technical professionals.

Cobb-Douglas production function model has been presented by the American economist Paul H. Douglas and C.W. Cobb. They based their conclusions on the empirical study of the American manufacturing industries between 1889 to 1922.

Cobb-Douglas had derived their formula by working on the manufacturing industries of U.S.A., Canada, Australia, Newzealand and South Africa through the medium of Time-series and Cross-section series.[46]

Cobb-Douglas production function model is appropriate in the context of manufacturing firms. Using various statistical procedures, Cobb and Douglas presented their model as:

$$Q = AL^{\beta 1} K^{\beta 2}$$

Where, Q = Production,

L = Labour,

K = Capital,

A = Constant,

$ß_1$ = Elasticity of labour

$ß_2$ = Elasticity of Capital

Cobb-Douglas Model is a linear, homogeneous production function of the first degree. Therefore, it takes into consideration only two inputs, viz. Labour and Capital for the entire output of manufacturing industry.

Assumption of Cobb-Douglas Model

The present model is based on certain practical assumption. The desired result cannot be obtained if these assumptions are neglected. These are as follows:

- The technique of production is constant and is the superior most.
- The units of labour and capital are homogeneous and are the substitutes of each other. But the quality of neither of the two can be zero.
- The analysis is possible only under a definite or constant period of time.
- Labour, capital and output is measured in terms of monetary values. Keeping inflation rate constant.
- There are only two inputs viz. Labour and capital.

Test of Cobb-Douglas Production functions Model with reference to IT companies of Madhya Pradesh.

Cobb-Douglas production function has been tested with reference to IT companies of Madhya-Pradesh. These are service-based companies located in Indore and Bhopal. An analysis of the model has been presented here. The worksheet of the model has been desired on the basis of the Table 4.14.

Analysis of Worksheet (Table 4.14)

The worksheet has been constructed mainly on the basis of general linear regression equation. There are seven columns in Table 4.14. First column shows the six IT companies of Madhya Pradesh. Second column shows the output/production. This has been presented in monetary form that means total mean revenues during last financial year from 1997-98 to 2001-2002. Third column shows the labour, data of labour is presented here in monetary terms that means their average salaries, perks etc during last financial year from 1997-98 to 2001-2002. Fourth column shows Capital invest during last financial year from 1997-98 to 2001-2002. Fifth, sixth and seventh column shows the natural logarithmic value of output, labour and capital respectively.

Table 4.14: Worksheet for Model: $Q = A L^{\beta 1} K^{\beta 2}$

IT Companies	*Output* *Q*	*Labour* *L*	*Capital* *K*	*Y* $L_n Q$	X_1 $L_n X_1$	X_2 $L_n X_2$
Policy Management System	2459.99	583.86	889.89	7.81	6.37	6.79
Horizon Infotech	33.00	14.07	15.13	3.49	2.64	2.72
Viscus Infotech	1.99	1.315	0.69	0.69	0.27	–0.37
Impetus Infotech	213.00	105.45	90.43	5.36	4.66	4.50
Oswal Data Processor	65.9	33.26	26.57	4.19	3.50	3.39
Suvi Information System	233.386	108.16	93.56	5.45	4.68	4.54

Source—Based on Survey.

From the help of above worksheet the our Cobb-Douglas Production Function Model of six IT companies will be in following form:

$Q = A L^{0.17} K^{0.84}$ where, $A = e^{0.83}$

$\log_e Q = 0.83 + 0.17 \log_e L + 0.84 \log_e K$ $\quad R^2 = 0.99$

S.E. = (0.37) $\quad$ (0.32)

t* = (0.459) $\quad$ (2.625)

From the above estimated model, it is observed that output elasticities of labour and capital are 0.17 and 0.84 respectively. In other words, holding the capital input constant, one per cent increase in labour input leads on the average to about 0.17 per cent increase in output. Similarly holding labour input constant, one per cent increase in the capital input leads on the average to about 0.84 per cent increase in the output.

From the statistical viewpoint, the estimated model fits the data quite well. The R^2-value of 0.99 means that about 99 per cent of the variation in the output is explained by the labour and capital. However on the basis of estimated standard errors labour (β_1) input coefficient does not appear to be statistically significant. The above analysis shows that the capital inputs are more effective compare to labour.

Notes and References

1. our_profile.htm at www.suviinfo.com visited on March 12, 2002.
2. our_profile.htm/company_overview at www.suviinfo.com visited web site on March 12, 2002.
3. http://www.diaspark.com/ visited web site on March 12, 2002
4. our_profile.htm/skill_set at www.suviinfo.com visited web site on March 12, 2002
5. our_profile.htm/fact_sheet at www.suviinfo.com visited on web site March 12, 2002
6. our_profile.htm/Verticales at www.suviinfo.com visited on web site March 12, 2002
7. our_profile.htm/Product_and_services at www.suviinfo.com visited on web site March 12, 2002
8. clientele.htm at www.suviinfo.com visited on web site March 12, 2002.
9. clientele.htm at www.suviinfo.com visited on web site March 12, 2002.
10. offshore.htm at www.suviinfo.com visited on web site March 12, 2002.
11. company_overview.htm at www.impetus.com visited on web site January 17, 2002
12. impetus_people.htm at www.impetus.com visited on web site January 17, 2002
13. success_stories.htm at www.impetus.com visited on web site January 12, 2002
14. success_stories.htm # Resource Manager Framework at www.impetus.com visited on web site January 17, 2002
15. success_stories.htm # tools and framework www.impetus.com visited on web site January 12, 2002
16. about_us.html at www.issinfotech.com. visited on web site January 12. 2002
17. service.html at www.issinfotech.com. visited on web site January 12, 2002

18. technology.html at www.issinfotech.com. visited on web site January 12, 2002
19. alliances.html at www.issinfotech.com. visited on web site January 12, 2002
20. aboutus.htm at www.webdunia.com. visited on February 15, 2002.
21. clients.htm at www.webdunia.com. visited on February 15, 2002.
22. products.htm at www.webdunia.com. visited on February 15, 2002.
23. Main.htm at www.ruchigourp.com. visited on February 21, 2002.
24. Service.htm at www.ruchigroup.com. visited on February 21, 2002.
25. Service.htm # software development at www.ruchigroup.com visited on February 21, 2002.
26. Service.htm # software training at www.ruchigroup.com visited on February 21, 2002.
27. Service.htm # networking solution at www.ruchigroup.com visited on February 21, 2002.
28. Service.htm # internet and internet services at www.ruchigroup.com visited on February 21, 2002.
29. Service.htm # RandD at www.ruchigroup.com visited on February 21, 2002.
30. Service.htm # facilities management at www.ruchigroup.com visited on February 21, 2002.
31. Service.htm # client/server solution at www.ruchigroup.com visited on February 21, 2002.
32. Service.htm # e-commerce at www.ruchigroup.com visited on February 21, 2002.
33. Service.htm # multimedia at www.ruchigroup.com visited on February 21, 2002.
34. Service.htm # support centre abroad at www.ruchigroup.com. visited on February 21, 2002.
35. Oxenfeldth A.R., *Cost-Benefit Analysis for Executive Decision Making AMACOM,* American Management Association, 1979, p.51.
36. Elias M. Awad, *System Analysis and Design*, Galgotia Publication (P) Ltd., 1999, p.238.
37. Software Technology Park of India, Electronic complex, Perdeshipura, Indore and www.stpi.net.

38. Ibid.

39. Miller, Jene (2000): *Sustaining Software Teletrade in Bangalore: Fostering Market Agility through Economic Competence,* EPW, Vol. XXXI, June 24. 2000, p.2253-2262.

40. Heeks, R (1999): *Software Strategies in Developing Countries,* University of Manchester.

41. Miller, Jene (2000): *Sustaining Software Teletrade in Bangalore: Fostering Market Agility through Economic Competence,* EPW, Vol. XXXI, June 24. 2000, p.2253-2262.

42. Gideon, S and Nett, Roger, *A methodology for Social Research,* Rawat Publication, New Delhi, 1992.

43. Sinha V.C., *Unnat Aarthic Sydhant-(Hindi),* National Publishing House, New Delhi. P.285.

44. Samulson P.H., *Economics,* M'Cgraw Hill Book Comp, New York. P.512.

45. Stigler G.J., *The Theory of Price,* M'Cgraw Hill Book Comp, New York., P.106-110

46. Sundaram and Verma, *Principal of Economics,* Sultan Chand and Sons Publication, New Delhi, P.231-234.

5

Problems and Prospects of Information Technology Industry in India Line of Action and Conclusion

5.1 Problems of IT industry

There is, of course, much more to business success than access to the internet. Firms exist in an environment that is either supportive of their competitive efforts, not supportive, or something in between. Even with a completed high-speed fiber optic network connecting most cities and with much-improved international gateways, both expected within the next two years, India's economic environment could, at best, be ranked as "something in between." For purposes here, it is unnecessary to run through the litany of well-known difficulties businesses face (continued government interference at both national and state levels, remaining protection, even in the IT sector, inadequate public investment owing to high fiscal deficits, the associated 'crowding out' effects in capital markets, government subsidies, sectors reserved to very small firms, labour laws, etc.).

The fact is that today few firms in India outside the software, textile and chemical industries are truly competitive internationally, especially among locally controlled companies. Even within the IT sector, domestic manufacturers of personal computers, peripherals and other equipment are concerned that opening markets in response to India's joining the World Trade Organisation (WTO) could be devastating if and when lessened levels of effective protection are introduced. Adjusting to increased international competition, in other words, could present difficult problems for many Indian companies. Two negative factors affecting the growth and success of the internet in affecting productivity improvement seem particularly important. The first has been mentioned earlier, poor physical infrastructure for moving products within the country and, for export and imports, through ports. The inability to ship goods easily and cheaply is a major constraint in building a true national marketplace in India and a constraint that will not easily be overcome. Some efforts have been made to improve ports through private sector initiatives, but much remains to be done both here and, particularly, in highway construction. Given low public investment and the apparent discomfort in relying on private methods of financing infrastructure projects, this constraint is likely to persist for some time to come.[3]

The other factor that ultimately promises to compromise success, certainly as compared with several other Asian nations, is educational achievement. Fewer than per cent of Indian children complete the fifth grade and 45 per cent are illiterate. These per centages compare poorly with such competitive countries as Thailand, Indonesia or, especially, the Philippines.[4] Although lack of literacy has not thus far been a major problem for those parts of the IT sector that have been successful, particularly the software industry, the much wider impacts from the internet that are anticipated across the economy will depend increasingly on availability of trained or trainable workers. In some ways, India appears bifurcated between an educated middle-class, from which the technical schools draw and the vast majority of the population with little, if any, formal education. For the software industry, such a bifurcation may still allow for rapid expansion, at least for a time. For other industries, however, servicing an increasingly 'wired' economy promises to require a workforce much more competent than is widely available at present.

As discussed in previous chapters, Madhya Pradesh IT industry are present focusing their attention mainly on custom computer programming, manpower training, consulting and developing of customised indigenous software packages receives very little attention. Systematic analyses of factors that explain such a specific pattern of growth are rare in the literature/ in order to bridge this gap, this

The only two areas where Information Technology found Madhya Pradesh falling behind its competitor were government initiative and size of domestic market. Given state's potential, question that naturally arises in this context is: why does Madhya Pradesh not diversify into production and sale of software packages? Obviously, there is no simple answer to this question and, hence, one needs to take a closer look at all possible problems towards moving in the desired direction.

Due to the constant flow of new entrants into the global software industry, profits for India industry from the sale of traditional services are likely to fall in the future; revenue growth would depend only on the growth in the number of software workers. In order to survive the increased level of competition in the world market, Indian companies would have to develop new products that are at the high end of the value chain. In may be noted in this context that while India's largest software services companies, Wipro and Infosys, reported a significant increase in profit in the year 2000, they experienced increasing competition from a number of low-cost Asian nations.[5]

Table 5.3: Problems Encountered By Madhya Pradesh IT Companies

Problem Factors	*Agree*	*Disagree*	*Not Sure*
Infrastructure			
Limited R and D Facilities	6	4	1
Lack of hardware capabilities	4	4	3
Poor quality control	5	5	1
Inadequate telecom services	7	3	1
High attrition rate	8	2	1
Regulation			
Inability to protect copyright	6	3	2
Non-conductive tech policies	3	6	2
Risk			
Long designing-marketing lag	8	3	0
Limited fund for investment in continuous innovation	7	4	0
Marketing and Distribution			
Limited domestic market	8	3	0
Poor internal distribution network	7	3	1
Absence of after-sales-services	7	3	1

Note—Column 2, 3 and 4 shows number of IT companies responses about problem factors.

Source: Compilation of survey results.

A viable demand estimates suggest that diversification into development and sales of software packages would open up a very large potential market, worth as much as US$150 billion in the year 2001.[6] However, there appear to be some major barriers to entry into the market. In order to have preliminary understanding of the factors that hander India firms from shifting the thrust of there production to standardised software packages, we asked the companies in our sample to identify the difficulties encountered within four broad groups of problem factors: infrastructure bottlenecks, regulatory constraints, risk elements and marketing and distribution. A summary of their responses is reported in Table 5.3.

As it appears from the table 5.3, a number of issues related to infrastructure development, regulation, estimated risks and marketing and distribution are together responsible for keeping Madhya Pradesh software developers from venturing into the packaged-software market. Seen from the standpoint of infrastructure development, lack of internationally compatible hardware capabilities, inadequate telecommunication services and limited research and development (R and D) facilities define the major set of constraints faced by IT companies of Madhya Pradesh. Also a high attrition rate has raised concern among a majority of producers.

Industrial infrastructure defining provision of power, water and transport is a preliminary requirement for production, irrespective of its specific form. The infrastructure that is of specific interest to the IT industry is the provision of a telecommunication network. Yet, IT companies in Madhya Pradesh encountered a number of telecommunication problems including shortages of telecommunication links, time lag in accessing such links, poor transmission and high cost of installation and use. Summarising the concerns of the IT companies, NASSCOM recently warned of a serious crisis in the IT industry over the next five years. Such limitations in telecommunication facilities have discouraged foreign clients from considering offshore software development as a feasible option.

Besides telecommunications, two other important elements in IT infrastructure are human resources and R and D facilities. While the growth of software services export has caused increased opportunities for employment growth, as is indicated by the survey, masks a major problem for the aggregate industry- that of worker turnover, especially the loss of workers to overseas markets facilitated by increased number of the onsite problems. The study given by our respondents suggest that IT companies were losing 10-15 per sent of their employee each year, but in some companies, the losses have been as high as 30 per cent in a single year. The high attrition rate has translated into slower growth, poor transfer of skills, reduced incentives for training investments and reinforced dependence on programming services.

Together with telecommunications and human resource management, low levels of R and D investment define a major problem of IT companies. Software developers, along with entrepreneurs in many other sectors of Madhya Pradesh industry, have experience poor levels of R and D investments. This has resulted in missed opportunities for the development of indigenous technologies and, hence, new software products.

With regard to regulatory problems, more than 75 per cent of the producers sampled consider poor enforcement of copyright protection laws, both at home and abroad, to be the most important reason for the insignificant market share of prepackaged software product of Madhya Pradesh. As seen by these producers, piracy of software in Madhya Pradesh in the rule rather than the exception. With pirated versions of sophisticated software frequently costing less then Rupees 500 (approximately US $12), domestic producer are affected negatively both in direct and indirect ways. While the direct effect defines the shrinkage in their market share, the indirect effect reflects the downward pressure on their prices. Together, the two causes reduced revenues for domestic producers.

Apparently, the perceived long lag from conceiving, designing, developing to marketing- in the production of packaged software products, together with the continuously changing nature of production technology and demand in this market, raise the associated risks of Madhya Pradesh producer to a very high level. In order to reduce the risk component, survive the competition and stay ahead of other producers in the market, Madhya Pradesh producers would need to invest significantly on continuos product and process innovation. On the other hand, since rapid diffusion of innovation prevents full appropriation of returns on investments, individual producers are unwilling to commit themselves to significant investment in these areas. The only way out, therefore, is to have a complementary investment programme supported by the government.

As suggested elsewhere, lack of a sizeable domestic market has long remained a major problem for Indian and Madhya Pradesh developers. Though the market grew by over 50 per cent during 1990-95, its size is still small to attract domestic producers to invest in indigenous software development. On the other hand, capturing a major share of the international market requires success in two area. Development of a global distribution network to respond effectively to clients needs and standards; and setting up of after-sales-service shops to provide support, maintenance and upgrades for the product line. India lags on both of these fronts because developing distribution capabilities and after-sales-service workshops are time-consuming and expensive.

Lack of a shortage of IT workers has long remained a major problem for Indian and Madhya Pradesh developers. There are 350,000 Indian software developers in India and 250,000 employed in the U.S. To illustrate the shortfall, Blueshift, a company in India needs 145,000 software specialists right now and that number will rise by 50 per cent very soon. Yet Indian universities graduate only 122,000 engineers a year, just 30 per cent of whom have computer-science degrees and almost all of whom end up in the U.S. and Europe.[7]

Analysts estimate that every year at least 15 per cent of the experienced engineers and managers in India's technology companies depart for foreign shores. "It's a major constraint to growth and every person gone is a missed opportunity", 'says Pavagada Indiresan, an adviser to the Indian government on matters of high technology and a former director of the Indian Institute of Technology in Madras.

Infosys, one of India's largest software-services company, increased salaries by 30 per cent in 1999 and 16 per cent so far this year. Still, there are many senior positions open. Lately, the company has been trying to fill positions by advertising in Singapore newspapers. At Wipro Corporation, a software-services company with $500 million in annual revenue, some 200 experienced personnel have to be replaced every year out of a staff of 7,500. "Everyone is short on IT talent," says Wipro Chairman Azim Premji.

From the above discussion we come to know the key problems faced by Madhya Pradesh IT companies are:

Lack of Entrepreneurial Spirit—The past and current Madhya-Pradesh education system set in a way that it does not promote creativity among students. Creativity is the key driver for innovation and entrepreneurship. The State government and IT institutes are waking up to this realization and are trying to change the curriculum to encourage entreprenuership.

Overseas Demand—According to Heeks[8], one of the key factors to a country's and state's (Madhya Pradesh) strength in an industry is strong customer support. However, in the case of Madhya Pradesh the domestic market overall is fairly weak and the state does not have a strong home customer base. In addition, the absence of a strong domestic market can cause hindrance to the growth of competition with leads to innovation and competitive pricing. In addition, it also shows that state is dependent on overseas demand for the growth of its IT industry, which, could be a major downfall if the demand for IT services overseas decreases.

Poor Communications Infrastructure—Currently only every 3 out of 100 people have access to a telephone line, computer penetration per family is fairly low as well. Overall, State's data communication infrastructure is expensive and limited. In order to see itself grow as IT super power, the state definitely has to cross some major hurdles in terms of its communication infrastructure.

Funding—It is only recently that the country has changed policies to encourage overseas and private funding. This has been another hurdle for the development of IT as the government has to realize the role private funding plays in the development of new innovative technologies.

Weak Management System/ Cultural Barriers—The current Indian system promotes managers on the basis of seniority rather than skill. Most clients view this as a big problem along with unwillingness of Indian software professional to point out problems up front and a general unwillingness to say no to clients for fear of offending them.

5.2 Line of Action

Drawing on some of these similarities and differences across the regions of Madhya Pradesh, several policy recommendations have been designed by us to boost Information Technology and Information Technology industry in Madhya Pradesh. These suggestion include:

1. Efficient conduct of telecommunication systems, strengthening the ability of the departments to face irreversible change, will only be possible with full autonomy.
2. Publications (newspapers, magazines and academic journals) which are not yet online must be encouraged to publish their information on the web. Content must also be provided in the business sector, geared towards creating a business market space. Constantly updated telephone/e-mail directories and yellow pages for businesses in each city and town must be made available online.
3. Special attention must be paid to the export/import sector. Directories of exporters, product catalogues customs

information, shipping/transport agencies, insurance agencies and third party audit. Verification information must all be compiled online for one-stop access by importers and exporters. Linkages must be provided to exiting trade databases published by organisation like government and non government agencies.

4. Content from non-profit organisations, public health groups and social services agencies must also be published online; a special grant should be setup for this purpose.
5. Special measures must be taken for providing online content rapidly during times of disaster like earthquakes and floods.
6. Government departments and agencies must publish extensive content online, geared towards citizen services like and registration, tax information, appointments with officials, transparent accounting practices and employment opportunities, etc.
7. Initiatives must be launched to publish education-related content and services at all levels. Online educational content and instructional delivery must be used to extends the scarce resources of educational content and instructional delivery must be used to extend the scarce resources of educational institutes across the country.
8. Content generation must take place in Hindi and English languages. The development and standardization of local language software, fonts and web publishing tool must be promoted aggressively.
9. Where possible, use of freeware and shareware packages and tools, such as the use of the Linux operating system and Apache web server for digital publishing should be encouraged, instead of relying on costly proprietary software solutions.
10. Training centres and seminars should be set up for generation of internal and intra-organisational Internet content, via intranet document management systems and Extranet-oriented flow of information. Computer courses and curriculum in schools and colleges must be augmented to go beyond basic word processing and programming to include web page design and online database management.

11. Legal developments concerning content classification, regulation and enforcement in Madhya Pradesh. Regional representatives from the industry, academia and government should try to be present in National and International forums dealing with cyberspace content issues lice intellectual property rights, copyrights, copyright protection, online privacy, online crimes and digital watermarks. Draconian content laws which require censoring of material published on web sites in India and abroad should be avoided.
12. Online forums and periodic seminars/briefings must be conducted at the national and regional levels to invite participation in policy making regarding national and state online content laws.
13. A key focus on content should be making a difference to the way service is delivered. In areas like making government procedures transparent, a lot of political will and muscle will be needed. For instance, in areas like land records and getting power connections, some unscrupulous middlemen tend to get involved; openness and transparency will threaten them, but the government must display the political will to clean up these processes via open content publishing.
14. To promote access to illiterate people, internet radio stations in local dialects should be encouraged and devices as well as channels should be found to distribute this locally e.g. via cable TV networks.
15. World-class hosting infrastructure must be created in Madhya Pradesh so that locally generated content will be predominantly hosted in the region and not outside, thus saving lucrative foreign exchange revenues and safeguarding information sovereignty.
16. It is too obvious that with visa relaxation, there will be a further increase in the demand for Madhya Pradesh IT professionals. This would lead to competition in the labour market between Madhya Pradesh IT exporting companies and their foreign counterparts for skilled manpower.

17. To examine the resource movement effect we shall focus on those sectors of the economy that require technical manpower. These are divided into two broad sub-sectors: (a) those engaged in the production of software services and (b) those engaged in the production of tradables and competing for technical manpower. This includes goods-producing sectors like hardware, communication and control instrumentation and service-producing sectors like research and training. The arguments that follow have been on the assumptions on which specific factor model and the Dutch disease models have been developed. The Dutch disease syndrome is explained in terms of two symptomatic effects o export boom, namely, the 'resource movement effect' and the 'spending effect'.[9]

18. Suggestion to Government Policy include policy changes in antiquated laws at several levels- in terms to investment opportunities, rental charges, fostering a liberal climate regarding connectivity, investment and licenses for small and medium scale establishments. They also include the need to take suitable steps to introduce state-of-the-art infrastructural facilities and support them with more liberal policies. Another important area was the need for changes in data collection tools and methods so that disaggregated data on the service sector and on gender within each sector may be collected. The need for evolving cyber-laws as well as the need to keep a balance regarding the different interests that are involved in IT enable services has also been expressed. This includes evolving a legal framework in order to address newly emerging issues such as health problems, lack of grievance redressal procedures and employee/subcontractor participation, protection of workers, especially IT professionals.

19. Infrastructural facilities or the lack of these have often been underlined as crucial in terms of the future of work and the economy itself. These include good roads and other means of communications. Some other crucial points that have come form the prevalence survey are need for ensuring uninterrupted power supply, improvement in the telecommunication

infrastructure, dealing with operational difficulties like low band width for VSNL facility, lowering of the cost of telecommunication services, relaxation of certain regulations of the VSNL like the small capacity assigned to each user, which results in difficulty in transferring and receiving large volumes of data and also facilitated like unlimited Internet access. Other related suggestions were that in areas of small-scale industries, there should be provisions for telelink facilities such that several small-scale units could share the facilities and at the same time retain crucial aspects like secrecy. This could take the form of tele-cottages. This will facilitate possibilities like sharing the skilled workforce, so that each unit does not have to independently recruit such a workforce. It is also felt that it is necessary to build on the existing resources especially for a resource scarce country like India. One needs to make use of public premises like schools, post offices, banks, etc, to begin tele-kiosks in rural areas too. These could take the form of community centres that provide for he educational, informational and entertainment needs of the people of the community. These would be especially useful for people who lack the possibilities of mobility either due to their own disabilities or because of caring responsibilities.

20. Line of action related to research, information and awareness includes systematic dissemination of information about teleworking and what its implications are foe the industry, the economy and for the quality of life of people. This could include elements like teleworking employment news, which gives information about the type of job opportunities that are being created in different sectors of the economy. Besides, research based on desegregated data is necessary so that policies and action will be more informed. Several establishments in the survey seemed little aware of the possibilities of telewokking. This may be rectified by regular dissemination of useful information.

21. From Mapping Agility of Information Technology companies study (chapter 4.4) we recommends that the government should

work together with industry in order to develop a coordinated approach to policy-making across a broad waterfront of political domains. These should include strategies for growth, skills and training, domestic and export trade, knowledge sharing and learning between firms and projects, remote and proximal work practices, social equity and protection from exploitation.

22. From our analysis of Cobb-Douglas Production Model in chapter 4.6, we suggest that private enterprise and government policies more capital input compare to labour in Madhya Pradesh.

23. Training that is useful to industry is most likely to be useful to people who undergo the training. The courses need to be constantly updated and geared to the demands of the labour and technology market. It is also necessary to devise mechanisms that curb the proiiferation of dubious computer instruction and courses. These courses tend to play on the insecurity of students and parents and offer them expensive courses that fetch hardly and skills or employment prospects. One of course needs to be careful about such mechanisms themselves. Special facilities need to be all section of society. Grievance redressal mechanisms, associations of IT professionals and labour protection need to be emphasized. Such forums can ensure long-term and sustainable partnerships and development with a firm basis of grass roots participation. All new attempts are aimed at increasing the quality of life of people. This is simple fact; but it is often forgotten and hence needs to be emphasized. For IT enable service to contribute to such and aim, several changes are needed in both the mind-set of several sections of people as well as changes in legislation and social relations.

Based on our empirical study we developed the Model for Information Technology Industry in Madhya Pradesh (Opportunity, Security and Strength) in figure 5.1. The enhanceing information to IT enable services and IT industry can be possible by IT resources base and across to internet and website, improving efficiency of IT enable services get strengthen by bandwidth quality and access to internet web site. The main cities of Madhya Pradesh like Bhopal, Gwalior, Indore and Jabalpur have high degree of opportunity for enhancing and improving efficiency of IT and

IT enable services. This opportunity will strengthen by right to accessing information, government policy and venture capital investment. However, there are some constraints for the growth of Information Technology industry. To overcome these constraints reduce the vulnerability to change in functioning of industry by stable power supply and sound IT infrastructure.

We discussed the Model for IT industry in Madhya Pradesh in figure 5.1. For sustain growth of IT industry development park should be designed by government and private enterprise as in the case of Bangalore

Figure 5.1—Suggested Model for Information Technology Industry in Madya Pradesh (Opportunity, security and Strength)

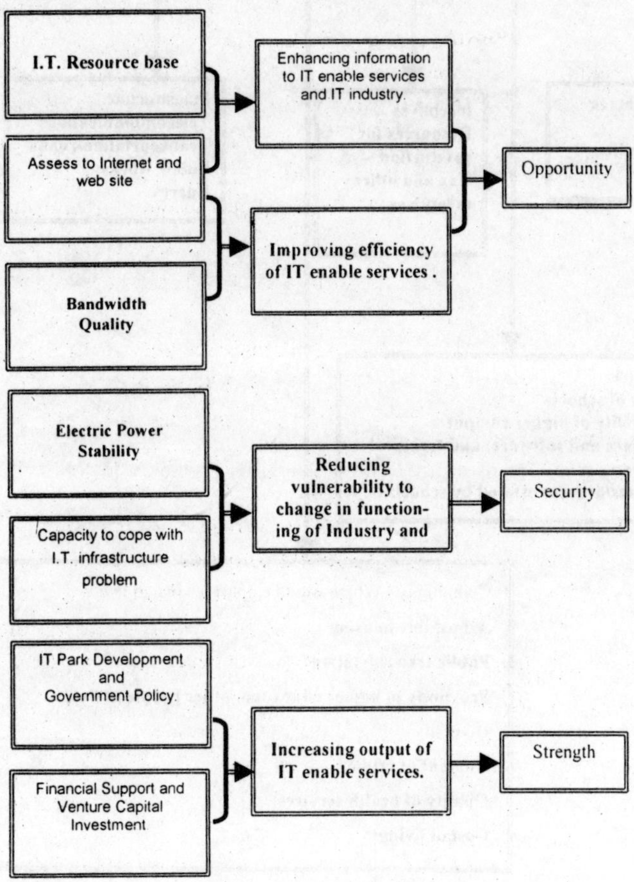

and Hyderabad Information Technology Development Park. We established a suggested model for Government of Madhya Pradesh in figure 5.2. In this model, firstly government create an environment for IT industry by developing infrastructural facilities like telecommunication, transportation, energy, etc. The main factor input of IT industry is skilled

Figure 5.2— Suggested Model for Information Technology Industry Development Park

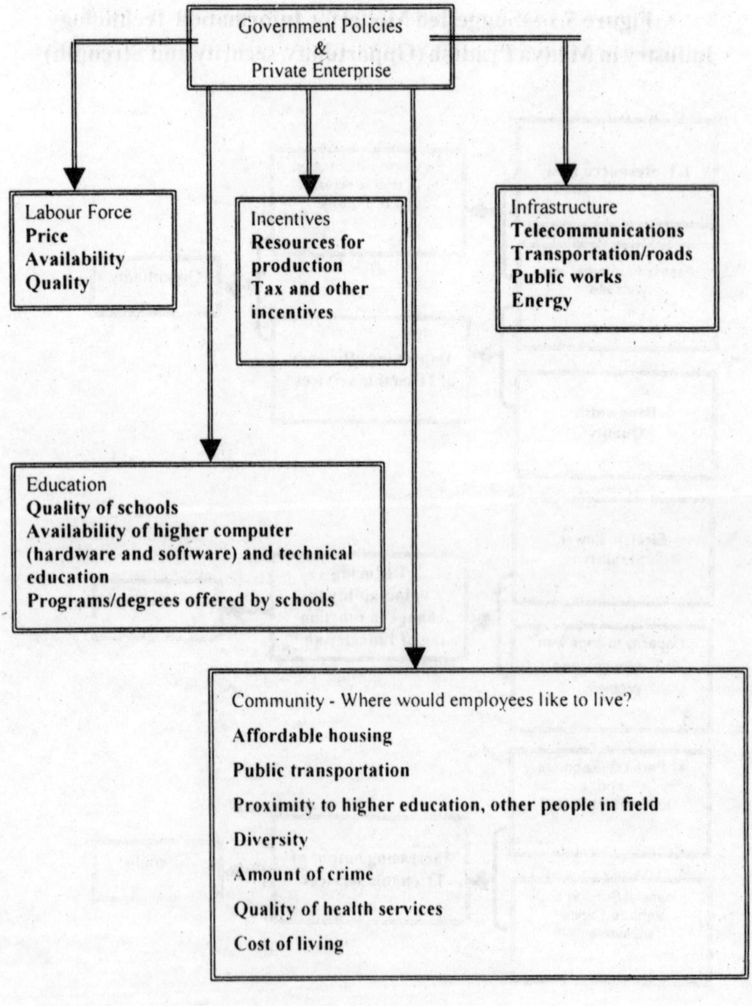

labour force, do higher computer education related with hardware and software courses is the need of Technology Park. This will also stop the inflow of brain drain from other states. Moreover, better salary packages and intensive to IT companies will increase the growth of IT industry in Madhya Pradesh.

5.3 Prospects of IT industry in Madhya Pradesh

Information Technology has been largely understood as a new kind of media or telecommunications infrastructure, which allows the dissemination of information, commands. As it appears from the breakdown of industry revenue by products, prepackaged software accounts for less than 30 per cent of total export revenue[10]. Yet it is common knowledge that prepackaged software, by its very nature, is the mast profitable segment of the industry's product groups. By being copied at no extra cost, standardised packages allow for increasing returns to scale immediately after their initial stage of development. Hence, this particular product group offers a significant advantage over all other product groups in the software industry; especially, over the customised product group. It is also interesting to note that in the resent past, Information Technology has surveyed potential markets and concluded that India and Madhya Pradesh could be rated above all of its competitors as a software development location. Information Technology rated India above most competitors on availability of a skilled labour force, widespread use of the English language and competitive labour costs. The score was above average on areas of technical competence, education and training and telecommunication infrastructure. The IT policy has classified IT applications which are likely to have direct relevance to large number of people at different levels in the country into the following categories:

1. Electronic Governance

Government and its numerous agencies are the largest service providers in the country. It is obvious that in order to have a visible impact of the benefit of IT on people, government must select major services at different levels such as Ministries/ Departments of Central Government and State Governments, District Administrations, Municipal Services and services related to local governance at Block/ Panchayat level and re-engineer them through extensive use of IT.

While over the years, there has been considerable progress in the use of IT in government services, most of these applications have been confined to back-office computerization. As a result, the improvement in quality of service to public has not made sufficient impact. It is, therefore, necessary that each one of the government agencies involved in providing public-oriented services should identify at least one area and use Information Technology in a highly intensive manner so that all aspects of delivery of service to people should transform into an IT based service. While doing so it would obviously be necessary that for sustainability of good quality of service to citizens, back-office component of the concerned agency for the identified application is fully computerized. However, the approach for computerization and IT induction should be from front-office applications to back-office and not the other way. This will ensure that there is sufficient pressure on the government agencies from public to sustain the quality of service using IT. Back-office computerization alone, which has very little impact on the public interface, is not sustainable in the long run due to lack of such public pressure. Some of the applications, which would like government agencies at different levels to undertake on priority are:

(i) Computerization of land records all over the country with computerized land/ property documents to be made available to people at all levels including in villages in a time bound manner.

(ii) Payment of bills / municipal taxes.

(iii) Computerization of information related to court cases particularly the ones related to land/ property disputes and extensive use of computers in courts at all levels in the country for office-automation and judicial applications.

(iv) All government regulations, notifications and forms for various services at all levels of government up to municipal / local government agencies to be made available to people on Internet.

2. Enabling Literacy and Education for Masses

In spite of Literacy Mission launched by the Government more than a decade ago, India continues to have largest population of illiterates in the world. The per centage of illiterates is considerably higher amongst women in the country. In an information driven society where socio-economic growth depends on capability to acquire and effectively utilize information, it is necessary that citizens not only be fully literate but also be educated in true sense (not just limited to formal education) so that they could fully exploit the benefits of technological advancements in various fields.

Information Technology with convergence of various technologies related to communication and delivery of information such as video, audio, telephone, television, newspapers, computers etc. into one unified framework, provides for the first time a unique opportunity to spread literacy and education at a mass scale in the country at affordable cost. The convergence enables ease of providing educational material, which is one of the pre-requisites to spread literacy and education in the country. We need to look at the concept of Community Information Centres, Community Library Centres and Panchayat Centres across the country in a completely new way with the availability of IT tools and services. These community centres could be major hubs of educating (not just providing information to) people on a mass scale. Unlike the earlier experiment using television as a means of educating people, the convergence of IT tools enables interactive learning alongwith broadcasting medium such as television and radio. Experience has shown that any exercise for educating people necessarily requires interactivity.

3. Fulfilling Local Information Needs of people

One of the major drawbacks of IT based systems developed in many areas is that its information content is generally not directly relevant to people for whom these are developed. The contents are generally planned by people who have themselves not lived in those areas particularly in semi-urban/ rural areas. As a result, these systems have a heavy urban-bias. Such systems, therefore

have limited utility and soon become commercially un-viable. It is a myth that people in rural areas like to have free delivery of information. Some of the surveys have shown that if information has direct relevance to people even in rural areas and will result in commercial gains and thus improvement in their economic conditions, people will be willing to pay for such services. We need, therefore, to launch a scheme, which would enable the process of large-scale self-employed youngsters across the country to set up and develop contents for Information Kiosks, particularly for rural areas. It has to be ensured that such schemes have large scale private participation and are not dependent on government funding alone. From the Government side, we have to ensure that any one who wants to set up Information Kiosk at any place in the country is not only freed from all government regulations and licenses but also is encouraged through evolving simple and attractive financing schemes offered by banks and financial institutions.

The model of growth evolved in the country by Cable TV operators could be used as a base for evolving such a scheme where initially for many years government had not at all intervened. The sector grew with large number of cable operators operating in neighbourhood.

4. Enabling better Economic Condition of People

The Working Group feels that in the ultimate analysis Information Technology must ensure improvement in economic status and purchasing power of the people at all levels. Some of the areas which have direct relevance / impact on economic status of the people and are expected to be addressed by IT in a big way are as follows:

(i) ***Employment Generation:*** *Large scale utilization of Information Technology in a manner that it will facilitate its reach to masses will result in massive new opportunities for employment generation. Some of the indications in this direction are already available in the manner in which two major industries have grown in the country in the last few years.*

(a) Cable industry, where large number of operators operate in the neighbourhood to solve any problem faced by the users. Each one of these Operators employ a small number of people who are generally semi-skilled and learn on-the-job.

(b) The other area is the off-shoot of large scale spread of cable TV reaching 30 to 40 million homes in the country. This has resulted in large number of TV channels with multilingual programming. As a result of such a massive programme requirements, the demand of TV programmes and as a result that of professionals who could work in various areas related to production of TV programmes such as journalists, music artistes, visual designers, scripting, acting etc. The success of TV channels depends directly on the viewership of its programme in the country. As a result TV programming has to cater to the taste of its target viewers, an issue which is not that well understood by IT industry yet. This development has resulted in large-scale employment generation in areas which were earlier not considered even employable. With the growth of Internet and its reach to masses in the country, such opportunities are expected to grow manifold. Millions of students and youngsters who remain jobless in spite of doing graduation and post graduation could be made employable by making them capable of handling IT tools. The technological developments in IT are ensuring that such tools do not require extensive knowledge of computer science. Moreover, as these tools become available in Indian languages with at least as much ease of operations as presently in English, the application development in IT would become very widespread and thus create massive employment opportunities.

(ii) ***Direct Marketing of Rural/ Agro Products***—One of the important components of improving the socio-economic status of people in villages is to ensure that their products find right kind of markets and reach these markets in minimum time without number of middle men involved in it. The reach of IT to rural areas will provide unique opportunities to producers of rural products, agricultural/ agro- processing products, rural handicrafts etc. to have direct access to markets. Internet will enable advertising of rural products produced even in the remotest villages to global markets.

5. Educating Citizens about their duties

Internet based information delivery systems in combination with conventional broadcast media, TV and Radio, could act as a major vehicle to educate citizens regarding their duties to the nation. This will immensely help in people's participation in programmes like family welfare, conservation of environment, preservation of ethical, moral and cultural values.

6. Social and Economic Implications of Information Technology

To maximize the benefits of new Information Technologies (IT) and infrastructures to the entire United States, research is needed to develop new knowledge about the underlying processes by which their development and use influence and transform society and by which society simultaneously influences their development and use. Especially encouraged are proposals that suggest fundamental advances in our ability to a) understand the particular societal values embedded in design proces es and products, b) model the co-evolution of IT and social groups, c) e olve new information technologies to better fill societal requirements and d sustain distributed

nd local use of critical infrastructures and networks over the l ng term. Advances in knowledge to overcome various social, economic, cult ral and managerial barriers related to the use of IT and infrastructures are undamental to maximizing societal benefits. These include, for example: IT a cess equity; universal participation in networks, infrastructures and digital economies; privacy issues related to new uses of digital informa ion and archived communications; surveillance, monitoring and tracking of network activities; the development of trust in distributed social settings and exchanges with strangers; intellectual property issues and rights related to electronic publishing, digital libraries, fair use in educational settings, etc.; and cross-cultural issues related to any of the above.

Specific areas of emphasis include: the economic and technical systems that comprise the digital economy, electronic markets and Internet commerce, etc.; the causes and effects of unequal participation in IT by different social groups; the interdependence of technologies, institutions and communities; and the evolution and functioning of IT-based collaboratories and distributed work environments. Also relevant are studies of how laws, ethics and social norms may be changing in relation to IT, of public access to government information and of the involvement of IT in public decision-making.

Development of new data and indicators that would facilitate tracking IT use and creation of new research methodologies to study the socio-economic implications of IT are also appropriate in this category.

7. Information Technology Labour Market

India has seen tremendous growth in its Information Technology sector mainly due to the global shortage in skilled labour force that the country has been in an advantageous position to provide for this shortage. One of the most obvious examples is the transfer of workforce to the United States which is currently facing a shortage in the IT labour force. Thus, making Information Technology a major driver of bilateral relations for India with United States and other countries such as Germany and Singapore.

India has fast become the IT hotbed, mainly due to its ability to churn out highly skilled workers every year. There are several reasons for the highly skilled work force such as the Indian education system. The education system has traditionally placed great emphasis on mathematics and science, resulting in a large number of science and engineering graduates. Mastery over quantitative concepts coupled with English proficiency has resulted in a skill set suitable for the IT industry.

Currently, India's universities are pumping out 120,000 engineering graduates a year and the number reaches nearly 1 million when polytechnics and the country's 3,000 computer-training institutes are included. This skilled labor has enabled the country to see $5.7 billion in exports of software products and a one-quater growth in India's $400 billion economy. However, even with such impressive numbers of skilled workforce, India is said to face a shortage of IT workers by 2008, according to a study done by McKinseyandCo. and India's National Association of Software andService Companies (NASSCOM). This is due to the fact that the country faces a severe brain drain with most of its skilled workers opting to move overseas for better pay and living conditions.

India IT Super Power Group Setup- the Ministry Of Information Technology (MIT) recently elected people to lead an IT Super Power group that is going to address issues about women in technology and technology development in rural areas. In view of the growing demand for software professionals around the globe and likely shortfall in human resources in IT sector, the government is taking initiatives to increase the number of technology students to double its current capacity. The government is sponsoring technology institutes (Indian Institute of Technology Management) in the same lines as the successful Indian institute of technology. There has been active support given to private institute, polytechnics and colleges that provide IT training. The DOEACC society has been formed which accredits institutions in the non-formal sector for four levels of courses.[11]

8. Export Prospects of IT Industry

Looking at future prospects both the domestic and international markets for IT products and services are growing at a rapid rate. To take advantage of the opportunities generated by expanding markets, Indian software developers would need to shift the thrust of their production from contractual programming and designing to indigenous prepackaged software products. Such a shift, however, requires major reforms in several areas including infrastructure planning, regulatory policies, risk management and marketing and distribution framework.

Talking about the performance Mr. Kiran Karnik[12], President, Nasscom, said, "Not only is the Indian Software and Services industry growing quantitatively but also qualitatively. We are seeing multi year contracts coming to India, which reflect confidence in our abilities. Further, Indian companies now service nearly 220 global 1000 customers. Indian vendors are also increasingly beginning to participate in large global bids against worldwide IT majors."

"The industry today has become one of the biggest contributor of Indian exports with its share going up to 16.5 per cent. The 29 per cent export growth is enviable in view of the 2 per cent export growth for the economy", Mr. Karnik[13] added.

Some of the interesting trends witnessed by the Indian Software and Service Industry in Financial Year 2001-02 includes:

- Offshore projects grew nearly 70 per cent while onsite grew only by 10 per cent.
- When adjusted for offshore billing rates, industry growth is nearly 60 per cent (offshore billing rates are only 1/3rd of onsite)
- Industry growth is increasingly polarized. Top 5 players contributed 55 per cent of growth of industry while top 10 players accounted for 73 per cent of growth. Some SME players grew more than industry average.

- There was increased vendor consolidation by customers which led to customers reducing the number of vendors they outsource their projects
- There was an increase in the number of fixed price multi-year contracts with many large players winning high value global projects
- There was an emergence of new service lines such as package software implementation, systems integration and network management
- The geographic mix of software exports is shifting with many Indian IT companies targeting countries apart from the USA such as Europe, Asia Pacific and Latin America
- India has emerged as the most preferred destination for BPO and almost every Fortune 100 CEO looking at outsourcing operations to India
- Indian productivity-quality-cost model has emerged as a unbeatable value proposition for the software and service industry

The above discussion underline the future prospects of IT industry in Madhya Pradesh. Some of the important prospects are as follows:

Education System— The Madhya Pradesh education system places strong emphasis on math and science, resulting in a large number of sciences and engineering graduates. Mastery over quantitative concepts coupled with English proficiency has resulted in a skill set that has enabled the country to take advantage of the current international demand for Information Technology.

Cheaper labour— Compared to the wages demanded by IT professionals in the United States, Indian programmers demand much cheaper wage rates. It is cheaper for international companies to outsource their work to companies in India.

Quality: Indian programmers are known for their strong technical skills and their eagerness to accommodate clients. In some cases, clients outsource work to get access to more specialized engineering talent, particularly in the area of telecommunications.

Indians Abroad— The large influx of Indians settled outside the country provides companies within the country with lifelines abroad by matching suppliers to buyers. This community of immigrants has been very supportive of its home countries ventures in IT. They are also the key people that gather information about new technologies and go back to the country to invest in new ventures related to IT.

Government—After realizing the potential of state as a major IT powers, the government has taken several initiatives to promote the development of IT. The Ministry of Information Technology is playing an active role to develop the infrastructure that supports the development of information technology.

The image one gets of the Madhya Pradesh IT industry is a mixed one. On the one hand, there is a great deal of excitement, in its rapid growth and its export success. On the other hand, the kind of work being performed is fairly mundane with only limited potential for sustained growth. An increase in offshore software development will also benefit Madhya Pradesh firms investing in providing software development and consultancy services of various kinds. As some Madhya Pradesh IT firms have noted, stricter visa restrictions will help with the drain of trained professionals to the US, holding down software wages and salaries in Madhya Pradesh. Insofar as Indian and Madhya Pradesh firms succeed in developing the competencies required to increase productivity, their clients in the US and elsewhere are likely to benefit as well from an increased supply of such competencies. Some of this would be at the expense of mid-level to small consulting firms that currently provide services similar to those provided by Indian and Madhya Pradesh IT companies at present or in the near future. In other words, our sense is that trade related restrictions are not the answer to the problem from the U.S perspective although such a cap would benefit Indian firms with large off-site facilities. These observations are consistent with the other research in this area (e.g., Heeks[14], 1996, D'Costa[15] 1998). Both of these authors have argued that the export orientation and routine tasks that exports involve have limited learning potential for Indian firms. Heeks has noted that the reported export revenues are misleading insofar as a substantial fraction of these are accounted for by onsite work, that in turn requires that a substantial fraction of the revenues be spent outside India. D'Costa has highlighted the limited potential for leapfrogging of most export-oriented activities in which Indian software firms are currently engaged. The responses by clients (self selected by the Indian firms) convey the sense that their Indian suppliers are competent (by and large) at providing a limited range of services but have not moved to where the suppliers offer solutions to client problems.

Much IT companies of Madhya Pradesh have offered two components. First, they hope to use their existing links to acquire domain knowledge and knowledge about the businesses that their clients are in and to use that knowledge to move up the value chain. In essence, they hope to become IT consultants offering business solutions. The second component is the creation of proprietary tools, methods and reusable software code that can be customized according to the clients' needs. This "productisation" of what was formerly a service will, it is hoped, increase the revenue per employee and will counteract the increasing shortage of skilled software professionals and rising wages.

However, our optimism about the beneficial impact of the IT industry of Madhya Pradesh on the state economy in the long run is not based entirely on the quantitative importance of the relatively smaller number of successes among software service exporters. We think that in the shadow of the much more prominent software services IT companies; we shall find IT companies developing a variety of new software products, components and technologies. Further, the software service firms are exemplars of organisational forms and practices that are relatively new to India. A large number of software firms are *de novo* startups, indicating that the supply of entrepreneurial talent appears to be forthcoming when the opportunity arises, even in new and technology intensive sectors.

These IT companies are relatively flat organisations, with young management teams, informal but professional management styles and with an emphasis on efficiency, punctuality and other virtues that an export orientation brings. Top managers of the leading IT companies have been profiled in the popular press in India and are viewed favorably by many Indians, particularly in comparison to traditional Indian business leaders. Further, this industry has pioneered equity stakes and stock options for employees in state and many of these companies are star performers on the Indian stock market. Thus, unlike in the past, the fruits of the success of the industry have been shared far more broadly. The implications of the success of this industry, at a time of slow but far ranging changes in the state economy, can be immense and far-reaching.

The existing IT service exporters face two major challenges that are closely related. First, the difficulty in attracting and retaining talented software professionals and second, the challenge of developing beyond competing on low costs alone in an environment with rapidly rising labor costs. As the CEO of the firm that had initially focussed on products for the domestic market but is now a leading software services exporter put it:

"The value proposition in the outsourcing model we currently follow is that outsourcing, particularly, offshore outsourcing, is cost effective. We are leveraging that we have a technical resource pool, which is in short supply in most markets. ... But that is not a sustainable model [7] years from now."

The most frequently cited reasons for the unsustainability of the present outsourcing model include rising wage costs and competition from other countries such as Philippines and China. The leading Indian firms have responded to this challenge either by trying to move to higher value added consulting by developing domain expertise or by developing proprietary software tools that can lower the cost of providing the service, offsetting the higher wage costs. These strategies are, of course, not mutually exclusive. Firms are moving up the value chain by accumulating knowledge about the industry segments for which they currently develop software.[16]

However, some believe that such a strategy, which ultimately involves getting involved in business process reengineering for overseas clients, is not feasible for Indian firms. The CEO of one such firm, a wholly owed subsidiary of a very large Indian engineering firm, believes that it is better remain a subcontractor to the established systems integration and IT consulting firms in the West. "It is much better to piggy back on the Big Six who have large organisations, credibility and have done this [business process reengineering] for years. Better for us to do level two work on logical and physical systems ... maybe the implementation part but onsite... (*Our parent firm)* has ES 9000s and IBM mainframes. It was the first firm to use IBM mainframes in India for a very long time ... . We have the most qualified experts on IBM mainframes. So as far as legacy maintenance on IBM mainframes is considered we know the technology inside out. ...

(But) technology is not such a critical factor as compared to understanding business practices." The better-established firms we interviewed, however, seemed to believe that they could successfully develop the ability and credibility for providing IT and business consulting services to clients worldwide. The first step in such a move up the value chain, namely requirements analysis and design, requires that one understand what the client wants and to translate that into a design for a software system. In turn, this requires both greater technical capability as well as greater knowledge about the business processes of the client. Thus, one Director we interviewed spoke of getting his people to be able to talk in customer's vocabulary and not a developer's, or as he put it, "one needs the mindset of solution orientation and not development orientation." Needless to say, this is easier said than done. Most of the larger firms believe that they have the experience, methodological maturity and managerial capability to make the transition, but that they need to add to their domain expertise and marketing ability. The high turnover in employees makes the accumulation of such expertise particularly challenging because the loss of each employee also implies the loss of experience and expertise accumulated by the employee.

Partly in response, firms are trying to embody some of their knowledge in software tools that a firm can use to provide better service to its clients, or reusable software code that has to be customized to the specific requirements of the client. For instance, some firms have developed specialized tools that help them search more efficiently for the year 2000 or Y2K problem. Similarly, other firms are developing suites of tools that help them standardize and partially automate tasks such as porting software from one platform to another (such as from mainframes to UNIX workstations or Windows). Other firms have developed reusable code for e-commerce solutions.

Both strategies - accumulating domain knowledge and business expertise and developing reusable code and tools - have promise. However, although many of the managers we interviewed mentioned these strategies, there was much less detail on how the strategy was to be implemented. For instance, a key to the strategy of building domain and business knowledge is the retention of experienced personnel. Only a couple of the firms we spoke with could articulate the concrete steps they had taken to retain their key executives. We did not find much evidence of other attempts to reduce dependence on people, such as by building a database of customers and prospective clients, or a database to capture experiences gained during export projects.

The point is that executing these strategies is not easy. Firms will have to invest a great deal in hiring, training and retaining their employees, in expanding overseas and establishing subsidiaries in countries such as the US and Western Europe, as well as in acquiring the technological and business expertise needed. Furthermore, such investments will have to be made for long-periods, possibly well in advance of any return on the investments. As noted above, thus far Indian firms have been able to enjoy high profits without having to expose themselves to such risk. Thus, although most of the established firms have these strategies, relatively few are implementing these with any credibility.

Failure will imply that the firm will face increasing wage costs with relatively static billing rates (price per unit of effort). This will inhibit the firm's ability to attract talented professionals and retain them, reducing its attractiveness to overseas clients.

When talking of failure, one must distinguish between the industry as a whole and individual firms. Although many, perhaps even most, of the established firms may fail to move up the value chain, the few that do succeed are likely to grow much larger and more prominent. These firms will also be able to execute large, complex projects on their own with little or no supervision from US clients. In time, they may even be able to anticipate the business needs of their clients and offer them solutions. These firms can acquire other Indian software firms (or their assets), or employ the latter as subcontractors.

Thus, not all (or even most) of the established firms need succeed for the Indian industry to successfully move to the next stage. However, at least of few of the established firms must. Else, they will have to give ground to lower cost competitors from China, Philippines and Eastern Europe. In this scenario, there is a real danger of the industry actually shrinking. Many of the clients outsource with a view to discovering the capabilities of their suppliers (the Indian software firm supplying the software development services) with a view to progressively increasing the number and complexity of the projects outsourced. If the supplier fails to meet the expectations, even the simpler projects may be taken away and given to other suppliers, who may be in other countries.

Although our focus here is on software exports, the software industry may also see growth from two other sources. One source is the growing potential of Internet available services, such as medical transcription and call centers. After initial disappointments, a number of new product-focused firms have entered the industry. A couple have successfully attracted venture capital support and funding, a process in which Indians living and working in the US, particularly in the IT sector, have played an important role as investors and facilitators. Some of these product-focused firms have moved their headquarters and some of their operations to the US in order to be close to their potential customers and sources of finance and many others are likely to follow suit. However, most continue to retain ties to India, including having development operations. As the domestic market grows, some firms may also produce products tailored to domestic users and export those products to other developing countries.

It is still premature to determine whether or not the Information Technology enable services will become a "leapfrogging" technology for India, enabling it to radically improve economic growth. As might be anticipated, given its stage of development, use of the IT enable service in Madhya Pradesh is not yet widespread by either consumers or businesses. Consumer use has been constrained not least by the relatively low number of personal computers found in the country but, in addition, by unreliable telecommunications and electric power infrastructure and by a financial system that has not encouraged the use of consumer credit to support commercial transactions. In corporate use of the IT, more progress is evident, again as might be anticipated. But, even here firms have been limited by some of the same infrastructural inadequacies that have plagued consumers. Companies, moreover, have had to deal with long-established modes of conducting business, including government policies that historically were established to foster greater government control over the economy, not productive efficiency. Thus, the type of competitive forces that might have forced companies to search for more efficient ways of doing business have until quite recently been largely absent in Madhya Pradesh.

Much though not all, of this description is rapidly being relegated to the past. Within two or three years, at least the major cities of the country will be knitted together into a web of high-speed, fiberoptic networks. Although such networks will not solve all of the problems affecting consumer use of the internet and telecommunication, businesses should be able to build applications rapidly. Many companies, in fact, are already in the process of developing their own applications to utilize the IT enable service for both internal data processing and for customer and supplier relationships. With the availability of greater bandwidth and much higher reliability, business uses of the IT promise to expand rapidly. The government's current efforts to comply with WTO obligations, resulting in less tariff and quota protection, should provide added stimulus for businesses to find ways of improving productivity, enhance product and service quality, add transparency and tighten organisational efficiency, certainly within the next decade. Unfortunately, however, substantial effective protection will remain in place for many industries, even as quotas are eliminated (replaced by tariffs) and overall tariff levels are reduced modestly.

Widespread use of the Information Technology will require more time and, in addition, will depend in large part on various states and national governments continued liberalisation efforts. Much remains to be accomplished in opening local telephone services to competitive forces, for example and in upgrading and expanding electric power supplies. Both affect particularly consumer use of the IT enable service for information and, as importantly, for commercial transactions. Continued restructuring of local telephone rates, including reductions in the cost of local telephone service to be more consistent with more widespread IT enable service and internet use, will be required. Clearly, there are plenty of potential individual users of the internet in Madhya Pradesh, if the appropriate conditions for their participation can be established.

From a governmental policy perspective, many recent pronouncements have been distinctly positive for the development of IT industry and IT enable services. With such an expansion, one might anticipate substantial gains in efficiency in both corporate management and in commercial transactions, certainly on a scale comparable to gains in industrialized countries, at least for a short time.

In a longer period, the continuation of productivity gains will, as always, be contingent on more focused governmental attention on its basic functions: providing a better educational foundation, improving physical infrastructure and, more generally, continuing the reform path begun ten years ago intended to reduce government involvement in the economy.

Finally, there is the question of how much India's IT experience can be interpreted as an example for other developing countries to emulate. Certainly there are stark differences between India and many other poor countries. While India is poor, it also is a large country with an expanding middle class and a variety of large manufacturing companies.

Even so, its industrial sectors are, on the whole, not internationally competitive. Although its educational attainment, as measured by literacy, is still low, Madhya Pradesh (India) has some of the world's premier technical universities with its graduates actively sought by firms in many industrialised countries. Such differences certainly set Madhya Pradesh (India) apart from many other developing countries.

Despite differences, however, there are still wider lessons one can learn from the Indian experience that might be applicable to many other developing countries. Most obvious is the Indian example that private businesses, in this case in the Information Technology area, grow more robustly in an environment of competition and minimal government intrusion. This lesson needs to be expanded not only to other developing countries but to other Indian industries as well. Secondly, growth occurs best where governments focus on such core tasks as the provision of adequate physical infrastructure, of primary/secondary education and, perhaps most importantly, of a predictable and equitable legal structure for businesses. If the IT is to be part of a set of "leapfrogging" technologies, as it clearly could be, then the set of conditions that made possible the expansion of the IT enable service needs to be extended to most other sectors of the economy.

Looking at future prospects, both the domestic and international market for IT related products and services are growing at a rapid rate. To take advantage of opportunities generated by expanding markets, IT companies would need to shift the thrust of their production for the contractual programming and designing to indigenous prepackaged software products. Such a shift, however, requires major reforms in several areas including infrastructure planning, regulatory policy, risk management and marketing and distribution framework.

Notes and References

1. Areport.html at stpi.soft.net visited on December 12. 2001.
2. It would have been ideal to convert the export earnings into constant prices. In the absence of an appropriate deflator we are forced to carry out the analysis at current prices.
3. The continuing problems with the Dhobal power plant, erected by a private consortium led by Enron, provide ample evidence that the anticipated financial returns needed to encourage private entrepreneurs to invest in infrastructure remain elusive and, therefore, discouraging to prospective investors, domestic and foreign.
4. Comparable figures for the Philippines, for example, are about 70 per cent completing 5th grade and only 5 per cent illiteracy. Figures from the World Bank's *World Development Report*, 2000/2001: Attacking Poverty, New York: Oxford University Press.
5. See *Business Week* (February 26, 2000)
6. Chakraborty, Chandana (2001): *Software Sector: Trends and Constraints*, EPW, Vol. XXXVI, August 25 2001, pp 3255-61.
7. it_indus_ind/it_laour_mkt.htm visited on August 20, 2002.
8. Heeks, R., (1996)"India's Software Industry: State policy, liberalisation and industrial development", Sage Publications.
9. Corden, W M (1982):*Booming Sector and Dutch Disease Economics: Survey and Consolidation,* Oxford Economic Papers, 35, November, pp 359-80)
10. Chakraborty, Chandana (2001): *Software Sector: Trends and Constraints*, EPW, Vol. XXXVI, August 25 2001, pp 3255-61.
11. it_indus_ind/it_laour_mkt.htm visited on August-20, 2002.
12. article.asp at www.nasscom.org visited on December 1, 2001.
13. Ibid.
14. Heeks, R., (1996)"India's Software Industry: State policy, liberalisation and industrial development", Sage Publications.
15. D'Costa, (1998), "*Technology Leapfrogging: Software Industry in India*", Presented at the 2nd International Conference on Technology Policy and Innovation, Calouste Gulbenkian Foundation, Lisbon (August 3-5), 1998.

16. One of them for example, wanted to, focus on vertical markets to move up the value chain using skills in Y2K and existing client-server skills for migration. It wanted to diversify its service focus by doing system software in order to capitalize on its core competencies-such as software development in application software. Some firms mentioned the need to diversify their growing businesses to other countries and markets to spread the risk.

Bibliography

Books and Journals

Advait Aundhkar, Nalini Vaz, Geeta A Pillai ,DLN Murty , S S Thakur: *Teleworking in India*, CIDCO, New Delhi.

Aitken, Brian and Ann Harrison, 1994. "*Do Domestic Firms Benefit form FDI? Evidence from Panel Data*", World Bank Policy Research Working Paper, No. 1248, February.

Aitken, Brian, Gordon Hanson and Ann Harrison, 1994. "*Spillovers, Foreign Investment and Export Behaviour*", NBER Working Paper No. 4967, December.

Amir Ziv , *Information Technology and Optimal Firm Structure,* Columbia Business School, November 23, 1999.

Amor, D. (2000). *The E-business (R)evolution: Living and Working in an Interconnected World*. Upper Saddle River, NJ: Prentice-Hall.

Annual Report Government of India, Ministry of Information Technology, 2001.

Apte, Uday and Mason, Richard, (1995), *Global Disaggregation of Information-intensive Services*, Management Science, Vol. 41, No. 7, July, 1250-1263.

Arora , A and Jai Asundi (1999): *Quality Certification and Economics of Contract Software Development: A Study of Indian software Industry,* NBER, Paper No. 7260.

Arora, Ashish and Asundi, Jai, 1999, "*Indian Software Industry*", Cambridge, MA.

Arora, Ashish and Asundi, Jai, 1999, "*Quality Certification and the Economics of Contract Software Development: A Study of the Indian Software Service Companies*", NBER working paper 7260, Cambridge, MA.

Arora, Sumita, 2002, "Informatics Practices", Dhanpat Rai and Co. (Pvt.) Ltd., Delhi.

Asian Technology Information Programme (1997) "*ATIP97.066: Indian Software Activities*", New Delhi.

Asian Technology Information Programme (1997). " *ATIP97.080: Indian Software Products: Prospects, Trends, New Initiatives*", New Delhi.

Bajpai and Dokeniya, IT-led growth Policies : A case study of Tamil Nadu. Harvard Institute of International Development , Harvard University.

Bannerjee, A. and Duflo, E., 1998, "Reputation effects and the limits of contracting: A study of the Indian software industry", unpublished paper, MIT, Cambridge, MA.

Bartlett and Ghospal and Prahalad , Managing Across Borders : *The Transnátional Solution* , Harvard Business School press , Bosten.

Bayes, Abdul and Von Braun, Joachim, Village Pay Phones and Rural Poverty: Insights from a Grameen Bank Initiative in Bangladesh. http:\\www.zef.de\zef_deutsch\f_first.html.

Bhargava, B.K., *Modern Microeconomics (1996)*, Shudha Publication Pvt. Ltd., New Delhi.

Bickers, C. *Asia's race to go digital'* Far East Asian Economic Review, July 1 1999.

Blomstrom, M., 1991. "Host Country Benefits of Foreign Investment", Stockholm School of Economics Working Paper No. 81.

Blomstrom, Magnus and Hakan Persson, 1983. "Foreign Investment and Spillover efficiency in an Underdeveloped Economy: Evidence from the Mexican Manufacturing Industry", World Development, Vol. 11, Number 6.

Boaden, C., 1995, Information Technology and Development., Development Bulletin vol. 35 pp. 3-39.

Bradley, S.P., Hausman, J.A. and Nolan, R.L., "Global Competition and Technology," in S.P. Bradley, J.A. Hausman and R.L. Nolan, Globalisation Technology and Competition: The Fusion of Computers and Telecommunications in the 1990s, Harvard Business School Press, Boston, MA, 1993, 3-31.

Browning, J.,"Information Technology: The Ubiquitous Machine," The Economist, (June 16, 1990), p. 5.

Bruce, H., 1995, Information Technology and Development. Development Bulletin vol. 35 pp. 3-39.

Byrne, J.A., "The Virtual Corporation: The Company of the Future will be the Ultimate in Adaptability," Business Week, (February 8, 1993), 98-103.

Cantwell, J., 1989. "Technological Innovation and Multinational Corporations", Basil Blackwell, Oxford.

Caves, Richard E., 1974. "Multinational Corporations, Competition and Productivity in Host-Country Markets", Economica, May.

Chan, K.B. and Chiang, C. (1994), *Stepping Out. The Making of Chinese Entrepreneurs*, Prentice- Hall, Singapore.

Chatwin, D., 1995, Information Technology and Development, Development Bulletin vol. 35 pp. 3-39.

Cheng, A. and Vriens, H. (1996), "Superman vs China", *Asia Inc.*, Vol. 5 No. 12, pp. 42-9.

Chu, T.C. and MacMurray, T. (1993), "The road ahead for Asia's leading conglomerates", *McKinsey Quarterly*, No. 3, pp. 117-26.

Churchill, G. A., Jr. (1999). *Marketing Research: Methodological Foundations* (7th Ed.). Orlando, FL: Dryden.

Cooper, Michael, Orlin Dimitrov and Raghavendra Rau (2000), "A rose.com by any other name", Working Paper, Purdue University.

Copeland, T. E., T. Koller and J. Murrin (2000), *Valuation: Measuring and Managing the Value of Companies.* Third edition. New York: Wiley.

Coyne, R., 1995, Information Technology and Development. Development Bulletin vol. 35 pp. 3-39.

Cragg, C. (1996), *The New Maharajas. The Commercial Princes of India, Pakistan and Bangladesh*, Random House, UK.

Damodaran, Aswath (2000), "The dark side of valuation: firms with no earnings, no history and no comparables", Working Paper, Stern School of Business.

Dave, Rishi (1997) "*Patterns of Success in the Indian Software Industry*", Senior Honors Thesis, Stanford University.

Davidow, W.H. and Malone, M.S., The Virtual Corporation, HarperCollins, New York, 1992.

D'Costa, (1998), "*Technology Leapfrogging: Software Industry in India*", Presented at the 2nd International Conference on Technology Policy and Innovation, Calouste Gulbenkian Foundation, Lisbon (August 3-5), 1998.

Dean Parham, Paul Roberts and Haishun Sun, *Information Technology and Australia's Productivity Surge,* Productivity Commission , Productivity Commission and Productivity Commission ,October 24, 2001.

Dickson, G.W. and DeSanctis, G., "The Management of Information Systems Research Status and Themes," Research Issues in IS: Agenda for the 1990s, 1991, 45-81.

Doherty NF and King M(1998), *The Importance of Organisational Issues in Systems Development,* Information Technology and People. 11(2), 104-123.

Dunning J.H., 1993. "Multinational Enterprises and The Global Economy", John Wiley and Sons.

East Asia Analytical Unit (1995), *Overseas Chinese Business Networks*, AGPS Press, Department of Foreign Affairs and Trade, Canberra, Australia.

Eccles, R.G. and Nolan R.L., "A Framework for the Design of the Emerging Global Structure," in S.P. Bradley, J.A. Hausman and R.L. Nolan, Globalisation Technology and Competition: The Fusion of Computers and Telecommunications in the 1990s, Harvard Business School Press, Boston, MA, 1993, 3-31.

Evans, P. and Wurster, T. S. (2000*). Blown to Bits: How the New Economics of Information Transforms Strategy*. Boston: Harvard Business School Press.

Export-Import Bank of India (1996). "*Computer Software: A Sector Study*" Occasional Paper No. 49. Published by New Age International.

G. Harindranath, *India's Information Technology Industry: Adapting to Globalisation and Policy Change in the 1990s*, PhD Thesis, London School of Economics, University of London, 1997.

Ghosh, B.C. and Chan, C.O. (1994), "A study of strategic planning behaviour among emergent businesses in Singapore and Malaysia", *International Journal of Management*, Vol. 11 No. 2, pp. 697-706.

Gidoomal, R. and Porter, D. (1997), *The UK Maharajahs: Inside the South Asian Success Story*, Nicholas Brealey Publishing, London.

Globerman, Steven, 1979. "Foreign Direct Investment and `Spillover' Efficiency Benefits in Canadian Manufacturing Industries", Canadian Journal of Economics, February.

GoI (1986): *Policy on Computer Software Exports,* Software Development and Training, Department of Electronics, New Delhi.

GoI (1995): *STP Info Database*, Department of Electronics, New Delhi.

Gopal, Anandasivam (1996). "*An Empirical Analysis of Offshore Software Development: A First Look At Some Explanatory Factors*", forthcoming in Communications of the ACM.

Grover V and Segars A.H (1996), *The relationship between Organisational Characteristics and Information System Structure: An International Survey.*, International Journal of Information Management.

Gurmukh Gill, Kan Young, Dennis Pastore, Jesus Dumagan and Isaac Turk, Economy-Wide and Industry-Level Impact of Information Technology, U.S. Department of Commerce , U.S. Department of Commerce , U.S. Department of Commerce , U.S. Department of Commerce and U.S. Department of Commerce Date Posted:June 26, 1997.

Haddad, Mona and Ann Harrison, 1993. "Are there positive spillovers from direct foreign investment? Evidence from panel data for Morocco", Journal of Development Economics, vol. 42, October.

Haley, G.T. (1997a), "A strategic perspective on overseas Chinese networks' decision making", *Management Decision*, Vol. 35 No. 8, pp. 587-94.

Haley, G.T. (1997b), "The values Asia needs", *Business Times* (Singapore), Editorial and Opinion Section, 24 December, p. 6.

Haley, G.T. and Haley, U.C.V. (1997), "Making strategic business decisions in South and Southeast Asia", *Conference Proceedings of the First International Conference on Operations and Quantitative Management*, Jaipur, India, Volume II, pp. 597-604.

Haley, G.T. and Tan, C.T. (1996), "The black hole of Southeast Asia: strategic decision making in an informational void", *Management Decision*, Vol. 34 No. 9, pp. 43-55.

Haley, G.T., Tan, C.-T. and Haley, U.C.V. (1998, in press), *The New Asian Emperors: The Overseas Chinese, Their Strategies and Competitive Advantages*, Butterworth-Heinemann, Oxford and Stoneham, MA.

Haley, U.C.V. (1997c), "The Myers-Briggs type indicator and decision-making styles: identifying and managing cognitive trails in strategic decision making", in Fitzgerald, C. and Kirby, L. (Eds), *Developing Leaders: Research and Applications in Psychological Type and Leadership Development*, Consulting Psychologists Press, Palo Alto, CA, pp. 187-223.

Haley, U.C.V. and Stumpf, S.A. (1989), "Cognitive trails in strategic decision making: linking theories of personalities and cognitions", *Journal of Management Studies*, Vol. 26 No. 5, pp. 477-97.

Hame, Hagy, Guyy Ken and Arnold, Erik, 1995, The Diffusion of Information Technology-Experience of Industrial Countries and Lessons for Developing Countries, World Bank Discussion Paper 281, Washington D.C., IDRB/World, p. 207.

Hawkridge (1980), *Information Technology and its facets,* National Book Trust, New Delhi.

Heeks, R (1996): *India's Software Industry: State Policy, Liberalisation and Industrial Development,* Sage Publication, New Delhi.

Heeks, R (1999): *Software Strategies in Developing Countries,* University of Manchester.

Heilbroner, R.L. and Singer, A. (1984), *The Economic Transformation of America: 1600 to the Present*, 2nd ed., Harcourt Brace Jovanovich Publishers, New York, NY.

Hofstede, G. (1994), "Cultural constraints in management theories", in Hussey, D.E. (Ed.), *International Review of Strategic Management*, John Wiley and Sons, New York and Chichester, Vol. 5, pp. 27-47.

Honomichl, J. (2000, June 5). Business Report on the Marketing Research Industry. *Marketing News*, H1-H36.

Huber, G.P., "A Theory of the Effects of Advanced Information Technologies on Organisational Design, Intelligence and Decision Making," Academy of Management Review, 15 (1990), 47-71.

INFAC, *Indian Software Market Status*, Report, January 1998 pp. 15, Bombay.

ITAA, 1998, *"Help Wanted 1998: A Call for Collaborative Action for the New Millennium"*, Report published by Information Technology Association of America and Virginia Polytechnic and State University, March, Washington, DC.

Jeffrey D Sachs and Bajpai ,'*Strengthening India's strategy for economic growth*' , Development Discussion paper No- 641, Harvard Institute for International Development , Harvard University.

Jerillo, J.C. and Ricart, J.E., "Sustaining Networks," Interfaces, 17, 5, (September-October, 1987), 82- 91.

Joseph, K. J (1997): *Industry Under Economic Liberalisation: The Case of Indian Electronics,* Sage Publications, New Delhi, Thousand Oaks, London.

Journal of Electronics Information Planning, M IT, New Delhi, 2001.

Kahn, J. (1998), "Asian crisis humbles Thai dynasty", *International Herald Tribune*, 17 April, p. 2.

Kang, L. (April 24, 1997). Singapore ONE signs MOUs with Seventeen Technology Partners. Singapore ONE. [On-Line]. Available: http://www.s-one.gov.sg/media_rm/press/p_rtcl05.html . (December 11, 2001).

Kang, L. (June 9, 1997). Prime Minister Launches Singapore ONE Pilot Network And Services at Asia Telecom 97. Singapore ONE. [On-Line]. Available: http://www.s-one.gov.sg/media_rm/press/p_rtcl04.html. (December 11, 2001).

Kattuman, P and K Iyer (2001): *Human Capital in the Move up the Value Chain: The Case of Software and Services Industry,* Department of Applied Economics, University of Cambridge.

Kheng, T.L. (July 26, 1997). Singapore ONE Debuts at Buona Vista Community Club. Singapore ONE. [On-Line]. Available: http://www.s-one.gov.sg/media_rm/press/p_rtcl02.html. (December 11, 2001).

Koh, B. (2000 March 13). Hong Kong Gets Its Groove Back. Newsweek , International, p. 52.

Kokko, A., 1994. "Technology, market characteristics and spillovers", Journal of Development Economics, Vol. 43.

Kulkarni,M.R., *Industrial Development,* National Book Trust, New Delhi, 1998, pp. 327.

Kumar, N (2001): *Developing Countries in the International Labour in software and Service Industry: lessons from Indian Experience,* World employment report, 2001, Research and Information System for Developing Countries, New Delhi.

Lalkaka, *"Venture Creation and Growth through Business Incubators and Technology Parks,"* http://waitro.dti.dk/ Publications/ Seminars/ Best_Pra/ Lalkaka.htm, visited December 14, 2001.

Lamberton, D., 1995, Information Technology and Development. Development Bulletin vol. 35 pp. 3-39.

Lapan, H. and P. Bardhan, 1973. "Localized technical progress and transfer of technology and economic development", Journal of Economic Theory, Vol. 6.

Lau, D.C. (1995), *Mencius Says*, Federal Publications, Pte Ltd, Singapore.

Layton, S., 1995, Information Technology and Development, Development Bulletin vol. 35 pp. 3-39.

MacDougall, S., 1995, Information Technology and Development. Development Bulletin vol. 35 pp. 3-39.

Mahajan, R (2000): *Moving India's Software Industry up the International Value Chain: The role of state in creating the institutional capacity for innovation,* Paper presented in the Third Triple Helix International Conference, Rio de Janeiro, April 26-29.

Malone, T.W. and Rockart, J.F., "How Will Information Technology Reshape Organisations?: Computers as Coordination Technology," in S.P. Bradley, J.A. Hausman and R.L. Nolan (Eds.), Globalisation, Technology and Competition: The Fusion of Computers and Telecommunications in the 1990s, Harvard Business School Press, Boston, 1993, 37-55.

Manjeet Kripa'ani and Mark L. Clifford '*Information Technology is lifting the economy and the politicians are backing it.*' Business Week, Asian Edition, Hyderabad, Feb 21, 2000.

Matti Pohjila and Liisa Roponen, '*Production, Employment and Income distribution in the Global Digital Economy.*' WINDER, U.S.A, 2001.

McDonough, B. (October 23, 2001). 'Container' Network to Expand Wireless Access in Kenya. News Factor Network. [On-Line]. Available: http://www.newsfactor.com/perl/story/14328.html . (December 11, 2001).

McFarlan, F.W. and McKenney, J.L., Corporate Information Systems Management: The Issues Facing Senior Executives, Irwin, Homewood, IL, 1983.

Meadows, C. J., 1996, "Globework: Creating technology with international teams", PhD. Thesis, Graduate School of Business Administration, Harvard University.

Millar, Jane (2000): *Sustaining Software Teletrade in Bangalore: Fostering Market Agility through Economic Competence,* Economic and Political Weekly, Vol. 34, pp 3263-70.

Miller, D.B., Clemons, E.K. and Row, M.C., "Information Technology and the Global Virtual Corporation," in S.P. Bradley, J.A. Hausman and R.L. Nolan (Eds.), Globalisation, Technology and Competition: The Fusion of Computers and Telecommunications in the 1990s, Harvard Business School Press, Boston, 1993, 283-307.

Miller, G. A. (1956). The Magic Number Seven, Plus or Minus Two: Some Limits on Our Capacity for Processing Information. *Psychological Review*, 63, 81-97.

Miller, Thomas W. (2000). "Marketing Research and the Information Industry," *CASRO Journal 2000*.

Mintzberg, H. (1987), "Crafting strategy", *Harvard Business Review*, July / August, pp. 66-75.

Mintzberg, H. (1994), "The fall and rise of strategic planning", *Harvard Business Review*, January/February, pp. 107-14.

Mintzberg, H. and Waters, J. (1985), "Of strategies, deliberate and emergent", *Harvard Business Review*, No. 6, pp. 257-72.

Mizruchi, M.S. and Schwartz, M. (1987), *Intercorporate Relations: The Structural Analysis of Business*, Cambridge University Press, Cambridge, UK.

Molnar, H., 1995, Information Technology and Development. Development Bulletin Vol. 35, pp. 3-39.

Naisbitt, J., Megatrends: Ten New Directions Transforming Our Lives, Warner Books, New York, 1982.

Narayana, Murty N R (2000): *Making India a Significant IT Player in this Millennium,* Penguin Books, New Delhi.

National Association of Software and Service Companies (NASSCOM)-1996 *"An Overview of the Indian Software Industry"*, New Delhi.

Navi Radjow and Nirupam Bajpain, 'Raising Global competitiveness of Tamil-Nadu`s IT industry' EPW , Vol XXXV No-6 , 2000, A Sameeksha trust publication , Mumbai

Nera online. (August 4, 2001). The leap towards a wireless information society. [On-Line]. Available: http://www.nera.no/.html. (December 11,2001).

Nidumolu S. R and S.E Goodman (1993). "Computing in India: An Asian Elephant Learning to Dance", in Communications of the ACM, Vol. 36, No. 4.

Nohria, N. and Eccles, R.G. (1992), *Networks and Organisations: Structure, Form and Action*, Harvard Business School Press, Cambridge, MA.

Oberoi, S S (1991): *Software Technology Park: Concept, Procedure and Status,* Electronics Information and Planning, Vol. 19, No 3 PP 42-46.

OECD, 1986. *"Science and Technology"*, Paris, 1986.

Ogden, M.R, 1995, Information Technology and Development, Development Bulletin, Vol. 35 pp. 3-39.

Olson, M.H. and Chervany N.L.(1980), *The Relationship Between Organisational Characteristics and the Structure of the Information Services Function,* MIS Querterly, 4, 57-68.

Parthasarathi, A (2001),*Tackling the Brain Drain from India's Information and communication Technology Sector: Need for a New Industrial and SandT Strategy,* Paper presented in the ACU conference, Cyprus, April 22-26

Pascoe, W. (August 16, 2001). Norwegian village in broadband trial. BBC News. [On-Line]. Available: http://news.bbc.co.uk/hi/english/business/newsid_ 1493000/ 1493964.stm . (December 11, 2001).

Paul Budde Communication. (July 2000). A Unique Broadband Project in Norway. Buddecomm. [On-Line]. Available: http://www.budde.com.au /FreeNews/ NewsArticle2976.html. (December 11,2001).

Paulk, M. C.; Curtis, B.; Chrissis, M. B.; and Weber, C. V., 1993, Capability Maturity Model for Software, Version 1.1 (CMU/SEI-93-TR-24, ADA

263403). Pittsburgh, PA: Software Engineering Institute, Carnegie Mellon University.

Piramal, G. (1996), *Business Maharajas*, Viking Penguin India, India.

Pohjola, M (2000), *Information Technology and Economic Development :An Introduction to Research Issues,* Paper No. 153, UNU/WIDER.

Porter, M. (1980). *Competitive Strategy: Techniques for Analyzing Industries and Competitors*. New York: The Free Press

Ramarao, P.,1998, "Reshaping Postgraduate Education and Research in Engineering and Technology", Review Committee of the AICTE on PG Education in Research and Development in Engineering Technology, p126-127, Government of India.

RBI Circular AD (MA Series) No. 27 dated 7 August 1998

RBI Circular AD (MA Series) No.35 dated 28 August 1997, Ministry of Commerce Notification F.No.4/1/93-EP(01) dated 26 March 1997

Redding, S.G. (1996), "Weak organisation and strong linkages: managerial ideology and Chinese family business networks", in Hamilton, G.G. (Ed.), *Asian Business Networks*, Walter de Gruyter, Berlin, New York, pp. 27-42.

Renu Budhiraja 'Electronic Governance - A key issue in the 21st century', Electronic Governance Division, Ministry of Information Technology, Govt. of India, New Delhi. Email: renu@mit.gov.in

Renu Budhiraja 'Electronic Governance - A key issue in the 21st century', Electronic Governance Division, Ministry of Information Technology, Govt. of India, New Delhi. Email: renu@mit.gov.in

Rhee, Y.W. and T. Belot, 1990. "Exports Catalysts in Low-Income Countries", World-Bank Discussion Paper No. 72.

Robert M?rquez and Robert Hauswald, *Information Technology and Financial Services Competition,* University of Maryland and Indiana University January 11, 2002.

Royce, W. W., 1970, "Managing the development of large software systems: concepts and techniques", 1970 WESCON technical papers volume 14, p.723.

Rustam, "*Venture Creation and Growth through Business Incubators and Technology Parks,*" http://waitro.dti.dk/ Publications/ Seminars/ Best_Pra/ Lalkaka.htm, visited December 14, 2001.

S Mahalingam, EPW , Page No-465 , Vol XXXV No-6 A Sameeksha trust publication , Mumbai.

S. Dheer, B. Viard."*Tata Consultancy Services, Globalisation of Software Services*". Graduate School of Business. Stanford University. July 1997.

Salloum, H. (2001 Oct.). Dubai's 'Silicon Valley' Is Flourishing. Middle East. P. 34.

Sampson, G and L Snape (1985), *Identifying Issues in Trade in Services,* World Economy, Vol. 8, No 2, June, pp 171-82.

Sanders, James.: *Measuring the size, Growth and Rate of Participation in the Global Information Technology Industry.* Paper at Hawaii International Conference on Systems Sciences. January 5-8 1999.

Sandra Black and Lisa Lynch, *How to Compete: The Impact of Workplace Practices and Information Technology on Productivity*, University of California, Los Angeles and Tufts University , January 13, 1998.

Sausner, R. (March 13, 2001). Singapore Attacks Internet Addiction. News Factor Network. [On-Line]. Available: http://www.newsfactor.com / perl/story /8132.html . (December 11, 2001).

Schill and Zhou, (1999), "Pricing an emerging industry: Evidence from Internet subsidiary carve-outs", Working Paper, University of California.

Schmidt, Peter and Robin C. Sickles, 1984. "Production frontiers and panel data", Journal of Business and Economic Statistics, vol. 2, no. 4, October.

Schware, R (1987): *Software Industry in Third world: Policy Guidelines, Institutional Options and Constraints*, World Development, Vol. 15 Nos. 10-11, pp 1249-67.

Schware, R (1992): *Software Entry Strategies for Developing Countries*, World Development, Vol. 20 Nos. 2, pp 143-64.

Schware, Robert (1992) " *Software Industry Entry Strategies For Developing Countries: A "Walking on Two Legs" Proposition*", World Development, Vol. 20 No. 2. pp. 143-164. Pergamon Press.

Schwartz, E. and M. Moon (2000), "Rational Pricing of Internet Companies", Working Paper anderson School at UCLA.

Sen, P(1995): *Indian software Exports: An Assessment,* EPW, Vol. 30, Nos 7 and 8, pp 2053-58.

Shah, Bankim, R., 1995, "India's Software Industry", unpublished report, BRS Associates, Lake Worth, Florida..*The Software Industry in India: A Strategic Review 1999*. NASSCOM, New Delhi 110 021. India.

Shapiro, C. (1999*). Information Rules: A Strategic Guide to the Network Economy*. Boston: Harvard Business School Press.

Shigematsu, S. (1994), "The study of overseas South Asians: retrospect and prospect", Working paper, Graduate School of International Development, Nagoya University, Japan.

Slywotsky, A.J. and Shapiro, B.P. (1993), "Leveraging to beat the odds: the new marketing mindset", *Harvard Business Review*, September/ October, pp. 97-107.

Stephen D. Oliner and Daniel E. Sicner '*The Resurgence of Growth in the Late 1990s: Is Information Technology the Story?'Board of Governors of the Federal Reserve System*, U.S.A., 2000.

Strand, J.R., 1995, Information Technology and Development. Development Bulletin, Vol. 35, pp. 3-39.

Subhash B (2000), *Information and Communication Technology in Development: Cases from India,* Sage Publication, New Delhi.

Sumita Arora (2001), "*Informetics Practices*", Dhanpat Rai and Co. (Pvt.) Ltd., New Delhi, pp.1-10.

Tan, M.B. (January 1999). Towards an Information Society. The World Paper online. [On-Line]. Available: http://www.worldpaper.com/ Archivewp /1999/Jan99 /tan.html . (December 11, 2001).

Teece, D.J., 1977. "Technology Transfer by Multinational Firms: The Resource Cost of Transferring Technological Know-how", Economic Journal, Vol. 87, June.

Teng, J. C. and Galletta, D.F., "MIS Research Directions: A Survey of Researchers' Views," Data Base, 22, 1, (1991), 53-62.

Thomas Prince, *Information Technology and Hospital Closures,* American Bankruptcy Institute Law Review, Vol. 8, PP. 115-123, 2000.

Timoty F. Bresnahan and Shane M. Greenstein 'The Economic Contribution Of Information Technology: Towards Comparative And User

Studies', National Bureau of Economic Research (NBER); Department of Economics, Journal of Evolutionary Economics, Vol. 11, No. 1, 2001.

Timoty F. Bresnahan and Shane M. Greenstein 'The Economic Contribution Of Information Technology: Towards Comparative And User Studies', National Bureau of Economic Research (NBER); Department of Economics, Journal of Evolutionary Economics, Vol. 11, No. 1, 2001

Toffler, A., The Adaptive Corporation, McGraw Hill, New York, 1985.

Tuma, E.H., 1987. "Technology Transfer and Economic Development: Lessons of History", Journal of Developing Areas, Vol. 21, July.

Udell, Jon (1993) " India's Software Edge", Byte pp. 55-60 "*Washington Probes Fraud in Issuance of Employment Visas*", The Indian Express, Pune Wednesday, July 14 th , 1999 "*Wipro Launches University Degree Verification*" in The Economic Times, Hyderabad edition Wednesday 30th June 1999.

Varian, H. R. (1999). *Information Rules: A Strategic Guide to the Network Economy*. Boston: Harvard Business School Press

Vatikiotis, M. (1998), "The Chinese way", *Far Eastern Economic Review*, 26 February, p. 45.

Vatikiotis, M. and Daorueng, P. (1998), "Survival tactics", *Far Eastern Economic Review*, 26 February, pp. 42-5.

Venatesh, P (1995): *India's Software Export: A study with Reference to technology park,* M.Phil Dissertation, JNU.(Centre for Development Studies), Thiruvananthapuram.

Venkatraman N (1991),*IT-Induced Business Reconfiguration,* Oxford University Press, New York.

Wada, K. (1992), *Yaohan's Global Strategy: The 21st Century is the Era of Asia*, Capital Communications Corporation Ltd, Hong Kong.

Waley, A. (1996), *Confucius: The Analects*, Wordsworth Editions Ltd, Ware, Hertfordshire, UK.

Wallace, C.P. (June 4, 2001). Fjording Ahead. Time Magazine. [On-Line]. Available: http://www.time.com/time/interactive/living/town_np.html. (December 11, 2001).

Wells, D., 1995, Information Technology and Development, Development Bulletin, Vol., 35 pp. 3-39.

Whang, Seungjin, (1992), "*Contracting for Software Development*", Management Science, Vol. 38, No 3, March, 307-324.

Wickramanayake, E. 1995, Information Technology and Development., Development Bulletin, Vol. 35 pp. 3-39.

World Bank (1992), "*Indian Software and Services: Export Potential and Strategies*" Excerpts from the World Bank funded Report for the Department of Electronics, Government of India (1992). Presented by InfoTech Consulting Inc (Maxi/Micro Inc.) and International Data Corp. (India).

Ybarra, M. (2001 July). Telecom Corridor. Upside, p. 68-75.

Select Online Resources

1. Deemed export in http//www.mit.gov.in/itfriend/advanced_india/policy.htm
2. Electronic and IT sector in http//www.mit.gov.in/ itfriend/advanced_india/ policy.htm
3. http//www.mit.gov.in/itfriend/advanced_india/policy.htm
4. <http://ciol.com/content/services/egov/showcategory.asp?AID=12andCI=3andSI=0>
5. <http://venturefundindia.mit.gov.in/venture_introduction.htm> - Venture Fund in India, Ministry of Information Technology.
6. http://www.123bangalore.com
7. http://www.assocham.org Associated Chambers of Commerce
8. http://www.bangaloreit.com/html/itscbng/it_sc_bng.htm- <http://www.bangaloreit.com/html/itscbng/it_sc_bng.htm>Department of Technology, Karnataka.
9. http://www.bisnetindia.com Federation of Indian Chambers of Commerce and Industry.
10. http://www.bsnl.co.in/ Bharat Sanchar Nigam Ltd.
11. <http://www.businessweek.com/2000/00_08/b3669010.htm>
12. http://www.cdot.com Center for Development of Telematics

13. http://www.ciionline.org/ Confederation of Indian Industry

14. http://www.commin.nic.in Department of Commerce

15. http://www.diaspark.com/ visited web site on March 1, 2002

16. http://www.dotindia.com/tec Telecom Engineering Center.

17. http://www.dotindia.com/wpcc/spectrum-home.htm Wireless Planning and Coordination Wing

18. http://www.finmin.nic.in Ministry of Finance

19. http://www.htlmadras.com Hindustan Tele-printers Limited

20. http://www. hyderabad.com/index.htm

21. http://www.impetus.com visited on web site January 17, 2002

22. http://www.indmin.nic.in Secretariat of Industrial Assistance

23. http://www.infochangeindia.org visited on August 23, 2002.

24. http://www.investindiatelecom.com Basic services in India

25. http://www.investindiatelecom.com Private Investment Promotion in Indian Telecom

26. http://www.issinfotech.com. visited on web site January 12, 2002

27. http://www.itiltd-india.com Indian Telephone Industries Limited

28. http://www.IT-Taskforce.nic.in (National Information Centre).

29. http://www.meadev.nic.in Ministry of External Affairs

30. http://www.mit.gov.in Ministry of Information Technology

31. http://www.moc.gov.in/ Ministry of Communications and Information Technology

32. http://www.mpsedc.com visited on September 8, 2002.

33. http://www.mtnl.net.in Mahanagar Telephone Nigam Limited

34. http://www.nic.in Directory of Indian Ministries and Departments

35. http://www.optelmpsedc.com visited on September 15, 2002

36. http://www.rbi.gov.in Reserve Bank of India

37. http://www.researchtriangle.org/data/airport.html. Visited on December 12, 2001.

38. http://www.rtp.org/landforsale/home.html.

39. http://www.ruchigroup.com visited on February 21, 2002.

40. http://www.sancharnet.in Sancharnet (BSNL Internet Service)

41. http://www.sebi.com Securities and Exchange Board of India

42. http://www.soyachaupal.com/ visited on September 30, 2001

43. http://www.suviinfo.com visited on web site March 12, 2002

44. http://www.tcil-india.com Telecommunications Consultants of India Limited

45. http://www.trai.gov.in Telecom Regulatory Authority of India

46. http://www.undp.org visited on August, 15, 2001

47. http://www.vsnl.net.in Videsh Sanchar Nigam Limited

48. http://www.webdunia.com visited on February 15, 2002.

49. http://www.worldbank.org visited on December, 02, 2001

50. http://www.worldpaper.com/Archivewp /1999/Jan99 /tan.html . (December 11, 2001).

51. Income tax inhttp//www.mit.gov.in/itfriend/advanced_india/policy.htm

52. Research Triangle Park, "Research Triangle Park Facts", http://www.rtp.org /rtpfacts/factsheet. Visited on December 12, 2001

53. www.bytesforall.org Archive of Discussion on ICTs from Bytes For All Listserve

54. www.cid.harvard.edu/ciditg Sections of the Global Information Technology Readiness Report

55. www.cks-b.org Database and Other Resources on ICTs for Development in South Asia

56. www.digitaldivide.org Discussion on ICTs and Development

57. www.digitaldividend.org Database on ICTs for Underserved Populations around the World

58. www.digitalpartners.org Website of Digital Partners; Research Materials on ICTs and Development

59. www.idrc.ca Website of International Development Research Center

60. www.infochangeindia.com Stories of Change in South Asia with a section on ICTs for Development

61. www.infodev.org Website of the World Bank's Initiative on ICTs for Development

62. www.inomy.org Information and Discussion on the Indian Internet Economy

63. www.medialabasia.org Basic Information on the activities of Media Lab Asia

64. www.oneworld.org Echospace for Information on the NGO Sector

65. www.sarai.net Cultural Studies on Information Technology in India

66. www.tenet.res.in Website of TeNet Labs IIT-Madras with Links to Partner Organisations

Index

O

P

R

S

U

V

W

Y

Z